I0759754

The Royal Pavilion Brighton

The Royal Pavilion Brighton

A REGENCY PALACE OF COLOUR AND SENSATION

Alexandra Loske

YALE UNIVERSITY PRESS
New Haven and London

Dedicated to the memory of John Dinkel (1942–91),
Keeper of the Royal Pavilion 1974–89,
whose work inspired me to write this book

(opposite, detail) The north front of the Pavilion, A.C. Pugin, watercolour and pencil on paper, *c.*1822 (detail). Behind the second window from the left on the ground floor was John Dinkel's office in the 1980s

First published by Yale University Press 2025
302 Temple Street, P.O. Box 209040, New Haven CT
06520-9040
47 Bedford Square, London WC1B 3DP
yalebooks.com | yalebooks.co.uk

For information about this and other Yale University Press publications, please contact:
U.S. Office: sales.press@yale.edu yalebooks.com
Europe Office: sales@yaleup.co.uk yalebooks.co.uk

Project Editor: Daphne Fordham-Smith
Designer: Isobel Gillan
Senior Production Controller: Leonie Kellman

Printed and bound in Italy by Elcograf

Library of Congress Control Number: 2024947865
A catalogue record for this book is available from the British Library.
Authorized Representative in the EU: Easy Access System Europe, Mustamäe tee 50, 10621 Tallinn, Estonia, gpsr.requests@easproject.com

Published with assistance from the Annie Burr Lewis Fund and the Albert Dawson Educational Trust.

ISBN 978-0-300-26666-5

10 9 8 7 6 5 4 3 2 1

Opening page: *(detail)* The centre part of the east front in *c.*1822, after Augustus Charles Pugin, aquatint from John Nash's *The Royal Pavilion at Brighton*, 1826

Title page, left: The Music Room central chandelier with the *Chinese Comedian*, derived from William Alexander's *The Costume of China* (1805)

Title page, right: *(detail)* Watercolour drawing of a fish, tassel pendant and a carved pole, from Frederick Crace's Sketchbook with 68 coloured designs from Chinese ornaments, *c.*1800–20

Opposite: A section of the recently restored Chinese yellow-ground wallpaper, *c.*1800 or earlier, now reinstated in Queen Victoria's Bedroom in the Royal Pavilion

CONTENTS

Foreword

By Hedley Swain, CEO, Brighton & Hove Museums

The Royal Pavilion is one of the most recognisable and spectacular buildings in the UK today. Its complex beauty is the result of George IV's boundless imagination together with the creative input of the many talented artists, designers and architects who have worked on it over the years, as well as the political and cultural circumstances of the time. Although well documented and explored in publications since its completion in 1823, there are many layers of this historic landmark to unravel.

Through years of academic research and a deep understanding gained by her curatorial work, Alexandra Loske was inspired to write this new account of the enchanting and often misunderstood palace, the most playful and fantastical of all historic British royal residences.

The Royal Pavilion estate was purchased by the Corporation of Brighton in 1850 and remained in their safe hands until 2020, when it came under the care of a new charitable trust, Brighton & Hove Museums. This book aims to capture the building's unique magnificence for a new audience and also stands as a tribute to all of those who have cared for the building so lovingly in the past 175 years. Since the 1860s, there has been a gradual process of attempting to return the Royal Pavilion to its original appearance as created by George in the early 1820s.

The building and garden remain challenges to conserve and manage, and to balance conservation with providing public access. The former is a core responsibility of any heritage managers, the latter both essential and a joy, but also increasingly a necessity to provide much needed income. 2025 will see the start of a major programme of restoration in the Garden, and the Royal Pavilion will also shortly require a major capital investment.

In the meantime, the stories we tell and the way in which we tell them evolve to reflect the society we live in. At Brighton & Hove Museums we look forward to continuing to care for this precious building for current and future generations while continuing to think of different ways to shine a light on its uniqueness. This book and the research behind it will be a powerful building block as we plan for the future.

(opposite, detail) One of the painted clerestory windows in the Entrance Hall (21st century reproduction by Anne Sowden)

'A Vision in a Dream'

A fragment?

The Royal Pavilion in Brighton, on the south coast of England, is perhaps the most daring and enchanting example of a building that expresses the European fascination with what in the early nineteenth century was considered the 'Orient', in particular China and India. With its sprawling assortment of domes, minarets, towers, upswept roofs, scalloped windows, arches and fretwork screens, the Pavilion forms an intriguing and unique roofline against the everchanging skies of the English coast (figs 0.1 and 0.2).

The Pavilion was created between 1787 and *c.*1823 by George, Prince of Wales (b. 1762–d. 1830), who became Prince Regent (1811–20) and subsequently King George IV (1820–30) (fig. 0.3). Over the course of more than 35 years – almost his entire adult life – he created a spectacular 'playground by the sea' that boasts one of the most colourful interiors of any historic building in the country.

George, who loved partying and entertaining, was generous as well as self-obsessed, sophisticated as well

0.1 *(previous page)* The north end of the west front of the Pavilion in *c.*1823, after Augustus Charles Pugin, aquatint from John Nash's *The Royal Pavilion at Brighton*, 1826

0.2 *(opposite, detail)* The west front of the Pavilion in *c.*1823, after Augustus Charles Pugin, aquatint from John Nash's *The Royal Pavilion at Brighton*, 1826

0.3 Mosaic portrait of George IV in garter robes by Dominico Moglia (after Sir Thomas Lawrence), 1829

0.4 *Brighthelmston, Sussex*, pencil, ink and watercolour drawing by Joseph Mallord William Turner, *c.*1824

as overly excitable. This helps us to understand the building, but its story is more nuanced than that. The Royal Pavilion sprang almost entirely from George's creative mind, but it also, as this book will show, reflects the cultural and philosophical mindset of his time. The building as we see it now, with its Indian-inspired exterior, was the work of the renowned architect John Nash (1752–1835), but several other gifted and inventive architects, artists and designers contributed, both directly and indirectly, to its appearance, and to how it was (and still is) experienced.

Today it looks like a fragile artefact carved in ivory, silhouetted faintly against the incongruous architectural urban clutter of twenty-first-century Brighton, but it has always been different and distinctive, displaying a dreamy, ephemeral quality that was captured in words and images by many writers and artists. Blink and you miss it in J.M.W. Turner's 1824 watercolour of Brighton as seen from a bobbing boat just off the coast (fig. 0.4), but it is there, making its presence felt in a subtle, bewildering way. Its bulbous domes, tent-shaped roofs and intricate minarets break up the predicable Georgian panorama and lure your eyes away from the dramatic waves and the imposing structure of the Chain Pier.

In 1951, Clifford Musgrave, the Director who steered the Pavilion through the difficult years of the Second World War, described it as resting 'on its lawns by the sea as though it had drifted down in a night of oriental enchantment',[1] like a jewel that had simply appeared, fully formed and perfect in its magical beauty. Musgrave was undoubtedly influenced by Samuel Taylor Coleridge's lines 'The shadow of the dome of pleasure / Floated midway on the waves' from his poem *Kubla Khan: or A Vision in a Dream*. Musgrave gave his book the title *Royal Pavilion: A Study in the Romantic* – changing it in a new, larger edition eight years later to *Royal Pavilion: An Episode in the Romantic* – and made a compelling case for it as 'one of the great monuments of the Romantic era'.[2] Musgrave was not the first, nor the last, writer who had noticed the romantic, dreamy character of the building, and the visual similarities to some of the best-known poetic works of the period.[3] It is uncanny how many of its elements seem to be a manifestation in stone, stucco and paint of Kubla's 'stately pleasure dome' in Xanadu as described in Coleridge's poem and in Samuel Purchas's seventeenth-century account of Marco Polo's thirteenth-century travels to China, which was Coleridge's inspiration:

> In the centre of these grounds, where there is a beautiful grove of trees, he has built a royal pavilion, supported upon a colonnade of handsome pillars, gilt and varnished. Round each pillar a dragon, likewise gilt, entwines its tail, while its head sustains the projection of the roof, and its talons or claws are extended to the right and left along the entablature. The roof is of bamboo cane, likewise gilt, and so well varnished that no wet can injure it . . .[4]

Although there is no proven direct link between the Royal Pavilion and descriptions of Kubla's palace, the time frame is intriguing: Coleridge's *Kubla Khan* was first published in 1816[5] (although it had been composed nearly two decades earlier), while William Marsden's translation of *Marco Polo's Travels* appeared in 1818, coinciding with the period in which Brighton's Pavilion was undergoing its most dramatic extension and redecoration. These and other Romantic literary sources may have directly influenced Nash, his interior designers, and even George, but the fanciful evocation of an 'oriental' pavilion in a lush setting was also more generally an expression of the Romantic imagination, which liberally used Asian metaphors, motifs and images. There is also a more personal connection between Coleridge and George: in 1825, the King granted the ailing poet a pension of £100 per year.

The Royal Pavilion is a building that draws you in, takes you on a journey, and plays with your senses. George's guests would have enjoyed a multi-sensory experience, encountering ever more colour, shimmer and sparkle the further they progressed through the building (figs 0.5, 0.6, 0.7 and 0.8). Soft, thick carpets in almost every room would muffle footsteps, but there would have been a cacophony of voices, the tinkling of crystals and ornaments on chandeliers and pagodas, the clatter of the serving of food and drink, and there was, of course, music. The state rooms were perfumed, and

0.5 The Octagon Hall in *c.*1823, after Augustus Charles Pugin, aquatint from John Nash's *The Royal Pavilion at Brighton*, 1826

0.6 The Entrance Hall in *c.*1821 or later, after Augustus Charles Pugin, aquatint from John Nash's *The Royal Pavilion at Brighton*, 1826

underfloor heating would have made the Pavilion a cosy and at times overheated place. Dinners, balls and concerts were the most exciting social events at George's court, and at Brighton he created the most dazzling interiors for these occasions. On a visit in January 1822, the sharp-tongued Russian Princess Lieven commented on the exuberant and intoxicating atmosphere at the Pavilion during an extended dinner: 'I do not believe that, since the days of Heliogabalus, there have been such magnificence and luxury. There is something effeminate in it which is disgusting. One spends the evening half-lying on cushions; the lights are dazzling; there are perfumes, music, liqueurs.' She reports that the Duke of Wellington's reaction to this decadence was, 'Devil take me, I think I must have got into bad company.'[6]

Although she was prone to exaggeration, her comments on the atmosphere in the Pavilion are crucial in understanding its creation, its design schemes, and its purpose: this was a building designed and destined to impress, to dazzle and to transport visitors into a different world, at least for a few hours. There are, at the same time, some darker and questionable aspects to the Pavilion and its creators, notably the conspicuous display of royal wealth and privilege and the murky area between cultural inspiration and appropriation. We may also interpret some of the Royal Pavilion's features as notions of colonial aspiration.

This book will look at how this poetic building floated into existence, and by what material and intellectual means George, his architects and his artists and decorators created a pleasure palace of such playful and stimulating aesthetics. It will focus mainly but not exclusively on how the building's interiors developed from the early 1800s to the mid-1820s. This is a period in the Pavilion's history for which we have rich visual and textual sources and documentation, and George commissioned a book that captured the Pavilion, the garden and the stables complex at the time, which suggests that he considered them complete and finished

0.7 The Long Gallery in *c.*1820-23, after Augustus Charles Pugin, aquatint from John Nash's *The Royal Pavilion at Brighton*, 1826

– although, had he lived longer, he would no doubt have made further changes (figs 0.9, 0.10, 0.11 and 0.12). The Pavilion was a royal residence and needs to be viewed in the greater context of court style. For George it was a place where rules were different and more relaxed than at the London court, and where he could and would push boundaries, and even go to extremes.

One of the most prominent aspects of 'oriental' interiors in general and the Pavilion in Brighton in particular was the use of colour. This will form a major thread running through this book, from George's lavish use of a vibrant new yellow pigment (fig. 0.13) in an entire suite of private rooms, to the subtlest of uses of a transparent red glaze on the inside of silvered wooden bells (fig. 0.14). Musgrave, writing in the catalogue of the first Regency Festival held in Brighton in 1946, recognised the importance of colour as a defining feature in the Pavilion and in the historical context of chinoiserie: 'A Chinese style had been adopted for the interior in 1803, but a more richly coloured and exuberant manner than the conventional "chinoiserie style" which had previously been fashionable.'[7] He also more specifically linked new attitudes to colour with Romanticism: '[The Georgian period] was then, as now, a period when art and decoration were moving out of a phase of strictness and severity into a more romantic and richer tendency, and Regency colour harmonies have inspired much of the philosophy of colour of our own day' (fig. 0.15).[8]

Building on the theme of royal tastes as well as wider cultural circumstances and fashions in architecture and interior decoration, this book will begin by providing an overview of the complex history of the Pavilion during royal ownership, from 1787 until the sale of the estate by Queen Victoria in 1850. Chapter 1, *Creating a Stately Pleasure Dome: The Development of the Royal Pavilion*, outlines the building phases and key people

0.8 The Music Room in *c.*1822, after Augustus Charles Pugin, aquatint from John Nash's *The Royal Pavilion at Brighton*, 1826

0.9 *(opposite)* The ground plan of the Pavilion estate in *c.*1823, after Augustus Charles Pugin, aquatint from John Nash's *The Royal Pavilion at Brighton*, 1826

0.10 *(below)* The centre part of the east front in *c.*1822, after Augustus Charles Pugin, aquatint from John Nash's *The Royal Pavilion at Brighton*, 1826

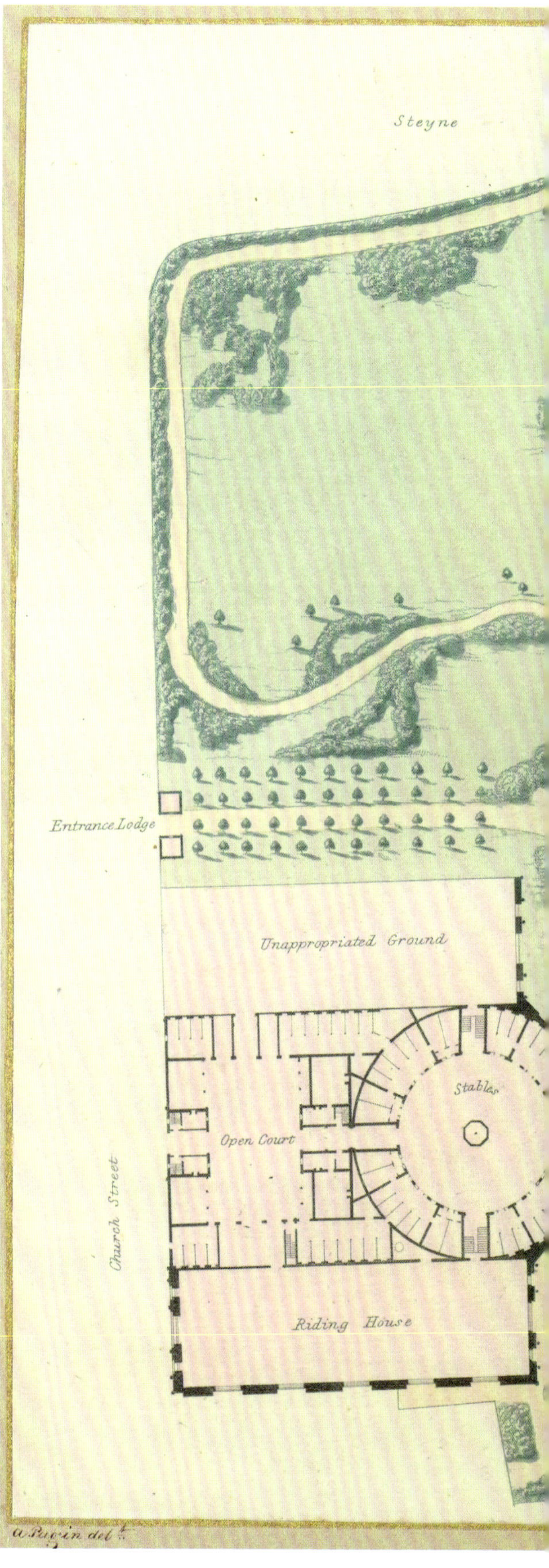

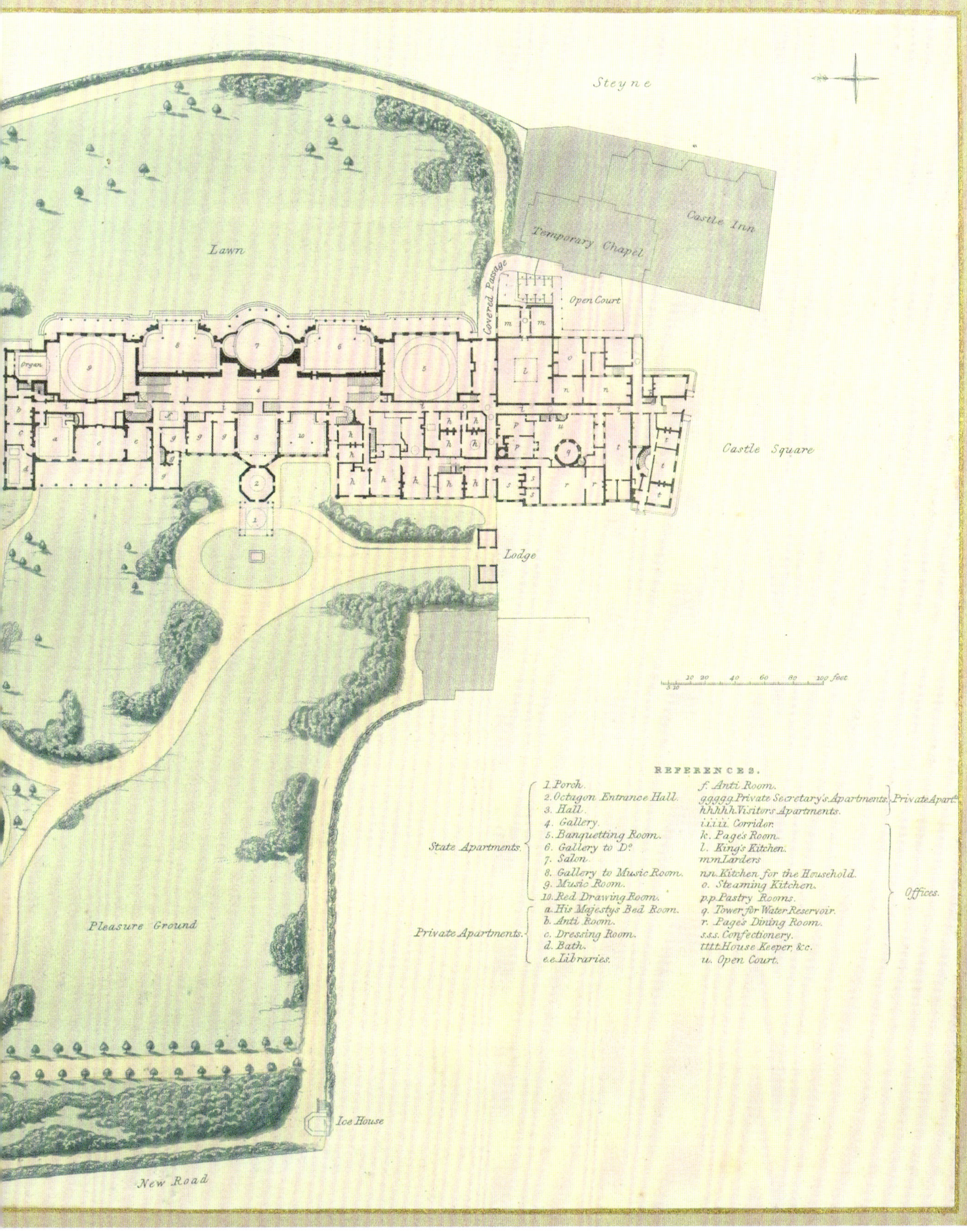

Steyne
Lawn
Castle Inn
Temporary Chapel
Covered Passage
Open Court
Organ
Castle Square
Lodge
20 20 40 60 80 100 feet
Pleasure Ground
Ice House
New Road
REFERENCES.
State Apartments.
1. Porch.
2. Octagon Entrance Hall.
3. Hall.
4. Gallery.
5. Banquetting Room.
6. Gallery to D^o.
7. Salon.
8. Gallery to Music Room.
9. Music Room.
10. Red Drawing Room.
Private Apartments.
a. His Majestys Bed Room.
b. Anti Room.
c. Dressing Room.
d. Bath.
e.e. Libraries.
f. Anti Room.
ggggg. Private Secretary's Apartments.
hhhhh. Visitors Apartments.
Private Apart^s.
iiiii. Corridor.
k. Page's Room.
l. King's Kitchen.
mm. Larders
nn. Kitchen for the Household.
o. Steaming Kitchen.
p.p. Pastry Rooms.
q. Tower for Water Reservoir.
r. Page's Dining Room.
s.s.s. Confectionery.
tttt. House Keeper, &c.
u. Open Court.
Offices.

0.11 *(opposite above)* The north elevation of the stables building in *c.*1823, after Augustus Charles Pugin, aquatint from John Nash's *The Royal Pavilion at Brighton*, *c.*1820

0.12 *(opposite below)* The garden front of the stables building in *c.*1823, after Augustus Charles Pugin, aquatint from John Nash's *The Royal Pavilion at Brighton*, *c.*1820

who contributed to the Pavilion's creation, beginning with a brief section on George as a collector, patron of the arts and mastermind of the Brighton project. The lesser-known first neoclassical phase (fig. 0.16) with some interiors by Biagio Rebecca (1734/5–1808) will be touched on, followed by a section on the changes that were introduced in the early 1800s. John Nash will be discussed in connection with his magnificent picture book *The Royal Pavilion at Brighton*, published in 1826 and based on artwork provided by Augustus Charles Pugin (1768/9–1832).

George's principal designers John Crace (1754–1819) and his son Frederick Crace (1779–1859) and their working practices will be introduced (fig. 0.17), as well as the elusive Robert Jones (active 1815–35) (fig. 0.18), designer of some of the greatest Pavilion interiors from 1815 onwards. Another key figure is Humphry Repton (1752–1818), a landscape gardener and designer who was commissioned by George to present a new scheme for the entire Pavilion estate in 1805 (fig. 0.19). This was never implemented, but

0.13 *(below)* The North Yellow Bow Room on the chamber floor

0.14 *(right)* A carved, silvered and glazed bell from the Banqueting Room, decorated by Robert Jones, *c.*1817

we owe to Repton some rare images and descriptions of the Pavilion in the early 1800s, and he influenced the later designs by Nash. The chapter finishes with a brief overview of the 'civic life' of the Royal Pavilion after it was sold by Queen Victoria in 1850 (fig. 0.20), and how it is used and presented today.

Chapter 2, *Escaping to Other Worlds: Chinoiserie and the Royal Pavilion*, will place the Royal Pavilion in the wider context of orientalism and chinoiserie in the decorative arts and architecture. The printed, visual and other sources that inspired chinoiserie designs generally will be outlined, along with those that influenced George, his architects and designers directly. The work of William Chambers (1723–96) will be discussed, as well as the images created by William Alexander (1767–1816) (fig. 0.21) a generation later, both of which left a mark on the Pavilion. George's own engagement with chinoiserie will be charted, from his seeing Chambers's buildings (fig. 2.2) at Kew and the inspiration he gained from his mother's and sisters' tastes, to his first experiments with chinoiserie at Carlton House in London (figs. 1.16, 1.17 and 3.45). A section of the chapter will examine George's direct involvement with designing and decorating the Pavilion.

0.15 *(opposite)* The west side of the Music Room

0.16 *(above)* The west front the Marine Pavilion, watercolour and ink drawing by Henry Holland, *c.*1787

0.17 *(below) The Royal Bird Foo Hum*, watercolour and ink drawing by Frederick Crace for the Royal Pavilion, *c.*1815

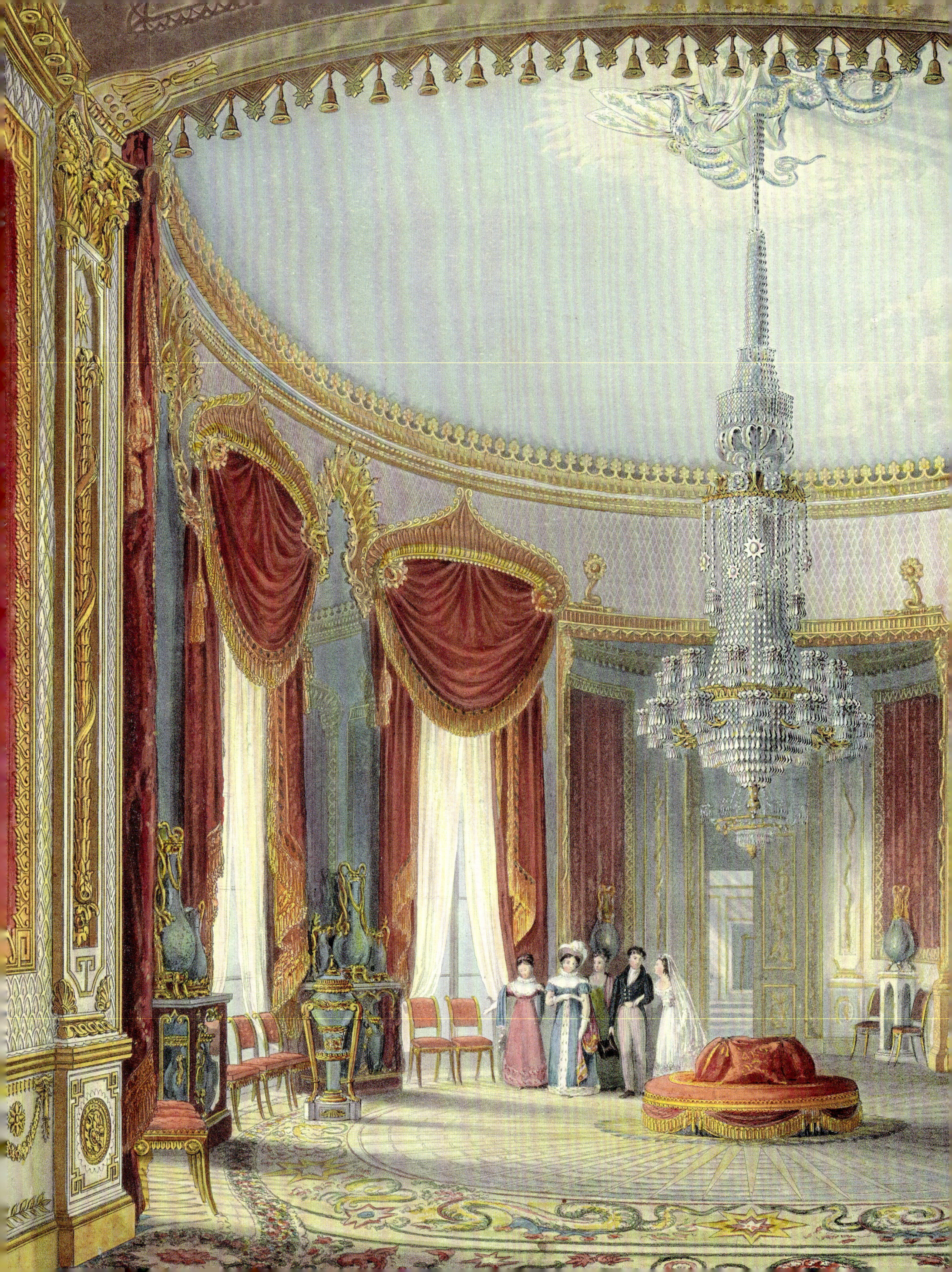

0.18 The Saloon as designed by Robert Jones in *c.*1823, after Augustus Charles Pugin, aquatint from John *Nash's The Royal Pavilion at Brighton*, 1826

One of the aims of this chapter is to site the Royal Pavilion at its particular point in cultural history, when Britain's fascination with what was considered the 'Orient', and in particular China, was gradually changing in response to political and cultural developments. The last part of the chapter will take the focus away from the inner realm of the court and the Pavilion's aristocratic guests, with a close examination of responses to the building in contemporary popular literature, and how its 'oriental' features were described, judged and interpreted in the nineteenth century.

In the final chapter, *'A Splendour of Light and Colour': Colour, senses and sensuality in the Royal Pavilion*, the interiors of the Royal Pavilion in their most complete and finished form in the mid-1820s will be described, along with how they were experienced. The focus will be on the crucial role that colour, lighting and reflective surfaces played in the experience and appearance of the Royal Pavilion, and its pioneering role in interior design. The chapter will also explain the historical background to the richly coloured and highly ornamented decorative schemes of the building (fig. 0.22), including new attitudes to colour that emerged in the Romantic Age and the availability of new, synthetic pigments, as well as a heightened sense of the psychological effects of colour and light. Colour and surface shine are discussed here as one of the key signifiers of 'oriental' and chinoiserie objects. The chapter includes a room-by-room imagined walk into and through the Royal Pavilion in the 1820s, focusing on how the carefully planned and balanced decorative schemes would have been experienced by visitors. It finishes with a detailed examination of the uses of silver as a harmonising colour and surface finish in the building, set in the greater context of silver in other European interiors and its significance in chinoiserie schemes.

0.19 *(below)* Design for the Royal Pavilion (*North Front towards the Parade*), aquatint from Humphry Repton's *Designs for the Pavillon at Brighton*, published 1808

0.20 *(opposite) Her Most Gracious Majesty Victoria 1st As She appeared at the Royal Pavilion, Brighton, previous to mounting Her favourite Arabian Horse*, coloured lithograph by H. Jones, 1838

H. Jones Lith.
Day & Haghe Lithrs to the Queen.
HER MOST GRACIOUS MAJESTY VICTORIA 1ST
As She appeared at the Royal Pavilion, Brighton, previous
to mounting Her favorite Arabian Horse.

*****

The Royal Pavilion has been in municipal ownership since 1850, when George's niece Queen Victoria sold the building and estate to the Town Commissioners of Brighton. Since 2020, the Royal Pavilion and its associated museums have formed an independent organisation, the Royal Pavilion & Museums Trust, going by the name of Brighton & Hove Museums. The Royal Pavilion Archives and the Fine and Decorative Art collections at Brighton & Hove Museums contain a rich and important array of original drawings, printed materials and other artwork, letters, manuscripts and documentation relating to the Royal Pavilion and its garden.

Among the manuscript sources are several inventories from the time of royal ownership, and various accounts relating to George's expenditure on buildings. The most reliable descriptions of the Royal Pavilion interiors are found in the Crace Ledger, an early-twentieth-century transcript of ledger entries from the books of Messrs Crace & Sons made during the time spent in the Royal Pavilion in 1802–4, 1815–19 and 1820–23. The original documents were once in the possession of Messrs Cowtan & Sons Ltd, who acquired them on taking over the business of Messrs Crace & Sons in 1899. The originals are now believed lost. Additional extensive archival material on the Royal Pavilion is available in the Royal Archives, the British Library and the Lord Chamberlain's bill books (National Archives, Kew).

The visual materials in the collections of Brighton & Hove Museums are equally important, as well as beautiful. Among them are hundreds of sheets and fragments of Chinese wallpaper and export paintings, and 40 original drawings by Augustus Charles Pugin, the latter dating

0.21 *(below)* 'The Habitation of a Mandarin', from William Alexander's *The Costume of China*, 1805 (plate first printed in 1799)

0.22 *(opposite)* The window side of the Music Room at clerestory level

0.23 *(overleaf)* South ('Blue') Drawing Room (later the Banqueting Room Gallery), watercolour drawing by Augustus Charles Pugin, before 1821

0.24 Exterior of the Royal Pavilion, watercolour drawing by Augustus Charles Pugin, *c.*1822

from between 1818 and 1823 (figs 0.23, 0.24 and appendix). In the absence of surviving architectural plans, Pugin's drawings and the engravings based on them provide the closest approach we will ever have to Nash's and George's complete picturesque vision.

John and Frederick Crace are represented by around 230 drawings as well as a sketchbook containing a further 68 drawings (fig. 0.25). These show that many of their designs were influenced by Chinese porcelain, enamels and embroidered textiles. While the more complete and more detailed Crace designs for the interiors are in the Cooper Hewitt, Smithsonian Design Museum in New York (figs. 2.39, 2.41 and 2.43), Brighton & Hove's collection of smaller drawings allows us to trace many of the motifs in the Pavilion and give us a sense of how the Craces worked. In addition, there are a few rare drawings by the artists Robert Jones (fig. 0.26) and William Alexander (fig. 1.74) and around 200 ground plans and designs by Joseph Henry Good (1775–1857), who surveyed the estate in the early 1830s (figs 0.27 and 0.28), as well as many more early printed books and drawings of the Royal Pavilion and Brighton (figs 0.29 and 0.30). Many of these designs were included in the encyclopaedic book by the former Museum Director John Morley, *The Making of the Royal Pavilion, Brighton* (1984), which remains the most meticulously researched work on the building and estate, but many of the original artworks have been newly photographed for the present book and are reproduced here for the first time in colour.

A note on terminology: many of the terms and labels associated with the Royal Pavilion and its stylistic features concern the wider history of colonialism and imperialism. The terminology associated with chinoiserie and orientalism is by nature complex, contentious and sensitive, and constantly needs to be re-evaluated and critically discussed when writing about a subject like the Royal Pavilion. Where terms and descriptions are used that are no longer appropriate or accurate, they

0.25 *(opposite above)* Watercolour drawing of a fish, tassel pendant and a carved pole, from Frederick Crace's Sketchbook with 68 coloured designs from Chinese ornaments, *c.*1800–20

0.26 *(opposite below)* Design for the Banqueting Room, watercolour drawing by Robert Jones, *c.*1816

will appear strictly in their historical context and, where necessary, will be contextualised or put in inverted commas (as, for example, in 'the East' or 'the Orient'). The identification of places, countries and regions of origin will, wherever possible, be referred to in a neutral and strictly geographical sense. The Prince of Wales, Prince Regent and later King George IV is, for the sake of neatness, referred to as George throughout, except where it is important to mention his current title. Likewise, the Royal Pavilion is referred to as 'the Pavilion' unless it is crucial to refer to its earlier incarnation as the 'Marine Pavilion', built by Henry Holland.

0.27 *(above)* Design for the North Gate area, watercolour, ink and pencil drawing by Joseph Henry Good, 1834

0.28 *(below) Elevation of the east side of a building proposed to be erected at the Royal Pavilion, Brighton*, watercolour, ink and pencil drawing by Joseph Henry Good, 1832

0.29 *(opposite above) The Steine Front of the Marine Pavilion*, watercolour drawing by James Bennett, 1797

0.30 *(opposite below)* The east lawns open to the public, shortly after the sale of the Pavilion, watercolour drawing by Joseph Nash, *c.*1850

卞堂爪喬司
觉叶各府右

CHAPTER 

Creating a Stately Pleasure Dome

The development of the Royal Pavilion

The Pavilion's history began in 1783, when the fun-loving Prince of Wales (figs 1.2 and 1.3), who had just come of age, first visited his uncle the Duke of Cumberland in Brighton. The old fishing town had in the previous three decades become a popular seaside town, or 'watering place', attracting wealthy and aristocratic visitors and investors. It was the closest seaside resort to London, just over 50 miles due south, and could be reached by coach and horses in just four hours (figs 1.4 and 1.5).[1] The architectural appearance of Brighton was changing, with the fishing industry and its traditional cottages being gradually overshadowed by new Georgian multistorey townhouses. George enjoyed spending time in Brighton and in 1784 rented a house through his German Clerk of the Kitchen Louis Weltje (1745–1810), on the site of the present Banqueting Room Gallery of the Pavilion. It overlooked the Steine (figs 1.6 and 1.8), a fashionable area to the north-east of the original medieval fishing village, and at a right angle to the nearby seafront. Weltje would later frequently go to France on

1.1 *(opposite)* One of the South Galleries on the chamber floor, with painted laylights

1.2 *(right)* Portrait of George when Prince of Wales (1779), oil painting on canvas by Alma Gogin (after Sir Joshua Reynolds), oil on canvas, early to mid-twentieth century

the Prince's behalf to buy furniture for his collection. In 1786 George hired the architect Henry Holland to build him a 'Marine Pavilion' (fig. 1.8), incorporating parts of the original rented house. This first building was a two-storey, symmetrical structure in a neoclassical style; elegant and sophisticated, but by no means 'exotic' in appearance in 1802. His Pavilion at Brighton became a place away from the strictures of London court life and his parents, King George III and Queen Charlotte.

In the early years of the 1800s, George began transforming the rather chaste-looking Marine Pavilion into one of the most comprehensive manifestations of an early nineteenth-century European vision of Asia. The first internal Chinese-inspired features were added to the original neoclassical structure by the gifted interior decorators and artists John and Frederick Crace. The greatest change to the exterior was made between 1815 and 1823, when the famous architect John Nash was hired to remodel the neoclassical building into an 'oriental' fantasy palace, inspired by Indian architecture, with a peppering of Gothic features (figs 1.7 and 1.9). Inside, George opted for an equally eclectic, irreverent and playful style. The two largest state rooms with their

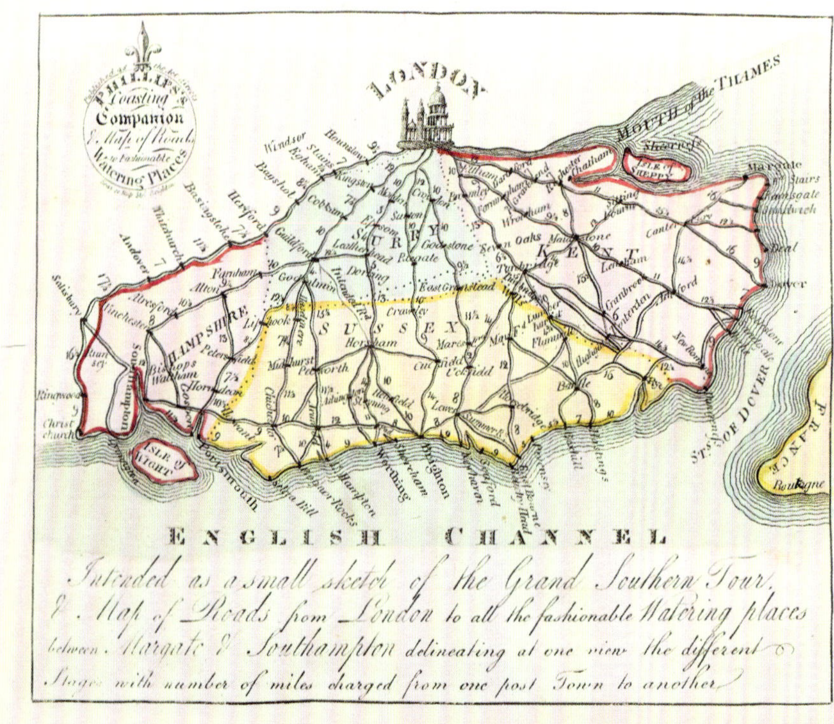

1.3 *(above) The Queen's —* , hand-coloured etching by Samuel William Fores, 1787

1.4 *(opposite)* Map of Brighthelmston, hand-coloured etching by Thomas Yeakell and William Gardner, 1779

1.5 *(left)* Map from *The Three Grand Routes from Brighton to London, and Topography of that Fashionable Watering Place*, hand-coloured etching, 1815

BRIGHTHELMSTON.

References
A. The Theatre
C. Quakers Meeting
D. Presbyterians Meeting
E F. Free Schools
G. Custom House
H. Post Office
I. The Bath
K. Castle Tavern
L. Old Ship Tavern

Church
North Row
Road to LONDON by LEWES
NORTH STREET
WEST STREET
MIDDLE STREET
SHIP STREET
BLACK LION STREET
EAST STREET
Castle Square
THE STEYNE
Road from Shoreham
Road to Rottingdean
Middle Street Cliff
Ship Street Cliff
Black Lion Street Cliff
Battery

A very fine Sand dry at Low Water

Scale of one Quarter of a Mile or Twenty Chains

…aved by Jeakell & Gardner Chichester

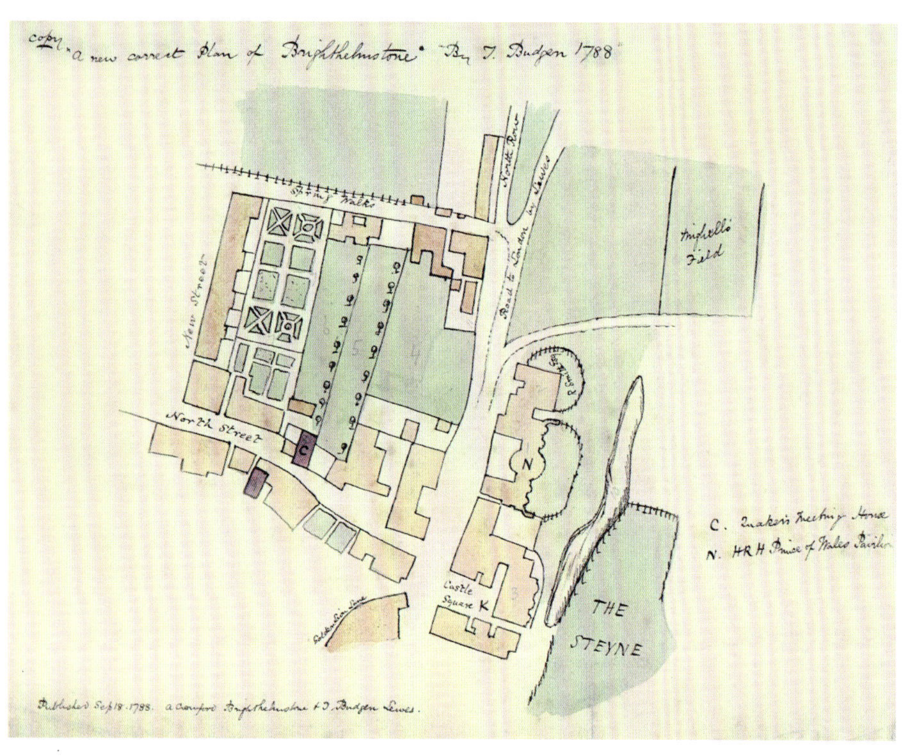

1.6 *(left) A New Current Plan of Brighthelmstone from 1788* by J. Budgen, twentieth-century copy, hand-coloured etching

1.7 *(below)* Outline engraving of the east front of the Pavilion, after Augustus Charles Pugin, from John Nash's *The Royal Pavilion at Brighton*, 1826

1.8 *(opposite above) Pavilion at Brighton* (the Steine front of Henry Holland's Marine Pavilion), engraving by E. Harding after W.N. Gardiner, 1801

1.9 *(opposite below)* The centre part of the west front in *c.*1822, after Augustus Charles Pugin, aquatint from John Nash's *The Royal Pavilion at Brighton*, 1826

PAVILION,

STEYNE FRONT.

GEOMETRICAL ELEVATION.

JOHN NASH, ESQ. ARCHIT. & INVENT.

PAVILION AT BRIGHTON

1.10 *(above)* Longitudinal cross section of the Royal Pavilion in *c.*1823, after Augustus Charles Pugin, aquatint from John Nash's *The Royal Pavilion at Brighton*, 1826

1.11 *(left) Le Kremelin*, engraving by Silvester, *c.*1820s (the print has been cut close to the lettering)

tent-shaped roofs were added by Nash to the north and south ends, whereas the onion-shaped domes and ornamental features in the centre of the Pavilion were built by Nash around and on top of the existing building, with cast iron used as a supporting framework throughout. In typical picturesque and Romantic fashion, rather than present a strictly symmetrical and orderly vision the building and its gardens play with your senses and encourage you to explore and investigate. On the inside, the Craces, whose involvement with the Pavilion began in around 1801, were in 1815 joined by the artist Robert Jones, and together they created a dazzling Chinese-inspired interior, with additional elements lifted from Indian, Egyptian and Japanese art and a sprinkling of Masonic motifs, the whole still underpinned by the French classical tradition (fig. 1.10).

John Nash, as excitable as George in matters of art and design, turned the exterior of the Pavilion into what the essayist William Hazlitt mockingly described as 'a collection of stone pumpkins and pepper-boxes'.[2] It was also frequently compared to the Kremlin – a curious misinterpretation of its Indian-inspired minarets, onion-shaped domes, and traceried balustrades (fig. 1.11). By the early 1820s the Pavilion's transformation was near-complete, and many contemporaries were in awe of this jewel-like building in the middle of a picturesque Regency garden, where newly imported colourful plants from China and India rubbed shoulders with English roses, trees

1.12 The garden front of the Royal Pavilion in *c.*1823, after Augustus Charles Pugin, aquatint from John Nash's *The Royal Pavilion at Brighton*, 1826

and shrubs (fig. 1.12). Although there were some critical and disdainful voices, many expressed their fascination and wonder at the sight of the Pavilion, comparing it to a 'fairy land'[3] or an enchanted palace from the tales of *One Thousand and One Nights*.[4] With his pleasure pavilion by the sea, George had almost single-handedly revived the fashion for chinoiserie, which had experienced the high points of its popularity in the late seventeenth and again in the mid-eighteenth century. Until George's Pavilion, very few Asian-inspired buildings had been created in Europe on this scale and with such confidence. The role and manifestation of the chinoiserie style at the Pavilion will be examined more closely in Chapter 2.

Following George's death in 1830, the Pavilion underwent several alterations under King William IV (r. 1830–37) and Queen Victoria (r. 1837–1901), before the entire building and estate were sold by the Crown to the town of Brighton in 1850 (fig. 0.20).

'THE GREAT JOSS AND HIS PLAYTHINGS': GEORGE IV AND THE ARTS

George was nothing if not daring, often verging on the reckless in his lifestyle, design ideas and spending habits. He is considered one of the great collectors and patrons of the arts in British royal history, with only King Charles I (r. 1625–49) to compare. He was a keen collector of art, in particular Dutch, Flemish and French paintings, but showed little interest in the Italian masters. In view of how and where George placed paintings in the interiors at Windsor Castle, Carlton House and other palaces, it is clear that his fine art collecting was often informed by the vision of a complete interior design scheme. Paintings would be hung in dedicated wall spaces, often on dark red or green backgrounds, framed by gilt mouldings or, in the case of the Chinese export paintings in the Pavilion, stuck directly onto the walls and incorporated into the wallpaper design, complete with trompe l'oeil frames (figs 0.13 and 0.23). The Pavilion never included a dedicated art gallery. Its interiors instead represent complete design schemes, where each decorative object and painting has a

1.13 *The Great Joss and his Playthings*, hand-coloured etching by Robert Seymour, 1829

predominantly decorative value and a specific place in the overall arrangement.

George was keen to promote innovations in architecture, and had an appetite for novelty, expressed in an interior design scheme that can be described as a theatrical spectacle, and was meant to impress. Significantly, a major exhibition at the Queen's Gallery at Buckingham Palace and the Queen's Gallery at the Palace of Holyrood House (2019–21) that showcased George as a collector and patron of the arts, was titled *George IV: Art and Spectacle*.

Early biographers such as Robert Huish[5] tended not to discuss George's collecting habits and architectural passions other than in the context of expenditure and excess, a critical attitude which is reflected in some contemporary caricatures. Robert Seymour's *The Great Joss and his Playthings* from February 1829 (fig. 1.13) is perhaps the caricature that most directly comments on George's extravagant building projects, of which the Pavilion is the most immediately recognisable. Here George is depicted as a rotund Chinese mandarin sitting on a teapot spouting public money, which pays for his expensive hobbies, such as a keeping a live giraffe, and various building projects, including the remodelling of Buckingham Palace, Windsor Castle and the Hyde Park Corner arches. The Pavilion is placed, unmistakably, right behind his head, and the print is embellished with further references to the exterior and interior style of the Pavilion.[6] A similar print by S.W. Fores from 1820, *New Baubles for the Chinese Temple*, again associates George's restless decorating and building activities and his taste for chinoiserie with childishness and immaturity. Various Chinese objects, including a large pagoda, dragons and Chinese figures, frame the scene in which George throws a tantrum after not being allowed an increase in his salary.[7] In *Moments of Pain* and *The Bill Thrown Out* (figs 1.14 and 1.15), both published in November 1820, a forlorn George, dressed as a Chinese emperor and surrounded by Asian porcelain and dragons, receives news of the defeat of the Bill of Pains and Penalties, through which he had tried to dissolve his marriage to Caroline of Brunswick

1.14 *(above left) Moments of Pain*, hand-coloured etching by Samuel William Fores, 1820

1.15 *(above right) The Bill Thrown Out. But the Pains and Pennalties Inflicted*, hand-coloured etching by Samuel William Fores, 1820

and deprive her of her royal titles. Criticism directly aimed at the Pavilion, and by extension the chinoiserie style, was common, and in the medium of caricature the Pavilion represents George's obsession with building and decorating projects of questionable taste and scale.

Twentieth- and twenty-first-century critical literature on George rightly shifted the focus to his role as patron, connoisseur, collector and builder. In his 2001 biography, *The Grand Entertainment*, Steven Parissien devotes two consecutive chapters to this aspect of his character, distinguishing between 'Architectural Patronage' and George as a 'Connoisseur of Fine Art',[8] in which he states that his 'love for art was another characteristic undoubtedly inherited from his father and, more particularly, from his grandfather [Frederick, Prince of Wales]'.[9] Stressing the influence of his father [George III] may seem surprising, given their lifelong differences, but while George III's tastes in art might have been different from his son's, his general attitude to connoisseurship clearly shaped young George's interests. The book that accompanied the abovementioned exhibition, *George IV: Art and Spectacle*, edited by Kate Heard and Kathryn Jones, provides the fullest and most thorough overview of George as a collector and patron of the arts to date, and acknowledges the unparalleled role he played in the history of British art and architecture, and of the Royal Collection in particular.[10]

Many of George's art purchases reflect his excitable nature and fondness for excess. Within the decorative arts, furniture, and silver gilt dominated and throughout his life he had a particular penchant for French art. He chose the Francophile Henry Holland as an architect for the first manifestation of the Pavilion, modelled very closely on the Hôtel de Salm in Paris. Even after the complete 'oriental' transformation of the interior and exterior of the building, French influences remained noticeable in certain decorative features and proportions, as well as in French cuisine as culinary preference. In 1817 he employed the famous French chef Antonin Carême, who made first use of the newly built Great Kitchen and Banqueting Room of the Pavilion.

At his London residence, Carlton House, the French presence was indeed all-pervasive. George was an avid collector of Sèvres porcelain and Boulle furniture. George's *marchand-mercier* Dominique Daguerre supplied and designed much of the furniture, with Holland providing many of the French-inspired exteriors and interiors (figs 1.16 and 1.17). This preoccupation with French art is perhaps best explained by a desire to emulate

1.16 *(above left) Carlton House. North Front*, aquatint after W. Westall, from W.H. Pyne's *The History of the Royal Residences*, 1819. University of Sussex

1.17 *(above right) Grand Staircase. Carlton House*, aquatint after Charles Wild, from W.H. Pyne's *The History of the Royal Residences*, 1819. University of Sussex

the splendours of the court of Louis XIV, and is one of the key themes and influences in the Pavilion. Megan Aldrich argues that the early chinoiserie interiors of the Pavilion, mostly designed by John Crace, are in fact developed from French neoclassical design aesthetics, specifically regarding the structural division of decorative surfaces and the use of bold base colours.[11]

George's largest purchase of decorative art objects came from the Watson Taylor sale on 28 May 1825, supervised by his then principal artistic advisor Sir Charles Long, later Lord Farnborough.[12] Although this sale took place after the completion of the Pavilion interiors, George's choice of purchases, for example several pieces of furniture decorated with Florentine pietra dura panels, confirms that his taste for colourful and highly ornamented objects had not changed. Hugh Roberts comments that 'George IV shared to the full the taste of collectors in the 1820s for furniture decorated in this costly and colourful manner, although in fact his interest in the subject long predated that of most contemporaries.'[13]

THE PEOPLE WHO SHAPED THE PAVILION: ARCHITECTS, ARTISTS AND DESIGNERS

The development of the Pavilion's interiors under George can be roughly divided into three stages: the neoclassical phase from 1787 to *c.*1802, the first chinoiserie scheme from *c.*1801/2 to *c.*1815, and the later chinoiserie schemes, which are concurrent with John Nash's transformation from *c.*1815 to *c.*1823. Within this last phase, several areas of the Pavilion underwent complex and frequent changes and redecorations. Several changes to the layout of the Pavilion and its interiors were carried out by both William IV and Queen Victoria, who visited five times between 1837 and 1845 (the first eight years of her reign)[14] before selling it to the town commissioners of Brighton in 1850 (figs 0.20 and 1.18). Both William IV and Victoria embraced the building's style and did not introduce any elements that were entirely different from the existing design schemes.

The neoclassical Marine Pavilion, *c.*1787–1815: Henry Holland and Biagio Rebecca

While the Pavilion is most famous for its Asian-inspired features, it is less widely known that for at least fourteen years (from the completion of Holland's Pavilion in the summer of 1787 until the introduction of chinoiserie interiors in *c.*1801/2) it was painted and decorated in a Pompeian or neoclassical style, reflecting the chaste and

Prince Albert driving the Queen & Princess Royal in their Sledge, at Brighton.

elegant exterior.[15] Holland's building, which incorporated some of the lodging house the Prince of Wales had been renting in the years before, consisted of a central rotunda capped with a flat dome and flanked by two wings to the north and south (figs 1.19–1.23). On the ground floor these wings are now occupied by the Banqueting Room Gallery and Music Room Gallery, but before *c.*1803 they were divided into several rooms.[16]

The building was clad in cream-coloured mathematical Hampshire tiles,[17] hung on a timber framework. The tiles contrasted with blue wooden shutters, as can be seen in some coloured images of the pre-1815 Pavilion. Most other buildings in Brighton, especially the more old-fashioned, were built with brick or flints, making this French-influenced Pavilion stand out as a stylish curiosity. Mike Jones suggests that the colour scheme of Holland's building was not accidental or simply an imitation of French style. 'The Whig colours were blue and buff', he points out, and 'the Prince had nailed his colours to the Steine for all to see, confirming his membership for the time being. . . . Later, as if to publicly distance himself from the Whigs, the new Marine Pavilion was to change colour on the outside and the garden became an enclosed space.'[18] There is no documentary evidence for George's use of colour as a political statement, but some buildings opposite the Pavilion on the Steine side are believed to have imitated the blue and buff colour scheme to express their allegiance to the Prince, and perhaps his political leanings as they were then.

Very little is known about the earliest design schemes and furnishings of the interior, since no detailed account books, images, inventories or descriptions survive from this important phase, but despite the professional connection between John Soane and Holland, these early interiors were not of the highly saturated colour varieties later found in Soane's own house in Lincoln's Inn (decorated between 1808 and 1823). The image that emerges from what documentation we have is that of a French-inspired, sober neoclassical style, where some brightly coloured ornamentation was set against a white or stone-coloured background.

An abstract of Weltje's expenditure incurred between 1787 and 1788 at the Marine Pavilion at Brighton was transcribed and published by Henry Roberts in 1935 and gives the impression of an elegant, but not necessarily lavishly furnished, building, which cost a total of £21,454 to build.[19] Both Roberts and Clifford Musgrave quote from an unpublished diary written by a young sightseer, Elizabeth Collett, in which she describes three rooms in the house rented by the Prince of Wales, from which Holland developed the Marine Pavilion: the Prince of Wales's bedroom, the Music Room and another,

1.18 *(left) Prince Albert driving the Queen & Princess Royal in their Sledge, at Brighton,* coloured lithograph by J.W.G., published by Dean & Co., 1845

1.19 *(right)* The Marine Pavilion, after Augustus Charles Pugin, aquatint from John Nash's *The Royal Pavilion at Brighton*, 1826

1.20 *(below left) H.R.H. The Prince of Wales's Pavillion at Brighton* (west front of the Marine Pavilion), watercolour and ink drawing by Henry Holland, *c.*1787

1.21 *(below right) Pavillion* (east front of the Marine Pavilion), watercolour and ink drawing by Henry Holland, *c.*1787

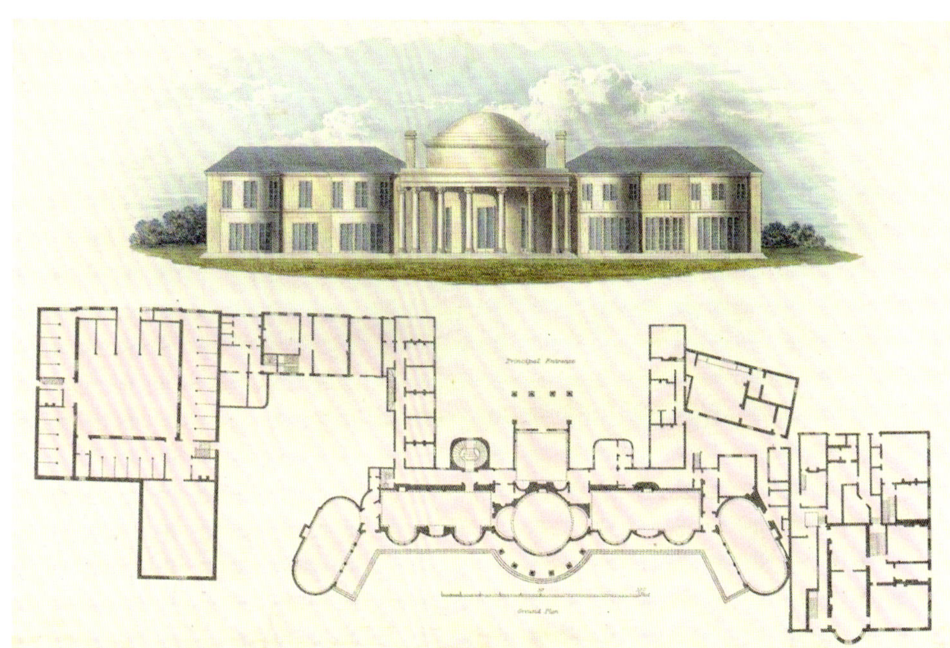

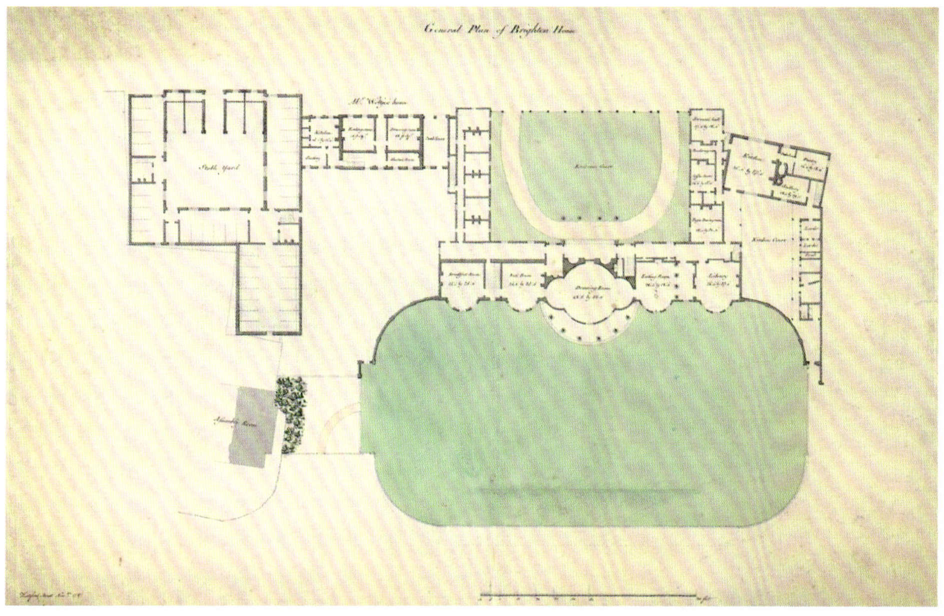

1.22 *(left) Ground plan of Brighton House* (the Marine Pavilion), watercolour and ink drawing by Henry Holland, 1787

1.23 *(overleaf) Brighthelmston. General Plan of the House and Stables with the Grounds next the Stein,* watercolour and ink drawing by Henry Holland, *c.*1787

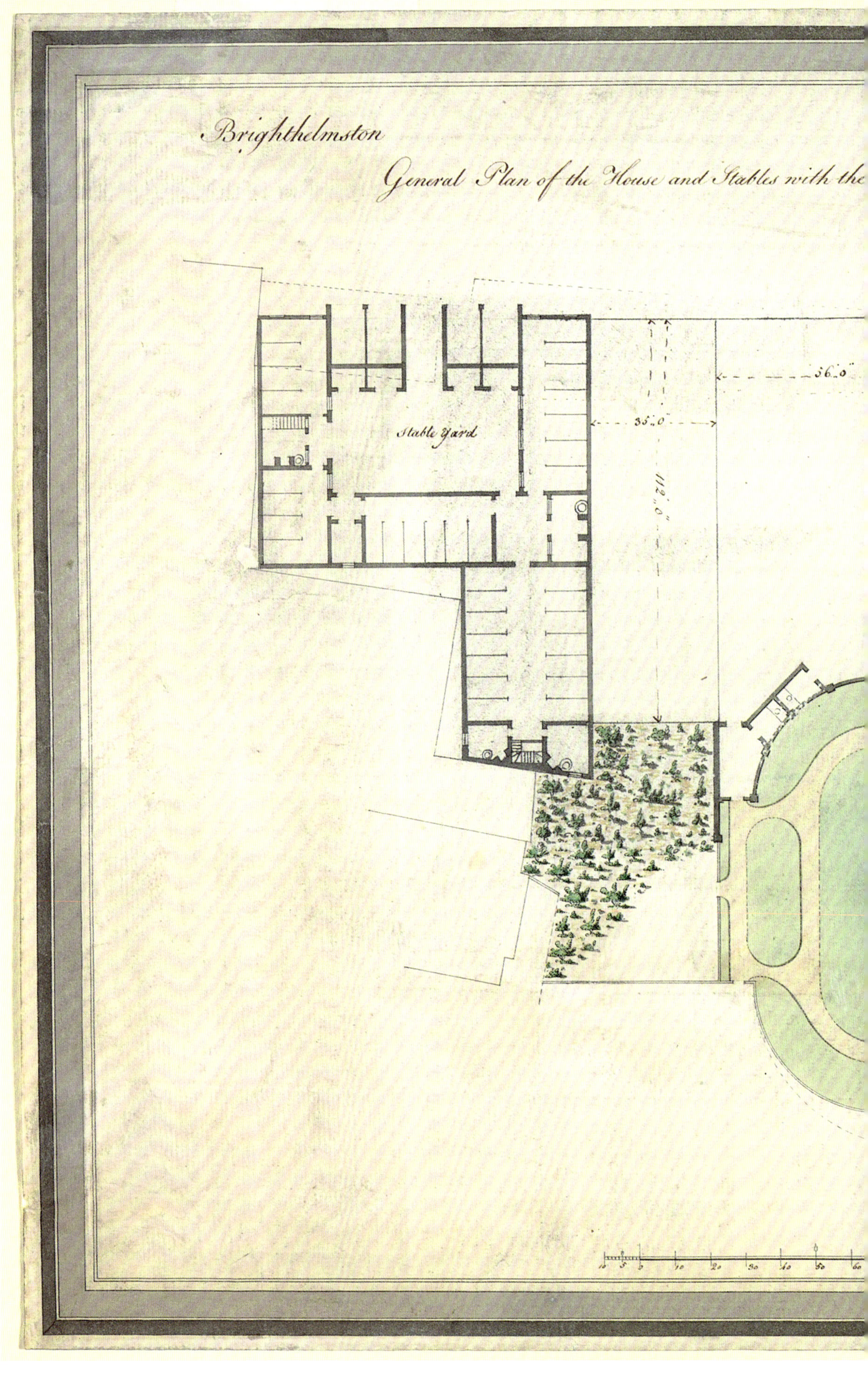

Brighthelmston

General Plan of the House and Stables with the

56.0"

35.0"

Stable Yard

112.0"

10 5 0 10 20 30 40 50 60

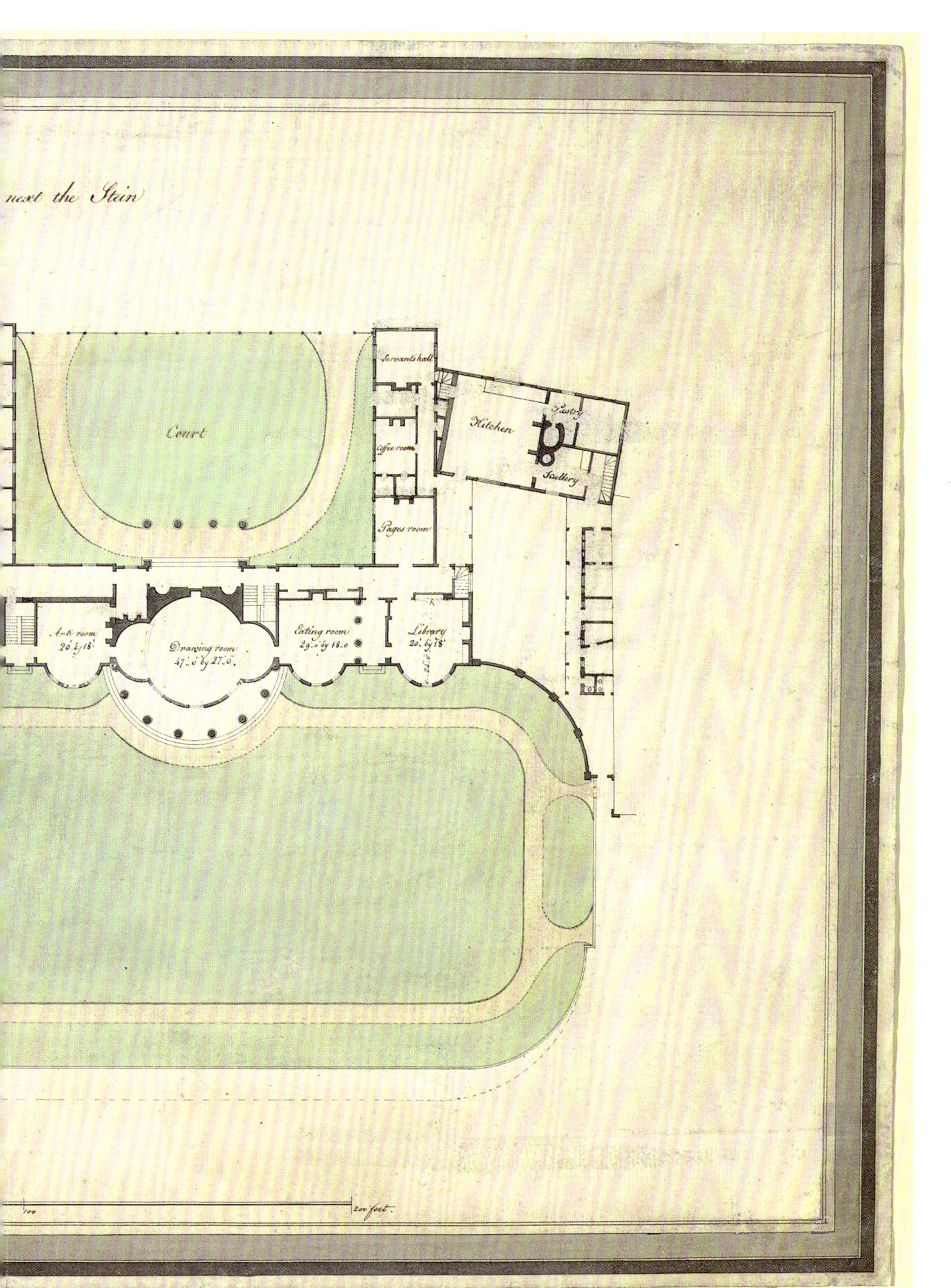

next the Stein
Court
Servants hall
Coffee room
Pages room
Kitchen
Pastry
Scullery
Anti room
20' by 18'
Drawing room
47' 6 by 27' 0
Eating room
29' 0 by 18' 0
Library
20' by 18'
100
200 feet

unidentified room. It is not clear how and why Collett would have gained access to the building, including the royal bedrooms on the chamber floor, but she provides details of some of the furnishings:

> This was really elegant but nothing extravagant, not when it is considered who the inhabitant is; a great deal of taste is displayed through the whole. The bed is placed in a kind of niche or recess and you go up it by steps; in the wall alongside of it is placed a large looking glass. Another room is really whimsical, being full of caricatures, some of which are truly laughable.[20]

There is some doubt as to whether the interiors described here are actually those of the lodging house or of the adjacent Grove House, which was also used by George. It is likely that the date of 1785 attributed to this diary is wrong, since the description of the bedroom is similar to one published in the *Sussex Weekly Advertiser* shortly after the completion of Holland's Marine Pavilion: 'The apartment in which the Prince sleeps is hung with quilted chintz, bordered with gimp; the bed-hanging is of silk, chequered green and white; and near it is a glass, so situated as to afford the Prince an extensive view of the sea and Steine as he lies in bed.'[21] In any case, the white and green fabric scheme and the materials mentioned by Miss Collett and the *Sussex Weekly Advertiser* are entirely typical of neoclassical furnishings and support the assumption that the first interior scheme of the Pavilion was classical and relatively restrained throughout, without any chinoiserie features.

Musgrave suggested that the interior, like the exterior, of Holland's building 'consisted of his characteristic simplification of Adam style, as seen, for example, in the interiors of Brooks's Club, St. James's, or Berrington Hall, Leominster', but also points out the French influence in the decorative scheme and the choice of furniture, the latter most likely acquired by Weltje at art sales in Paris.[22] Intriguingly, Musgrave also informed the reader that the wallpaper in the Library was 'fitted up in the French style' in a brilliant yellow, that the Eating Room was painted yellow and maroon with a sky-blue ceiling, the corridors were painted 'French blue' and the walls of the staircase were painted bright green, contrasting with a grey and white ceiling.[23]

Henry Wigstead's travelogue *An Excursion to Brighthelmstone, Made in the Year 1789* (published in 1790) provides the briefest of descriptions of the building and its interiors in the 1780s, just after their completion. The one room that is singled out is the Saloon, then the largest of the state rooms:

> The Marine Pavilion of HIS ROYAL HIGHNESS THE PRINCE OF WALES, on the West Side of the *Stein*, is a striking Object, and is admirably calculated for the Summer Residence of the Royal Personage for whom it was built; . . . The Furniture is adapted with great Taste to the Stile of the Building. The grand Saloon is beautifully decorated with Paintings by *Rebecca*, executed in his best Manner. The *tout ensemble* of the Building is, in short, perfect Harmony.[24]

The painter mentioned here was the Italian fresco artist Biagio Rebecca. Only very few views of Rebecca's interior survive, one of them a plate after a drawing by Rowlandson illustrating Wigstead's book (fig. 1.24). The image is not reliable regarding ornamental or architectural detail, but it does convey the liveliness and elegance of a grand neoclassical interior, with some typical visible elements, such as stuccoed walls, a domed ceiling composed of small squares and floral swags, oval roundels in the centre of wall compartments, and what appears to be a pale base colour on walls and ceiling. Tinted versions of the prints exist (fig. 1.25), but while they cannot be considered an accurate representation of the Saloon's colours, they do give a good impression of a typical neoclassical colour scheme, comprising a white, grey or stone block wall colour, a shade of green often referred to as pea-green, and contrasting colours introduced by soft furnishings.

Two coloured architectural drawings of wall decorations for the Pavilion survive in the Prints and Drawings collection of the Victoria and Albert Museum, archived in a box with drawings by William Chambers. One of them is inscribed 'This Design for the Great

1.24 *(right)* Interior of the Saloon of the Marine Pavilion, watercolour and ink drawing by Thomas Rowlandson, *c.*1790

1.25 *(below) Saloon at the Marine Pavilion*, hand-coloured etching after Thomas Rowlandson, 1790

SALOON at the MARINE PAVILION

1.26 *(above left)* Decorative roundels, probably from the Saloon, distemper and oil on paper, attributed to Biagio Rebecca, *c.*1787

1.27 *(above right)* Decorative fragment, probably from the Saloon, distemper and oil on paper, attributed to Biagio Rebecca, *c.*1787

Saloon was received from M. Lignereux'.[25] However, there appears to be some confusion about the artist who executed these drawings. Musgrave discussed them as early as 1951, when he still entertained the idea that Chambers had been commissioned to supply designs for the Pavilion interiors.[26] In the new edition of his Pavilion book from 1959, he concluded that they were not in the style of Chambers, but most likely the work of 'one of the several French decorators who produced French grotesque ornament of this kind, such as André de Labrière, who worked for Holland when he built Southill for the Whitbreads'.[27] John Morley later described them as 'two early unexecuted designs . . . in the Etruscan or Pompeian style', probably intended for the wall and cove spaces to the left and the right of the fireplace of the Saloon in Rebecca's phase. In any case, the note referring to Martin-Éloi Lignereux on one of the drawings may simply mean that he was the supplier or sender of the designs. He was a *marchand-mercier* who had been selling Sèvres porcelain and other French objects to George, sometimes via Sir Harry Fetherstonhaugh of Uppark, West Sussex.[28] Morley pointed out that Lignereux was also once paid in association with Dominique Daguerre for work at Carlton House.[29] If Lignereux was the creator of the drawings, then Rebecca might have worked to his designs, but it is much more likely that he was simply importing examples and templates of French designs.

The Saloon decorations as depicted by Rowlandson bear no resemblance to these drawings, but two fragments of wall decoration were recently discovered in the Royal Pavilion Archives that appear to stem from the Rebecca scheme. They are three painted roundels with heads in profile, imitating white marble and in the style of cameos, against a dusty pink background (fig. 1.26), and a single mask-like face with an open mouth, wearing a laurel wreath (fig. 1.27). Their provenance and stylistic features – bright but not highly saturated colours and classical iconography – make it very likely that they are the only known physical survivors of Rebecca's neoclassical Saloon scheme.

An inspection of the V&A drawings revealed that these fragments can be linked to them with near-certainty. Single mask-like faces with wreaths appear in one drawing (V&A: 2216:4) at ceiling level on a frieze, while roundels with white heads in profile can be seen in the other drawing (V&A: 2216:37) on wall panels above the dado level. The overall tonality and figurative details match the Pavilion fragments. These are the only decorative elements that can give us a clearer idea of the colouring of this first interior of the Pavilion, confirming a brightly coloured, but not highly saturated, neoclassical scheme on mostly white ground colour, entirely representative of mid- to late-eighteenth-century French-inspired classicism. The fragments and drawings suggest the motifs and pale colouring associated with a light-toned variety of the Pompeian or Etruscan style, as found in many eighteenth-century British country houses, for example the Etruscan Room at Osterley House in West London, executed by Robert Adam.[30] Other hard evidence of Rebecca's decorations of the Saloon is a layer of green oil paint identified by a microscopic cross-section examination of a piece of original paint from the south apse ceiling.[31] What is known of this first interior design scheme therefore forms a stark contrast to the highly saturated colours and reflective finishes of the 'orientalised' interiors that were to follow in the Pavilion.

Holland's Marine Pavilion may have been relatively modest, elegant and built in a classical style, yet, surprisingly, it was described in the *New Brighton Guide, Or, Companion for Young Ladies and Gentlemen to All the Watering-places in Great Britain* in 1796 as:

> a nondescript monster in building [that] appears like a mad house, or a house run mad, as it has neither beginning, middle, nor end; yet to acquire this design, a miserable bricklayer was dispatched to Italy, to gather something equal to the required magnificence, and actually charged two thousand guineas for his expenses – There are four pillars in *scagliola*, in a sort of an oven, where the Prince dines; and when the fire is lighted, the room is so hot that the parties are nearly baked and incrusted.[32]

It is a curious and somewhat irrational description by the author Anthony Pasquin that should not be taken too seriously, but one wonders whether George's reputation for experimental building and decorating projects had caused this harsh assessment of the eighteenth-century Marine Pavilion. It certainly gave a taste of what was to come in the next two decades.

All change in the new century: William Porden's Royal Stables

In the early years of the 1800s, George made several significant changes to the Pavilion and the garden and toyed with further ideas for a new look for his seaside residence. This was the period when he first introduced 'oriental' elements to the estate and began toning down the classical severity of the building. Between 1801 and 1803 the classical figures that graced the central dome of the Pavilion were removed, and some noticeable structural changes were carried out, including the addition of upcurved green metal canopies for the outside windows. Most importantly, two wings protruding at approximately 60-degree angles from the galleries were added at either end on the east side of the building (visible in the ground plan in fig. 1.19 and in some amateur drawings of the period). These are generally attributed to Peter Frederick Robinson, a pupil of Holland, but it is still unclear whether the designs were his or whether he was supervising the execution of Holland's designs.[33]

Between 1803 and 1805 a new stables complex was erected to the north-west of the Pavilion, to designs by William Porden, with room for at least 60 horses, as well as accommodation for stable staff on the upper level. It was one of the most ambitious and largest buildings of its kind in England, with an adjoining Riding House to the west (figs 0.11, 0.12, 1.28–1.32). The stables complex was inspired by both classical architecture and images of India created by the artists and travellers Thomas and William Daniell in the 1780s, and was the first building on site with external 'oriental' features. The main stable block was at the time the largest domed structure in Britain apart from St Paul's Cathedral in London, measuring 24 metres in diameter, with a height of nearly 20 metres. It dominated the skyline of Brighton in the early nineteenth century and made the Pavilion look rather small by comparison. After his visit in 1805, the landscape designer Humphry Repton described it thus:

> I found in the gardens of the Pavillon [*sic*] a stupendous and magnificent building, which, by its lightness, its elegance, its boldness of construction, and the symmetry of its proportions, does credit both to the genius of the artist and the good taste of his royal employer. Although the outline of the dome

1.28 *(above left)* The interior of Porden's stables (the Rotunda), watercolour and pencil drawing by Augustus Charles Pugin, *c.*1820

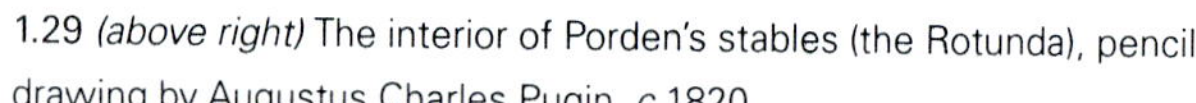

1.29 *(above right)* The interior of Porden's stables (the Rotunda), pencil drawing by Augustus Charles Pugin, *c.*1820

1.30 *(below)* The interior of Porden's stables (the Rotunda) in *c.*1823, after Augustus Charles Pugin, aquatint from John Nash's *The Royal Pavilion at Brighton*, *c.*1820

1.31 *(right) A Front View of His Royal Highness the Prince of Wales's Stables, Brighton,* English school, watercolour and ink drawing, *c.*1806–1811

1.32 *(below)* the interior of Porden's Riding House in *c.*1823, after Augustus Charles Pugin, aquatint from John Nash's *The Royal Pavilion at Brighton*, *c.*1820

> resembles rather a Turkish mosque than the buildings of Hindustan, yet its general character is distinct from either Grecian or Gothic, and must both please and surprise every one not bigoted to the forms of either.[34]

By contrast, Mrs Calvert, who visited in 1807, sharply remarked that the stables 'are a most superb edifice, indeed quite unnecessarily so'.[35]

Most of the original interiors of Porden's stables have been lost and the building has undergone two major internal and external changes since the sale of the estate, in 1867 and in 1934. However, the magnificent barrel-vaulted Riding House to the west of the stables retains many of its original structural features and was sensitively restored between 2018 and 2022. Both buildings are now public event venues.

The Pavilion that never was: Humphry Repton's designs

Humphry Repton visited Brighton at the end of 1805 for a particular reason. He had been commissioned by George to propose plans for the transformation of Holland's neoclassical Pavilion and its garden. Although his proposals were never realised, Repton is an important figure in the history of the estate. He published widely on architecture, design and landscape gardening, at times challenging aesthetic ideas of the picturesque, at other times embracing them.

Repton embarked on a career in landscape gardening in 1788, shortly after the death of Lancelot 'Capability' Brown in 1783. In the vacuum created by the death of Brown he quickly established himself in the field, working for a wide range of clients. Repton became known for lavishly produced portfolios known as 'Red Books' because many of them were bound in red Morocco. These comprised watercolour paintings of 'before and after' views of gardens, landscape settings and even buildings. For maximum visual effect the 'after' views (Repton's own designs) were typically revealed by lifting an overlay pasted onto the sheet.[36] André Rogger has identified a total of 123 Red Books, one of which is of the Pavilion estate and dates from 1806.

Repton had earlier tangible connections with the Pavilion. In *c.*1796 he went into partnership with the then relatively unknown John Nash,[37] and in 1805 he designed the gardens surrounding Samuel Pepys Cockerell's Mughal-style Sezincote House in Gloucestershire, thus forming a stylistic link to both Porden's contemporary stables in Brighton and the later Indian designs for the Pavilion by Repton and Nash. Repton was briefly involved with the Pavilion in the summer of 1795, possibly for the design of a conservatory and in collaboration with Nash,[38] and between 1797 and 1802 to advise on groundwork concerning the extensions to Holland's building.[39]

In November 1805, while Porden's stables were nearing completion, George once again invited Repton to produce designs for the transformation of the Pavilion gardens and the palace itself, having rejected earlier Chinese-style designs by both Holland (1801–2) (fig. 1.33)[40] and Porden (*c.*1805) (figs 1.34, 1.35 and 1.36).[41] Repton worked feverishly on this prestigious royal commission and presented the Pavilion Red Book to George just a month later. It consisted of ambitious, fantastical and elaborate Indian-style designs for the entire estate, complete with 'before and after' views. Two interior views were included: a thickly planted conservatory-style glass corridor, and a dining room with large windows and a highly ornamented plaster ceiling reminiscent of John Nash's style. According to Repton, the Prince responded enthusiastically to the designs, but despite giving Repton hope of 'immediate execution', the project was never realised.[42] Repton saw George again in 1807 in London where he was summoned to an event at Carlton House the following week to discuss plans for a great conservatory, but this project, too, after having been initially accepted, was superseded by another architect's designs.[43]

Short of commissions in the difficult years of the Napoleonic wars, Repton had the Pavilion designs engraved by J.C. Stadler in 1808 and, in a joint effort with Stadler to generate money, published the plans as *Designs for the Pavillon* [*sic*] *at Brighton*, together with a treatise on architectural styles, *An Inquiry into the Changes of Architecture*. The book was dedicated to George, perhaps in the vain hope of rekindling his interest in the designs. The Pavilion portfolio is the only one of Repton's Red Books that was ever published in its entirety, with only minor omissions of the original text (figs 1.37 to 1.54).

1.33 *Brighton Pavilion: Elevation towards the Steyne for the House adjoining the Pavilion/Elevation for decorating the front of the Stable building in the Garden*, ink and watercolour drawing by Henry Holland, 1802

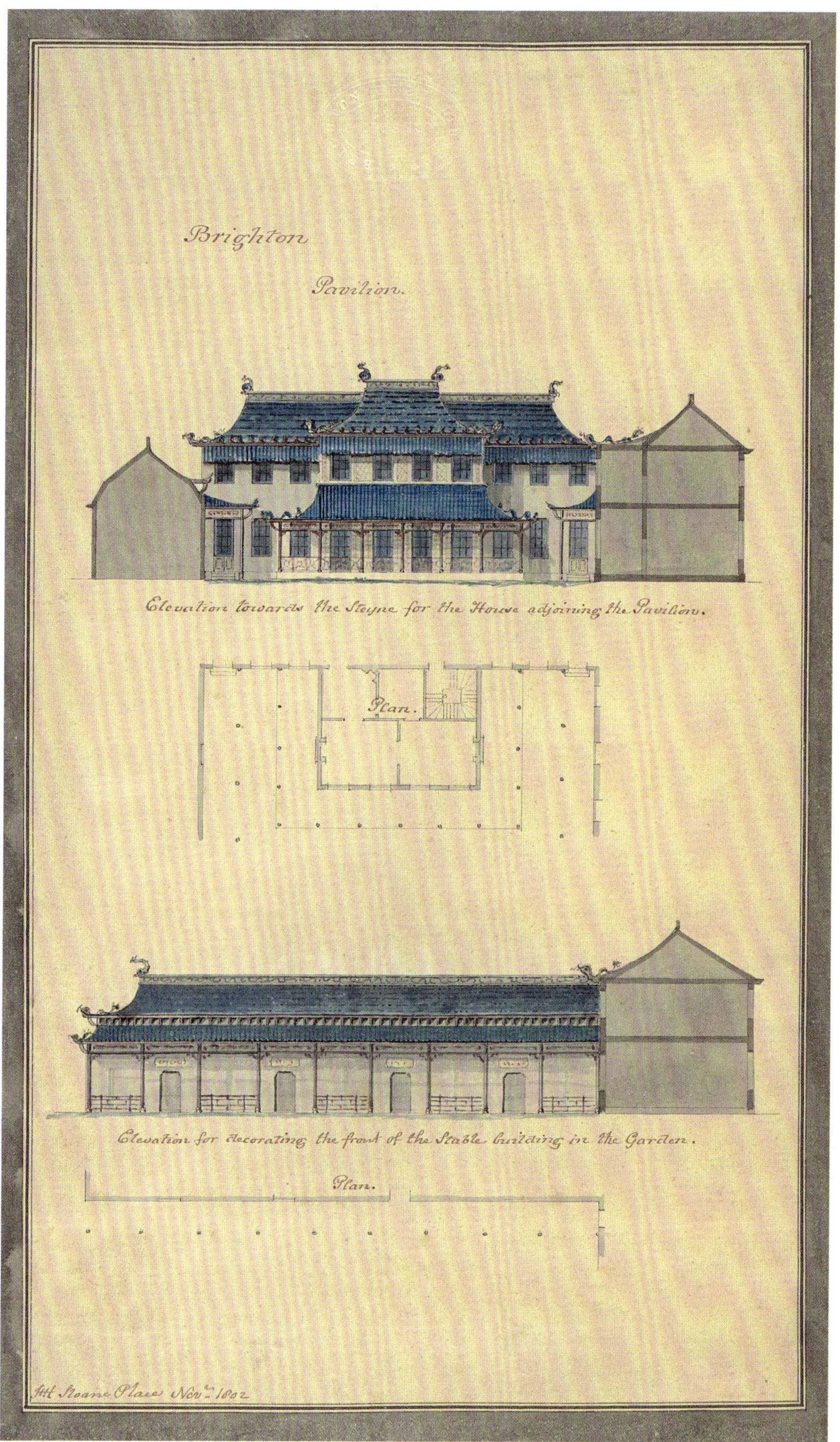
Brighton
Pavilion.
Elevation towards the Steyne for the House adjoining the Pavilion.
Plan.
Elevation for decorating the front of the Stable building in the Garden.
Plan.

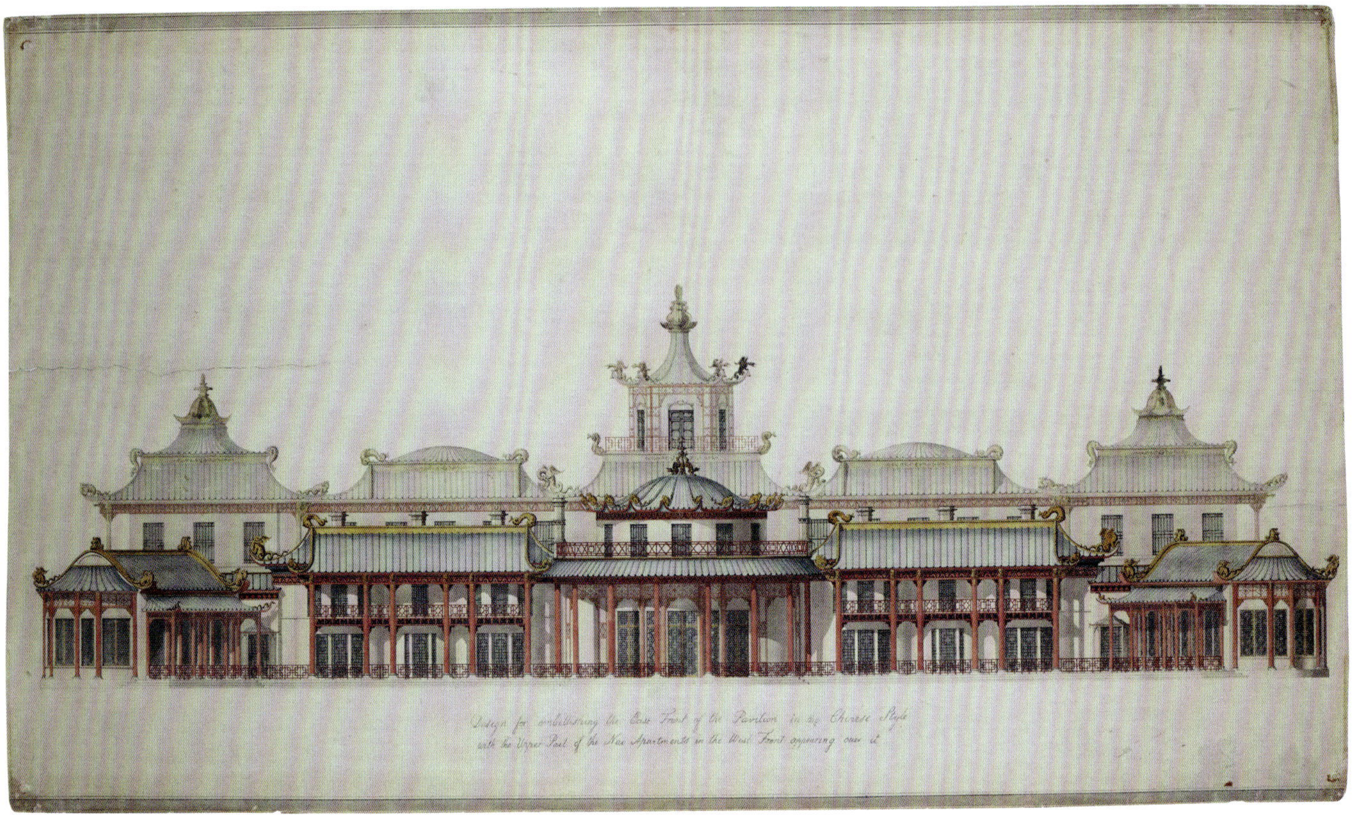

There are few references in Repton's Pavilion designs to interior decoration, but he advocates the use of coloured glass in architecture. In a passage from the Red Book that was not included in the published version, he recommends coloured glass for the purpose of vivid illumination of the interior, but also warns that colours might interfere with views of the surrounding landscape seen through stained-glass windows. His comments display a good understanding of coloured light and suggest that he had followed intellectual discourse on the topic:

> Perhaps more general use may be made of coloured glass in adorning your rooms . . . there is a charming effect of transparency which depends on colour and combination, without the aid of design . . . There is a curious effect from purple glass, of which little advantage has yet been taken; viz. all green objects seen through purple glass appear white and thus a beautified landscape illuminated by the midday sun of Summer will appear a perfect Winter scene covered with snow; the strange effect of contrast may perhaps be worth considering, in a room exposed to the Western sun.[44]

It is likely that Repton was aware of George's interest in coloured glass and illuminated interiors, since the early chinoiserie designs of the Pavilion from *c.*1801/2 included coloured glass in the form of many Chinese lanterns, as well as a 'Glass Passage', created sometime between 1801 and 1803 (pp. 148–151), that connected Holland's building with one of the new angular extensions. Coloured glass would also form a significant element in the post-1815 interior design schemes, including green clerestory windows in the Entrance Hall, painted laylights in the Long Gallery and the North and South Galleries on the chamber floor (see for example, figs 1.1 and 1.56), back lit stained-glass decorations on the North and South Staircase landings, and high-level multicoloured windows in the Banqueting Room and Music Room (fig. 1.55).

1.34 *(opposite above) Design for embellishing the East Front of the Pavilion in the Chinese Style, with the Upper Part of the New Apartments in the West Front appearing over it.* 1.35 *(opposite below)* Design for the Royal Pavilion. 1.36 *Elevation of the West Front for the Pavilion at Brighton, Designed for His Royal Highness the Prince of Wales*, watercolour and ink drawing by William Porden, *c.*1805

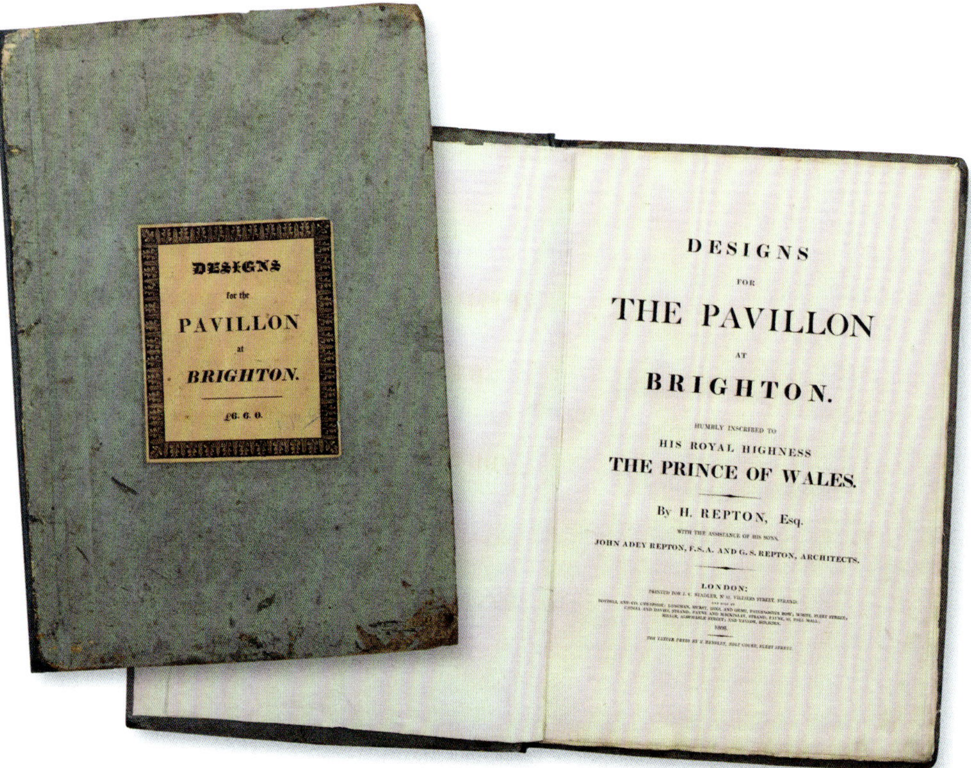

1.37 *(top)* Front board of Humphry Repton's *Designs for the Pavillon at Brighton*, 1808

1.38 *(left)* Title page of Humphry Repton's *Designs for the Pavillon at Brighton*, 1808

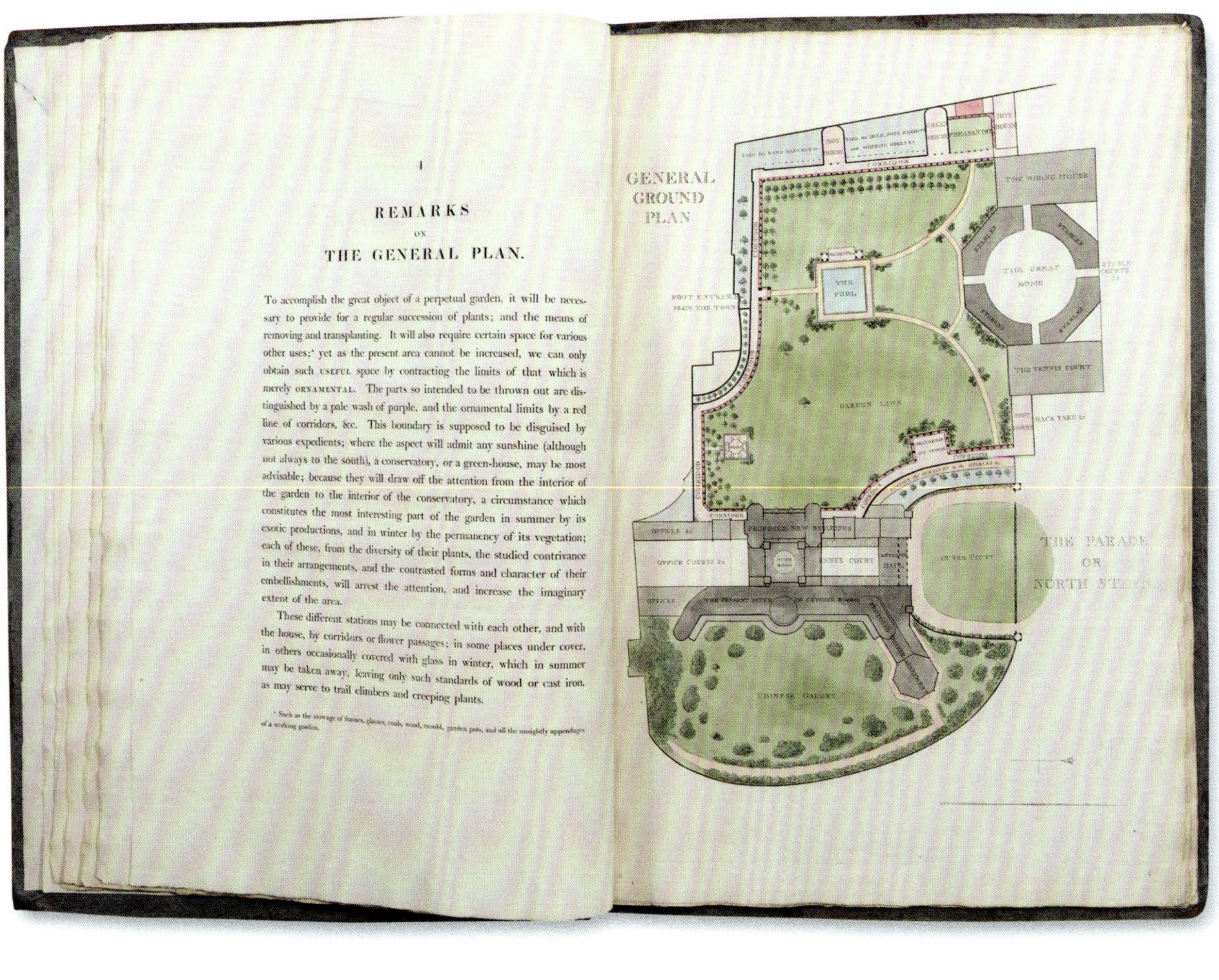

1.39 *(below)* Double page from Humphry Repton's *Designs for the Pavillon at Brighton* showing and describing the *General Ground Plan*, 1808

1

REMARKS
ON
THE GENERAL PLAN.

To accomplish the great object of a perpetual garden, it will be necessary to provide for a regular succession of plants; and the means of removing and transplanting. It will also require certain space for various other uses;* yet as the present area cannot be increased, we can only obtain such USEFUL space by contracting the limits of that which is merely ORNAMENTAL. The parts so intended to be thrown out are distinguished by a pale wash of purple, and the ornamental limits by a red line of corridors, &c. This boundary is supposed to be disguised by various expedients; where the aspect will admit any sunshine (although not always to the south), a conservatory, or a green-house, may be most advisable; because they will draw off the attention from the interior of the garden to the interior of the conservatory, a circumstance which constitutes the most interesting part of the garden in summer by its exotic productions, and in winter by the permanency of its vegetation; each of these, from the diversity of their plants, the studied contrivance in their arrangements, and the contrasted forms and character of their embellishments, will arrest the attention, and increase the imaginary extent of the area.

These different stations may be connected with each other, and with the house, by corridors or flower passages; in some places under cover, in others occasionally covered with glass in winter, which in summer may be taken away, leaving only such standards of wood or cast iron, as may serve to trail climbers and creeping plants.

* Such as the stowage of frames, glasses, coals, wood, mould, garden pots, and all the unsightly appendages of a working garden.

GENERAL
GROUND
PLAN

THE GREAT
DOME

THE TENNIS COURT

GARDEN LAWN

CHINESE GARDEN

OUTER COURT

THE PARADE
OR
NORTH ST

1.40 *(right)* Dedication page of Humphry Repton's *Designs for the Pavillon at Brighton*, 1808

1.41 *(top below)* and 1.42 *(bottom below)* *View from the Dome* with and without overlay, from Humphry Repton's *Designs for the Pavillon at Brighton*, 1808

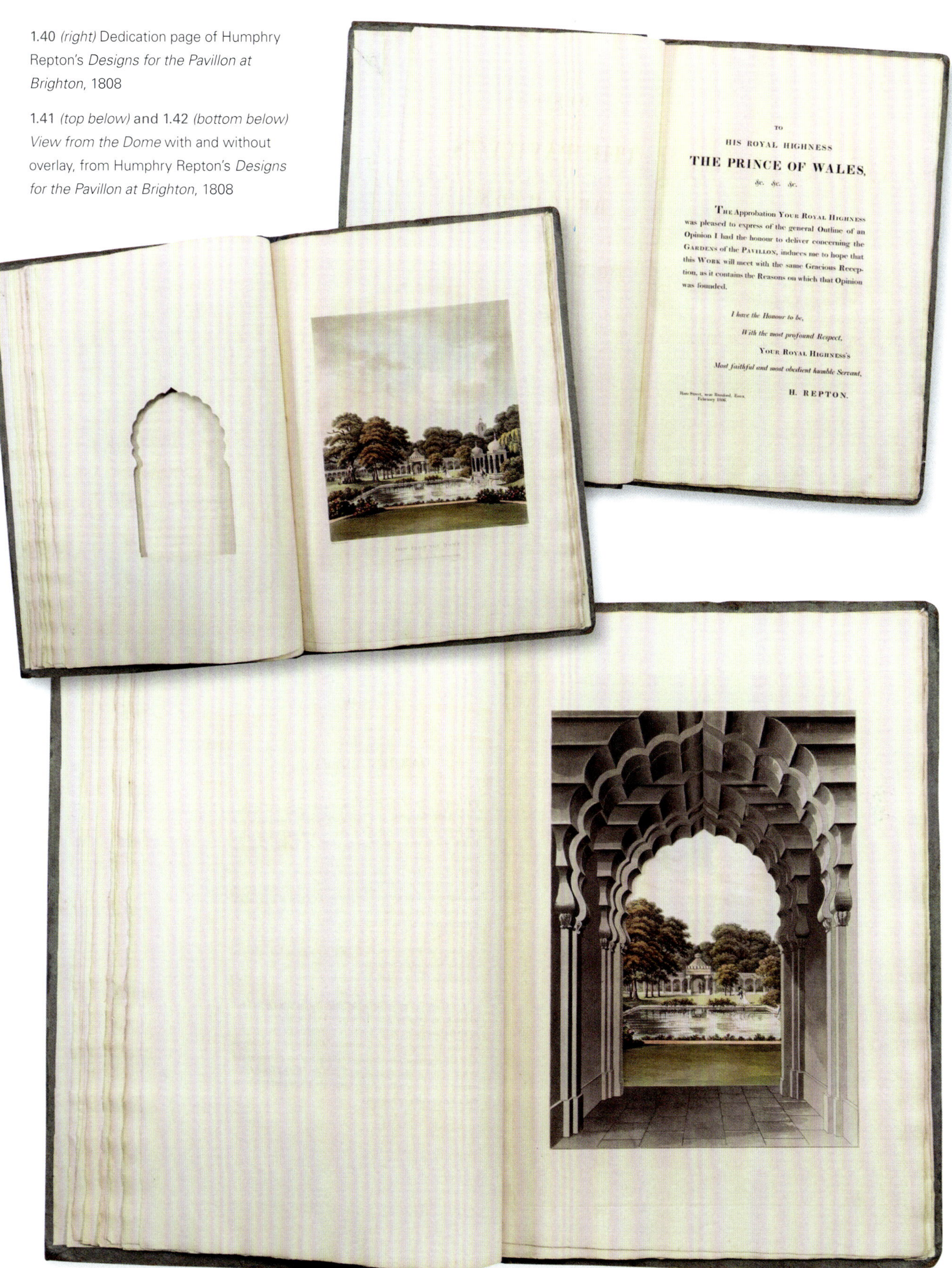

1.43 and 1.44 *The General View From the Pavillon* with and without overlays, from Humphry Repton's *Designs for the Pavillon at Brighton*, 1808

1.45 and 1.46 Page showing the *View from the Proposed Private Apartment* with and without overlay, from Humphry Repton's *Designs for the Pavillon at Brighton*, 1808

1.47 *Design for an Orangerie* with overlays (winter months), from Humphry Repton's *Designs for the Pavillon at Brighton*, 1808

1.48 *Design for an Orangerie* without overlays (summer months), from Humphry Repton's *Designs for the Pavillon at Brighton*, 1808

1.49 and 1.50 Page showing *View of the Stable Front* with and without overlay, from Humphry Repton's *Designs for the Pavillon at Brighton*, 1808

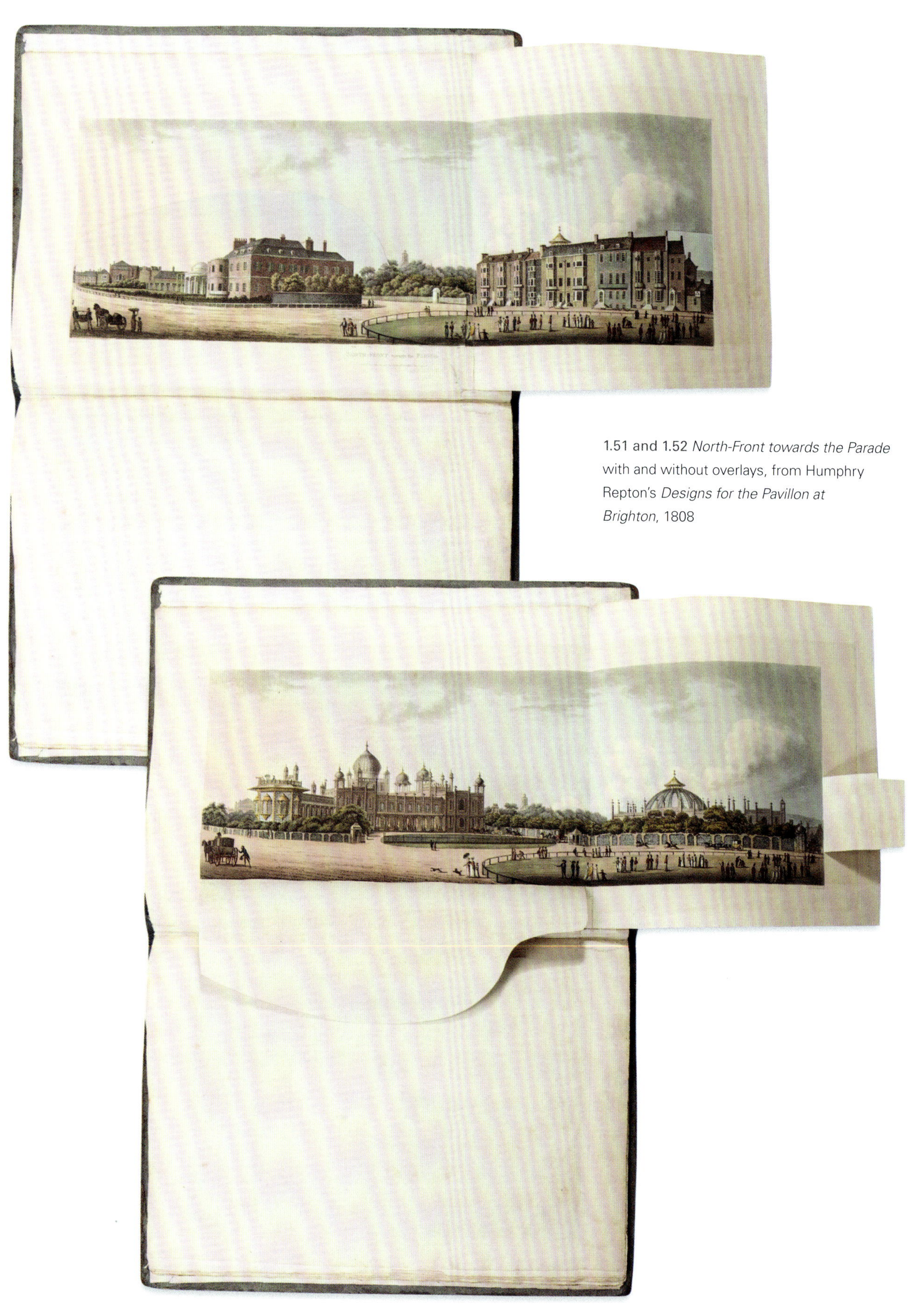

1.51 and 1.52 *North-Front towards the Parade* with and without overlays, from Humphry Repton's *Designs for the Pavillon at Brighton*, 1808

1.53 and 1.54 *West Front of the Pavillon Towards the Garden* with and without overlay, from Humphry Repton's *Designs for the Pavillon at Brighton*, 1808

1.55 *(overleaf)* Cornice, clerestory windows and part of the ceiling of the Music Room, with the central chandelier on the right

The first chinoiserie schemes and the arrival of the Craces: *c.*1801–*c.*1815

The introduction of Chinese-inspired interiors to the Pavilion created by the Craces is recorded in account books from 1802, but, as the dates of several Crace drawings show, it had been planned from at least 1801. This coincided with the structural changes in the form of the angled wings to either end of building. No complete views of these early chinoiserie schemes survive, but descriptions in the Crace Ledger suggest polychrome designs with highly polished and varied surface finishes, as this entry for a Music Room located south of the Saloon in 1802 illustrates:

> Molding and filletts round Architrave Red Blue &c
>
> Painting 20 Pannels red and varnished Yellow ornaments on D[itt]o and shadowed
> 36 Ornaments in Pannels of imitation Dado shadowed
> 10 Columns highly finished Scarlet ground to Shafts, fully enriched with yellow ornaments shadowed with purple and Dragons highly finished on D[itt]o with purple Capitals and enrichments D[itt]o. The bases stone color with ornaments and shadowed, the whole highly varnished at £5. 5. 0 each[45]

The Crace Ledger makes some references to flatted greys, whites, duck egg greens and fawn and slate colours in the Entrance Hall,[46] but these lighter colours were combined with saturated chinoiserie decorations in the same room:

> Chinese fret pannels blue 2ft wide
> Chinese fret railing blue 2'6"
> Columns scarlet and varnished
> Chinese fret frieze green ground red fret and shadowed dark green
> Red Margins twice cut in
> Chinese ornamented frieze to front of Landing
> Carved swag ornament red and varnished under D[itt]o [47]

The design schemes from this period were strongly informed by John Crace's literal, often flat chinoiserie style, busy with fret patterns, imitation trellis-work and large areas of marbling and woodgraining, as seen in many of the design drawings in the Royal Pavilion Archives. In this period the Pavilion is marked by the use of the primary colours yellow, red and blue as ground or dominant colours. The choice of bright, prismatic colours, arranged for maximum effect and according to the laws of colour contrast, is particular to two-dimensional designs found on Chinese export ware, a concept clearly understood by the Craces.

While the use of highly saturated colours was not as subtle or as gradual as it became after Nash's transformation, a deliberate structure in the distribution of dominant colours in each room can be observed. The Craces introduced a colour scheme that took into consideration the layout and use of the Pavilion as a whole, rather than treating each room separately. The Music Room Gallery was predominantly yellow, and the Banqueting Room Gallery blue, while the central Saloon featured a combination of vibrant red, yellow and blue. For these earliest chinoiserie schemes we do not have full and reliable illustrations, but a few drawings in the Cooper Hewitt Collection give a good impression of the relatively simple designs (figs 1.58 and 1.59). The chinoiserie scheme of the Saloon in *c.*1815, shown in the aquatint after Augustus Charles Pugin (fig. 1.60) is unlikely to be that of 1802, but probably retains elements of the initial Crace scheme. Traces of these schemes are still evident in the historic layers in the room today, now covered with a later scheme.

The Craces and their sources of inspiration

The Craces were a family of artists and designers who worked as gilders and interior decorators for five consecutive generations, from *c.*1750 until 1899, when John Dibblee Crace (1838–1919) closed the firm, which had been set up by his great-great-grandfather Edward in 1768. Royal patronage was secured early on, and Edward Crace was appointed Curator of the Royal Pictures in the mid-1770s. His son John joined the family firm in 1780 and was, with his own son Frederick, frequently employed by leading British architects, including Henry Holland at Carlton House and the Chinese Dairy at Woburn Abbey, John Soane at his house in Lincoln's Inn Fields and

1.56 *(opposite)* Painted laylight in one of the South Galleries

1.57 *(overleaf)* Clerestory windows in the Entrance Hall

1.58 *(above left)* Interior with Chinese wallpaper, drawing by John or Frederick Crace, 1802 or earlier. Cooper Hewitt, Smithsonian Design Museum, Acc. No. 1948-40-52

1.59 *(below left)* Design for wall with doorway, probably for the Ante Room of the Royal Pavilion, Brighton, drawing by John or Frederick Crace, 1802 or earlier. Cooper Hewitt, Smithsonian Design Museum, Acc. No. 1948-40-44

1.60 *(right)* The Saloon in *c.*1815, after Augustus Charles Pugin, aquatint from John Nash's *The Royal Pavilion at Brighton*, 1826. This hand-coloured print was mis-coloured: the blue wallpaper should be yellow, while the draperies should be yellow-green.

1.61 *(overleaf)* A design drawing of a floral border with scrolls and flowers, copied from famille rose Chinese porcelain of the Qianlong period, watercolour by Frederick Crace, *c.*1815

Pitzhanger Manor, and eventually John Nash. John Crace was the driving creative force in this first chinoiserie phase of the Pavilion, while from 1815 Frederick Crace took the artistic lead and was responsible for the large project encompassing the new Music Room, the Long Gallery and the redecoration of many other areas of the building.

The lives and work of the Craces are well recorded. They have been the subject of Megan Aldrich's comprehensive research over many years, leading to the retrospective exhibition *The Craces: Royal Decorators 1768–1899* at Brighton Museum and Art Gallery in 1990. Material produced by the Craces (predominantly Frederick) survives in great quantities and in a variety of formats and media, ranging from ink and pencil drawings to watercolour and gouache sketches, often with accompanying notes.

The Craces' interests and artistic range were wide, and they seem to have been studious and well informed. As Aldrich states in her doctoral thesis, 'a history of the Crace firm entails the study of coach painting, restoration and curatorial work, house decoration, the decorating of public buildings, furniture making, textile and wallpaper production, upholstery and drapery'.[48] John and Frederick appear not to have travelled to Asia, but they were familiar with the early chinoiserie interiors at Carlton House (see Chapter 2, pp. 139–143 and Chapter 3, pp. 220–224) and the Chinese export ware owned by Queen Charlotte. John Crace himself owned a large collection of Asian artefacts and the firm supplied clients with Chinese export ware. This allowed the Craces to study the design, ornamentation and colouring of Chinese art from authentic objects, as is evident in many of their

design drawings (see for example, figs 1.61 to 1.65). A good example of the use of objects as a source of inspiration is the Frederick Crace drawing seen in figs 1.64 and 1.65, which, in respect of motif, composition and colouring, was clearly inspired by Chinese court robes and rank badges seen on export ware such as the 'Nodding figures' prominent in the Long Gallery since at least 1815 (fig. 1.66). These individual motifs were then incorporated into designs for chinoiserie objects and entire schemes (see for example, fig. 1.67). Both Morley and Aldrich have pointed out that George and the Craces shared a passion for Chinese objects, and refer to a painting by Robert Dighton of Frederick Crace presenting a piece of Asian porcelain to George.[49] The Craces' design drawings reveal what Gordon Lang calls 'a very close, almost slavish adherence to original Chinese sources'.[50]

Other obvious sources of inspiration for the Craces were illustrated travel books. The Sotheby's sales catalogue from 7 July 1819 of John Crace's library lists fourteen books on China alone,[51] including William Alexander's *The Costume of China* (1805) (figs 1.68–1.72), which greatly informed the Music Room and other decorations in the Pavilion. The small drawing in fig. 1.73 is one of many examples where the Craces directly copy from Alexander's plates; it shows how they lifted one motif (a decorated shield) from Alexander's image of a Chinese soldier (fig. 1.71). One complete figure from Alexander's plates, the *Chinese Comedian*, found its way on to the central chandelier in the Music Room and also inspired the glass panels on the landings of the North and South Staircases, along with figures and motifs appropriated from other printed sources, for example William Chambers' illustrated books (see Chapter 2, pp. 122–126).

1.62 *(left)* A page showing a Chinese porcelain vase, from Frederick Crace's Sketchbook with 68 coloured designs from Chinese ornaments, *c.*1800–20

1.63 *(below)* A design for a laylight likely copied from a Chinese porcelain bowl or plate, watercolour by Frederick Crace, *c.*1815

1.64 *(right)* A design drawing likely inspired by Chinese silks and court robes, watercolour by Frederick Crace, *c.*1815

1.65 *(below)* A design drawing likely inspired by Chinese rank badges on court robes, watercolour by Frederick Crace, *c.*1815

1.66 *(opposite)* A Chinese 'nodding figure', *c.*1800, in the Long Gallery of the Royal Pavilion. Lent by His Majesty King Charles III (RCIN 26082)

1.67 *(below)* Design for a Chinese-style lantern suspended from a lamp-standard, watercolour by John or Frederick Crace, *c.*1815 or earlier

1.68 and 1.69 *(above)* Cover and the title page of William Alexander's *The Costume of China*, 1805

1.70 *(below) A Pagoda (or Tower)*, double page from William Alexander's *The Costume of China*, 1805

1.71 *(top right) A Chinese Soldier of Infantry*, double page from William Alexander's *The Costume of China*, 1805

1.72 *(bottom right) A Chinese Comedian*, double page from William Alexander's *The Costume of China*, 1805

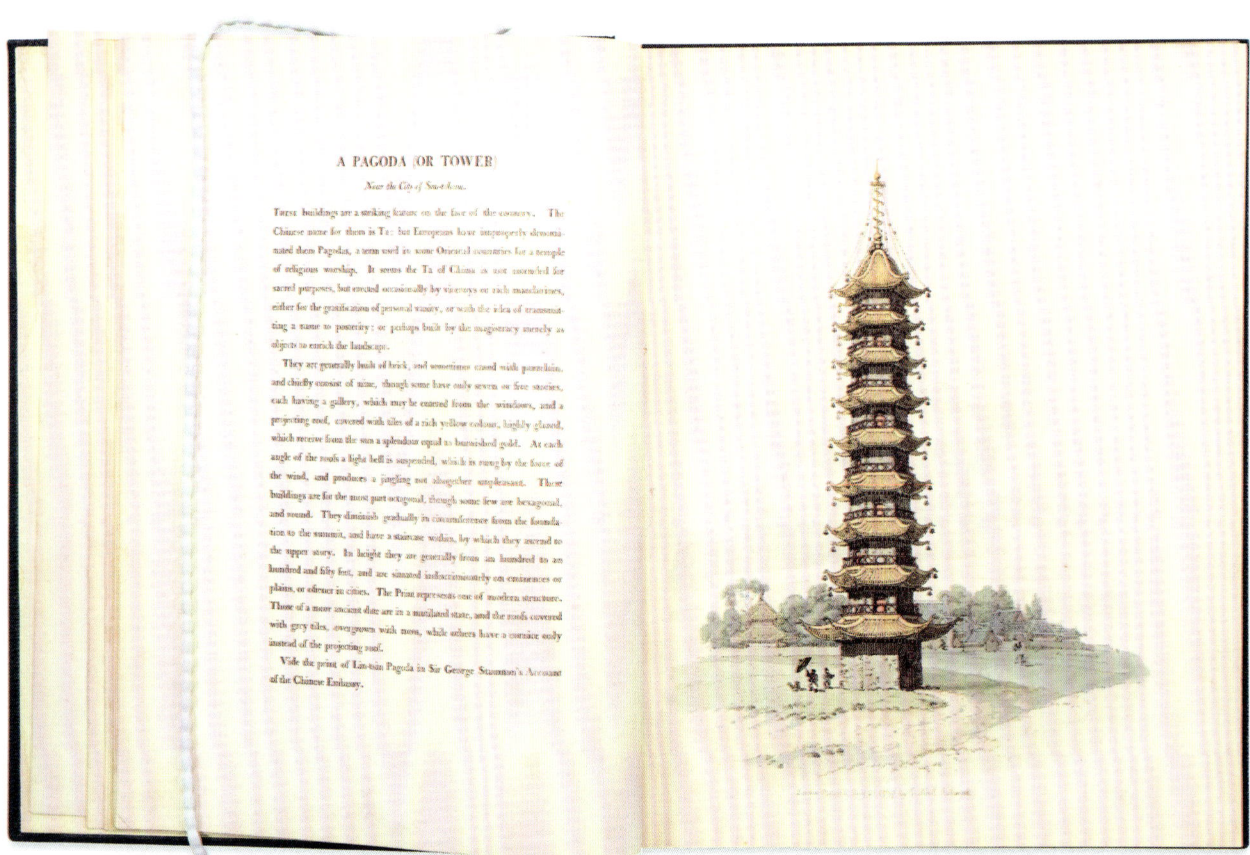

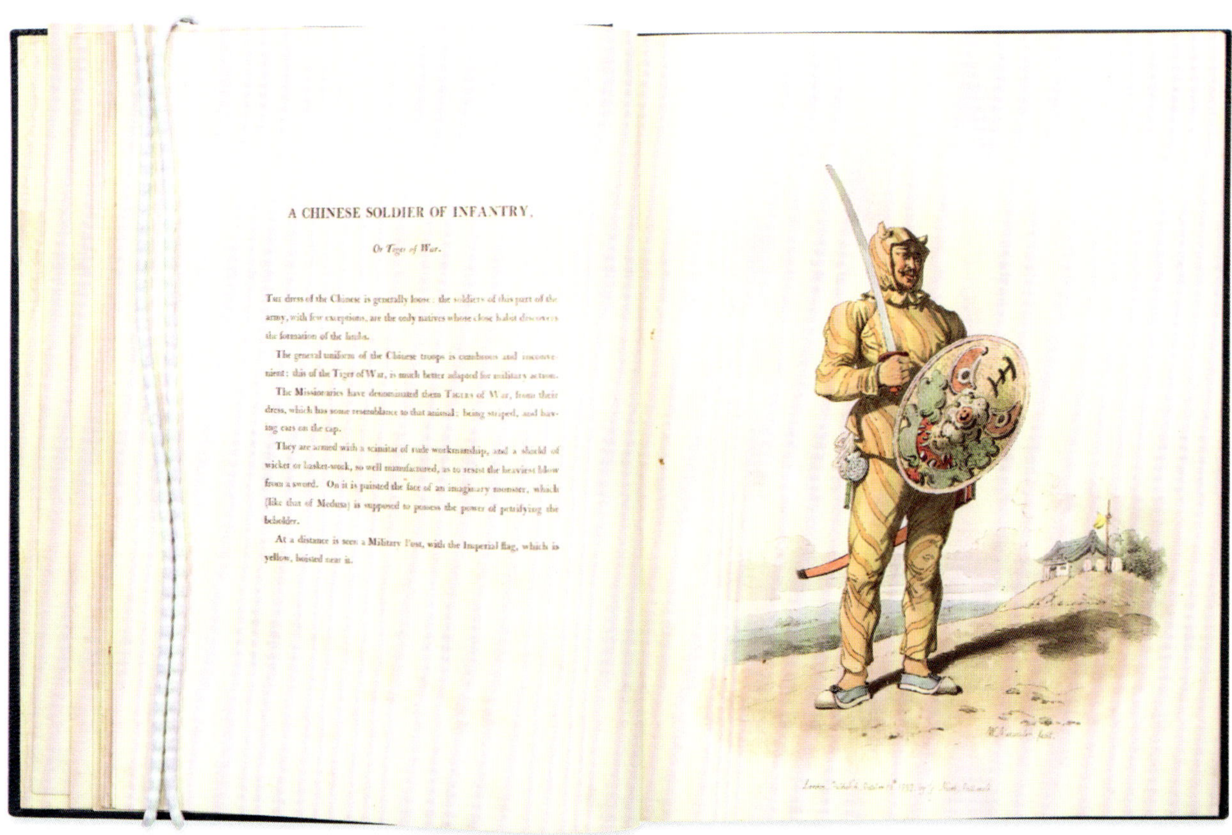

A CHINESE SOLDIER OF INFANTRY,

Or Tyger of War.

The dress of the Chinese is generally loose: the soldiers of this part of the army, with few exceptions, are the only natives whose close habit discovers the formation of the limbs.

The general uniform of the Chinese troops is cumbrous and inconvenient: this of the Tyger of War, is much better adapted for military action.

The Missionaries have denominated them Tigers of War, from their dress, which has some resemblance to that animal; being striped, and having ears on the cap.

They are armed with a scimitar of rude workmanship, and a shield of wicker or basket-work, so well manufactured, as to resist the heaviest blow from a sword. On it is painted the face of an imaginary monster, which (like that of Medusa) is supposed to possess the power of petrifying the beholder.

At a distance is seen a Military Post, with the Imperial flag, which is yellow, hoisted near it.

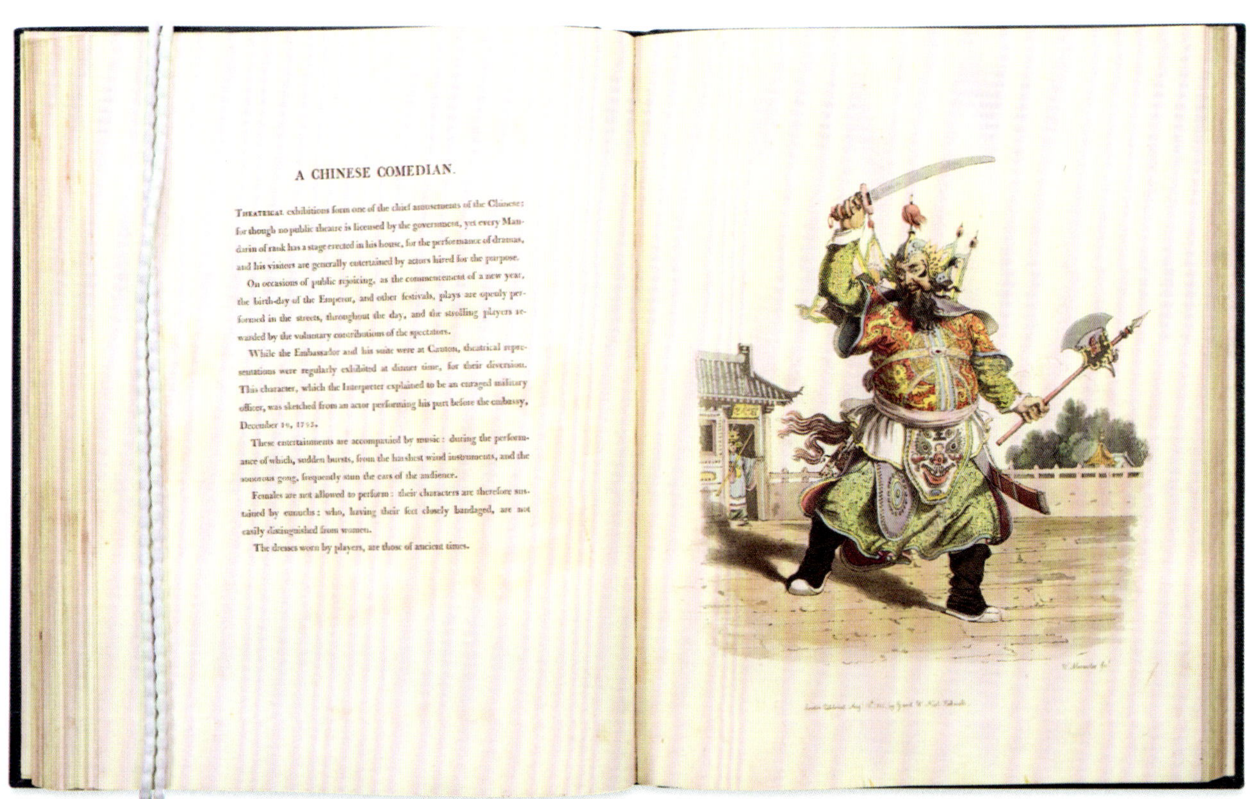

A CHINESE COMEDIAN.

Theatrical exhibitions form one of the chief amusements of the Chinese: for though no public theatre is licensed by the government, yet every Mandarin of rank has a stage erected in his house, for the performance of dramas, and his visitors are generally entertained by actors hired for the purpose.

On occasions of public rejoicing, as the commencement of a new year, the birth-day of the Emperor, and other festivals, plays are openly performed in the streets, throughout the day, and the strolling players are rewarded by the voluntary contributions of the spectators.

While the Embassador and his suite were at Canton, theatrical representations were regularly exhibited at dinner time, for their diversion. This character, which the Interpreter explained to be an enraged military officer, was sketched from an actor performing his part before the embassy, December 19, 1793.

These entertainments are accompanied by music: during the performance of which, sudden bursts, from the harshest wind instruments, and the sonorous gong, frequently stun the ears of the audience.

Females are not allowed to perform: their characters are therefore sustained by eunuchs: who, having their feet closely bandaged, are not easily distinguished from women.

The dresses worn by players, are those of ancient times.

1.73 *(left)* A Chinese shield in the form of a grotesque face, drawing by Frederick Crace, *c.*1815 or earlier

1.74 *A (left) Chinese Comedian*, pen, pencil and watercolour drawing by William Alexander, *c.*1793

1.75 *(opposite)* The Music Room central chandelier with the *Chinese Comedian,* derived from William Alexander's *The Costume of China* (1805)

John Nash's transformation and the later chinoiserie schemes *c.*1815–*c.*1823

Having discarded proposals for a new look for the exterior of the Pavilion by Porden, Holland and Repton, and following the sudden death of his preferred architect James Wyatt in a carriage accident in 1813, George, now Prince Regent, turned his attention to John Nash. Nash had worked for George at the Royal (formerly Lower) Lodge in Windsor Park and at Carlton House and had also designed several temporary structures for celebrations after the defeat of Napoleon in 1814. In January 1815 he was given the task of transforming the Pavilion, possibly carrying out work that had begun under Wyatt, but the exact sequence and origin of structural changes is unclear, since regrettably no original architectural plans of the Pavilion before *c.*1827 survive.[52] Like Repton, and possibly borrowing liberally from his 1806 designs, Nash also proposed an Indian-style cloaking for the classical Marine Pavilion, with the aim of linking it stylistically to Porden's stables. Having never been to India, he sought inspiration from the images produced by the artists William and Thomas Daniell, who had travelled to India and China in the 1790s. Between 1795 and 1807 Thomas Daniell published a set of 24 aquatints of palaces, temples, towns and landscapes around the rivers Jumna (Yamuna) and Ganges in India in *Oriental Scenery*. Nash borrowed the book from George's library at Carlton House before creating his designs for the Pavilion. His architectural drawings for the Pavilion do not survive, but the book of views of the Pavilion published in 1826 (see pp. 90–100) is the closest visual record of his vision. Nash's work on the Pavilion comprised the construction of a new kitchen and ancillary areas to the south and the widening of the spinal corridor (the Long Gallery) to the west. He also added the new Music Room to the north and Banqueting Room to the south. These are the largest and arguably most spectacular rooms of the Pavilion, identical in size and shape, with daring upswept tent-shaped roofs that were a nod to the rejected Chinese-inspired proposals and to the chinoiserie interiors. These large extensions were complete by 1817, with the original Holland building sandwiched between them. By 1818, Nash had cloaked the building in a Mughal-inspired dress of fretwork friezes and scalloped arches, topped with a large central dome and several smaller domes. By 1819 the outline of Nash's building was clearly visible, resembling, as David Beevers notes, 'an Indian-inspired palace conceived as a huge spreading tent' (see figs 1.7 and 1.12).[53]

A few amateur drawings and popular prints captured this intermediate stage in the architectural history of building (see for example, fig. 2.44), while newspapers were reporting regularly on the developments. On 17 October 1818, *The British Luminary and Weekly Intelligencer* in London published a lengthy update on proceedings, starting with critical comments on the cost of the transformation and an early comparison with the Kremlin, before providing a fascinating commentary on the erection and installation of Nash's central dome:

> PRINCELY ECONOMY! THE NEW KREMLIN, OR ROYAL PAVILION
>
> We can almost fancy the feelings with which those who have argued for economy and retrenchment in royal households will peruse the following account of the magnificent Works of our Great REGENT, and, of course, the magnificent addition now making to the expense already incurred upon that costly edifice, styled 'The Pavilion' at Brighton. His Royal Highness, though he should fail in rivalling the Czars of Muscovy, in the erection of a KREMLIN, seems in a way to rival in expense the most extravagant of eastern emperors. . . .
>
> Let us see how our money goes: First, then, the plan for the elevation of this Royal Edifice more and more develops itself every day, and the beauty, as well as grandeur of its architectural design, requires more than a cursory observation. It is premature to anticipate the extent of improvements which are only in part commenced, but while general remarks are made upon erroneous calculations, it becomes interesting to obtain a small portion of information upon the outline of a Royal structure, which will ultimately present an external appearance of magnificence, and exhibit a monument of the taste of its illustrious Possessor. We must take for the first division of our report the centre

1.76 Glass panels on the North Staircase landing with the *Chinese Comedian,* derived from William Alexander's *The Costume of China* (1805)

range of noble buildings that are to be finished this year. This includes a space from the north and south minarets (improperly called pagodas).The large minaret to the north is designed for the music-room, whilst that to the south is internally finished for the grand banquet or dining-room. Upon the angles of the north minaret are raised beautiful stone ornaments designated Kremlin. The elevation of them is nearly equal to the towering appearance of the centre . . . Having mentioned the large minarets with their auxiliary ornaments, we shall notice the centre elevation, which will more properly assume the appearance of a pagoda from its immense circular frame of massy iron work, with ribs and supporters of the same material. The workmen have this week begun the Herculean labour, and as we are unable to estimate its towering elevation, we must conjecture, from the first part of its stupendous shape, that it will rise considerably in splendid magnificence.[54]

One of the last structures to be added under Nash was an underground tunnel that connected the north end of the Pavilion with the stables, built in early 1822 at a cost of £1,783, and constructed of bricks, cement, clay and an unreliable material called mastic that was also used elsewhere in the building. It was thought to have provided easy and dry access to and from the stables, and for the delivery of coal, wood and other goods, without having to walk through the delicate garden. It was also used to allow access to the building for members of the King's Band.

Nash's new Music Room, Banqueting Room and kitchen area changed the layout of the building and the functions of several existing rooms (see fig. 1.10). The entrance area on the west, too, was greatly extended. These considerable changes to how the building operated, how it was entered, and the sequence of the rooms in general resulted in substantial redecoration of many of the existing rooms and the overall design scheme of the building. A subtle dialling-down of the exuberant chinoiserie designs after 1818 has frequently been linked to George's changed role as Prince Regent and, from 1820, King. The interiors of the Saloon and his private apartments after 1820 in particular have been described as a regal style more suitable for a newly crowned King (fig. 1.77). The design schemes of the transformed interiors of the 1820s, encompassing Frederick Crace's later chinoiserie design and the work of the artist Robert Jones, whose involvement with the Pavilion began in 1815, will be discussed in detail in Chapter 3.

A complete picturesque work of art: Nash and Pugin's *Views of the Pavilion*

The interior designs scheme of the Pavilion in what could cautiously be described as its most finished state under George was recorded in the 1820s in a series of watercolours and pencil and ink drawings by A.C. Pugin (see for example, figs 0.23, 0.24, 1.28, 1.29, 1.78, 1.79 and appendix). These were engraved by various artists and printed as aquatints with hand-coloured additions for what has become known as *Nash's Views* (referring to the lettering on the spine of the book). This was an elaborate volume entitled *The Royal Pavilion at Brighton* ('published by the command of & dedicated by permission to the King by John Nash'), comprising 35 folio views of the exterior and interior of the Pavilion as completed by Nash. It was commissioned by George and published in 1826 by Rudolph Ackermann, although it did not appear until 1827.

The volume provides a rich source of images of exterior and interior views, layouts and cross-sections of the Pavilion, the stables and the Riding House (figs 0.11, 0.12 and 1.28 to 1.31). Significantly, these include views of design phases preceding the final 1820s scheme (for example, fig. 1.19), indicating an interest in the design history of the building (with the notable absence of the first neoclassical interior). Most of Pugin's preparatory drawings and watercolours were created between 1818 and 1823 (see appendix), while Nash's great structural transformation was underway and the interior schemes were changed several times.

This being a royal commission, the aquatint plates are of very high quality, and were advertised in a prospectus from 1824 as 'Picturesque Views, highly finished in Colours, as facsimiles of the original Drawings, by AUGUSTUS PUGIN (educated in MR NASH's Office)'[55], stressing the authenticity of the coloured images.

1.77 *(opposite)* George IV as King, after Sir Thomas Lawrence, oil on canvas, after 1821

1.78 *(overleaf)* The Steine (east) front of the Royal Pavilion, watercolour drawing by Augustus Charles Pugin, 1823

Augs. Pugin
1823

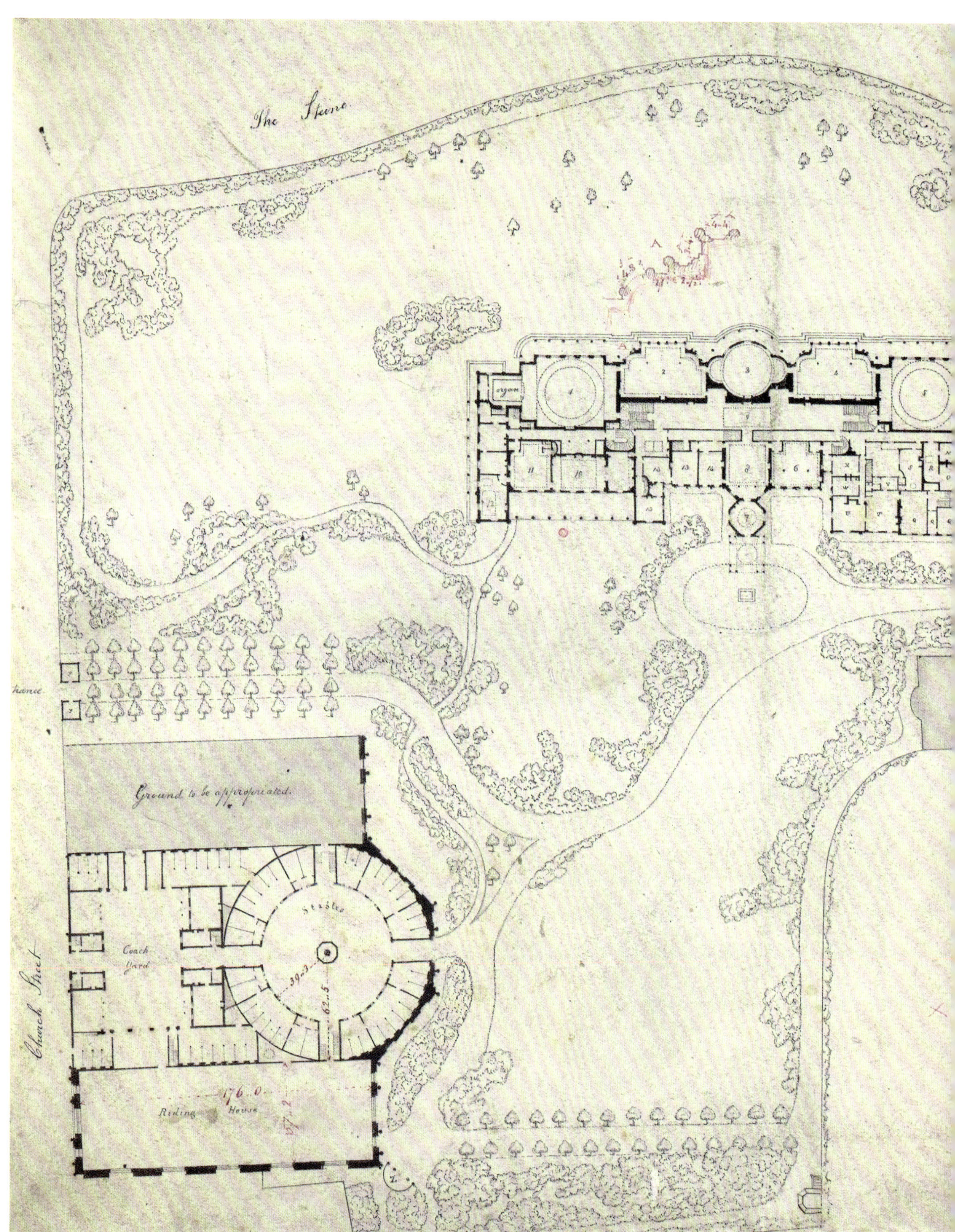
The Steine
organ
Ground to be appropriated.
Stables
Coach Yard
Church Street
Riding House
176.0

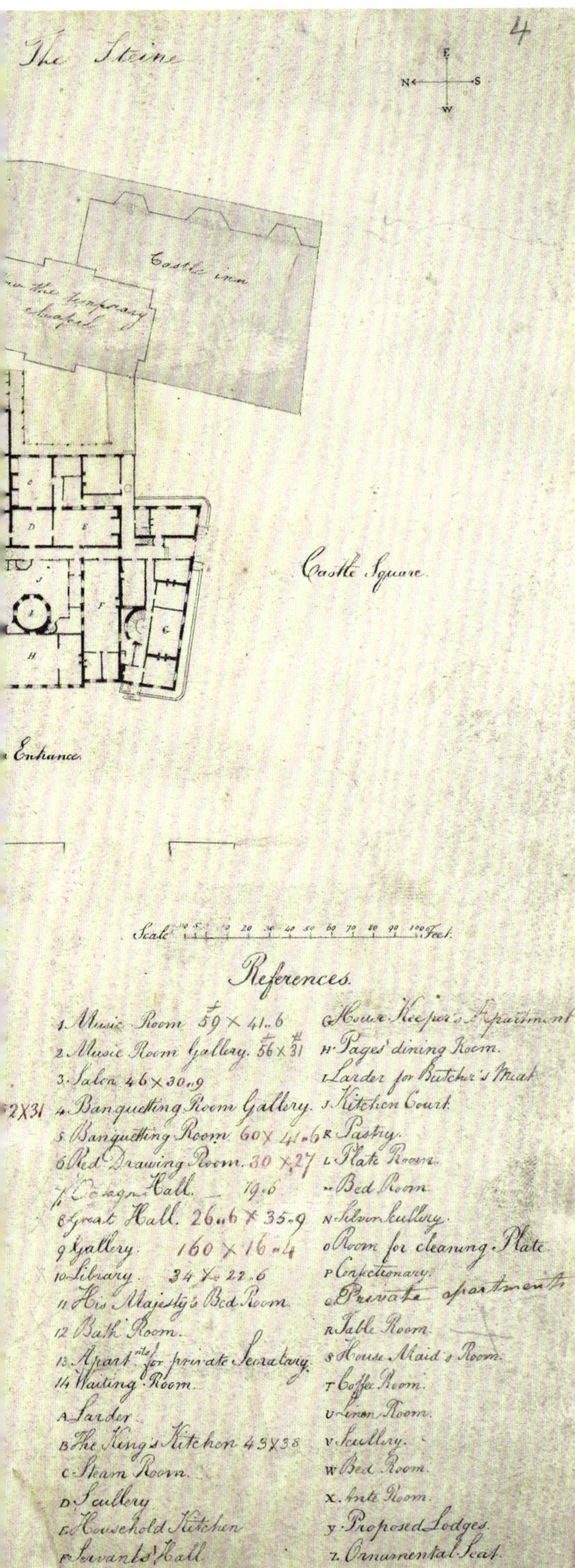

The prospectus further assured prospective buyers of the high quality of the publication by stating as one of the conditions that 'The Work will be finished in the first style of elegance, and only 250 copies printed, after which the plates will be destroyed.'[56] Of the 250, George bought 86 copies, bound in purple Morocco and embossed with the royal arms (fig. 1.80).

This elaborate picture book remains the principal source of reference for much of the current restoration work in the Pavilion, and Musgrave considers these detailed hand-coloured aquatints 'among the finest productions of an age in which engraved book illustration was at a high level'.[57] Figs 1.82 and 1.83 (detail view fig. 1.10) show the largest of the plates, an entire longitudinal cross-section of the building, folded and unfolded. The number of plates and images varies greatly between copies, but the general concept was to juxtapose a coloured aquatint that gave a vivid image of the look, feel and colouring of each part of the building, with a detailed line engraving of the same dimension and composition (for example, figs 1.81 and 1.84). Not all images of earlier stages were included in all copies of the book, while some copies include an additional set of lithographic versions of the views. Musgrave also notes that 'exquisite as they are, they do not compare with the original watercolour drawings of Pugin' (compare, for example.[58]

In style and scope, *Nash's Views* was possibly inspired by Repton's 1808 Pavilion book, as well as another invaluable visual record, William Henry Pyne's *The History of the Royal Residences*. Published in 1819, it was an ambitious publishing project in three volumes, containing 100 high-quality aquatints after watercolour drawings by Charles Wild, James Stephanoff (who later contributed many of the figures in Pugin's Pavilion drawings) and other artists. It did not include the Pavilion, possibly the building was undergoing Nash's dramatic transformation at the time the books were produced, or because the Pavilion was considered too ephemeral. In the context of the Pavilion, the images of Carlton House, Buckingham House (later Buckingham Palace) and Frogmore House (see Chapter 2) are of particular importance. An additional value of Pyne's volumes lies in its detailed descriptive

1.79 The ground plan of the Royal Pavilion estate, pencil, ink and watercolour drawing by Augustus Charles Pugin, *c.*1818–1823

1.80 The front board of John Nash's *The Royal Pavilion at Brighton*, bound in Morocco and embossed with the royal arms, 1826

1.81 A double page in John Nash's *The Royal Pavilion at Brighton*, showing an outline engraving and coloured aquatint of the centre part of the east front together, 1826

FIGS 1.82 and 1.83 The cross-section of the Pavilion (folded and unfolded), aquatint from John Nash's *The Royal Pavilion at Brighton*, 1826

1.84 A double page in John Nash's *The Royal Pavilion at Brighton*, showing an outline engraving and coloured aquatint of the Music Room together, 1826

1.85 *(opposite)* The carved dragon on the central chandelier in the Banqueting Room

text. By comparing the images in these three publications and their accompanying text (where present), it becomes clearer how the Pavilion related to other English royal residences at the time. *Nash's Views* did not contain any descriptive text, but in 1838 Edward W. Brayley reissued the plates under the title *Illustrations of her Majesty's Palace at Brighton: Formerly the Pavilion, Executed by the Command of King George the Fourth, Under the Superintendence of John Nash. To which is prefixed a History of the Palace.* While the quality of the illustrations in the edition is noticeably inferior to the 1826 edition, the added *History* is a valuable first stand-alone descriptive account of the Pavilion while still in royal ownership (see Chapter 2, p. 151 and Chapter 3, pp. 195 and 214).

The elusive Robert Jones

Between 1815 and 1823, throughout John Nash's time at the Pavilion, the designer and artist Robert Jones was one of the most significant contributors to the interior decoration of the building. He first appears in the Crace Ledger for October to Christmas 1815, which lists charges for 'Painting and coloring pannels white for Mr Jones and afterwards repairing and coloring D[itt]o in consequence of Mr Jone's [*sic*] paintings being removed', at the cost of £11 12s.[59] It is not entirely clear why these paintings were removed, but the entry suggests that they were installed some time before this date, thus placing Jones in the building before October 1815, the date previously considered as the start of his work in the Pavilion. That fact that he is named in this account and that Frederick Crace is carrying out preparatory work for him implies that Jones was acting independently rather than as an employee (employees being very rarely identified by name). An item in the same quarterly account of 1815 shows Crace 'Attending His Royal Highness with 9 assistants putting in patterns to Small Drawing Room, arranging the pictures, India paper &c in Yellow Drawing Room; putting in patterns to Entrance Hall and Gallery and arranging Mr Jone's [*sic*] pictures'.[60] Robert Jones does not appear thereafter in the Crace Ledger, despite his known involvement in the extensive works in the Pavilion over the next eight years.

Although none of Jones's own bills prior to 1818 are known to survive, there are numerous references to him in the accounts of other contractors which show that he was both designing and supervising the manufacture of a wide variety of furnishings for the Banqueting Room before this date, and in subsequent years he was also responsible for decorating the Saloon (the 1823 scheme), the Red Drawing Room, King's Apartments, Yellow Ante Room, Yellow Bow Rooms and various apartments on the chamber floor. The range of his activities is remarkable: he produced designs for chimneypieces, chandeliers, clocks, curtains, carpets, ormolu, wallpaper, decorative carving, gilding and furniture, as well as personally executing the Banqueting Room mural decorations.

In the Royal Pavilion Abstracts of Accounts, Jones is described as 'Robert Jones, Artist' throughout, and he refers to himself in the same way in the Robert Jones Accounts. In the Abstracts of Accounts Jones is first mentioned in relation to the furniture makers Messrs Bailey and Sanders in 1817, who made the six 'Pedestals for the Orlean Vases made to Mr. Jones design'[61] for the Music Room. In the same year Bailey and Sanders carved, prepared, silvered, and eventually installed the large central dragon in the Banqueting Room (fig. 1.85), as well as making a large sideboard, both designed by Jones. Again, Jones supervises some of the work, including making two additional models of the dragon, the whereabouts of which are unknown:

> To a very large Dragon for the Centre of the Room richly carved with extend'd Wings to suspend Chandeliers & prepar'g it for silvering
> To silvering it at Brighton
> To mak'g & alt'g at sundry times 2 Models of the Dragon originally designed by Mr. Jones and under his superintendence
> To a very large & superbly decorated Sideboard made of very fine Rosewood Snakewood and Satin Wood with 12 large Dragons & Ornam'ts richly carved and double Gilt in the very best manner to Mr. Jones's design.[62]

Authenticated drawings by Robert Jones are rare, but three signed designs for the Royal Pavilion's Banqueting Room and Saloon survive in the Royal Pavilion Archives (figs 0.26, 1.86 and 1.87)[63], while several drawings in the Cooper

1.86 Unexecuted design for the Saloon, watercolour drawing by Robert Jones, *c.*1821 or earlier

1.87 *Design for the Curtains Corners etc. - for the Saloon, approved by H– Majesty 3rd July 1821*, watercolour, ink and pencil drawing by Robert Jones, 1821

Hewitt Collection,[64] acquired with the Crace drawings in 1948, have been cautiously attributed to Jones. Two of his design drawings for the Saloon carpet are owned by Axminster Carpets (figs 1.88 and 1.89) and a large but faded fragment of the carpet itself is in the Royal Collection.[65] The drawings for the carpet are of particular interest with regard to his use of bright colours reminiscent of multicoloured Chinese export ceramics. Jones's style is distinctive in its bold, imaginative use of colour and choice of motifs, which derive partly from Chinese sources but also show Indian and Egyptian influences. His decorative painting reveals a number of distinctive painting techniques that use subtle combinations and gradations of colour, often with silver providing a unifying element (see Chapter 3, pp.213–219), and the combination of silver and gold in close proximity to saturated reds and blues.

While much of Jones's work in the Pavilion survives, there is little biographical information on this important figure. There is no confirmed date of birth or death, and he cannot be positively identified with any of the artists of that name working in Britain at that period. An effect of this obscurity is that he is rarely considered separately from the Craces; even in John Morley's substantial work *The Making of the Royal Pavilion, Brighton*, Jones is incorporated into the chapter on the Crace firm, although Morley does present him as, to a degree, their rival, noting that his designs are 'more *spirituelle* than Frederick Crace's: they have spontaneity and fire'.[66] In his time, however, Jones was far from obscure: George Smith, in *The Cabinet-Maker and Upholsterer's Guide* (1826), while admitting the superiority of the French in ornamental decoration, wrote:

> We have however in the present day many decorative artists (natives of our own soil) of great merit, some of whom possess uncommon versatility of talent; performing equally well both in oil and distemper colour, the three branches of decorative art; viz. figure, landscape, and ornamental painting in all its variety; as the numerous works of Mr. R. Jones (who stands at the head of his profession) sufficiently testify.[67]

1.88 and 1.89 Details from a scale drawing for a section of the Music Room carpet, watercolour and gouache drawing by Robert Jones, *c.*1823 or earlier. Axminster Carpets Ltd

At the same time as his Pavilion work, Jones was carrying out major works at Northumberland House (demolished in 1874) on the Strand in London, including the restoration and partial extension of Robert Adam's famous Glass Drawing Room,[68] and painting transparencies (to designs by Henry Howard RA) for Deane Franklin Walker's 'Eidouranion', a stage device similar to a planetarium which presented celestial phenomena to accompany lectures on astronomy.[69] Also concurrent with these activities were Jones's 1821 designs for the elaborate front cloth for George's coronation banqueting table.[70]. He continued to be employed on royal commissions of lesser extent throughout the 1820s and into the 1830s, including the restoration of the panels in the Banqueting Room in the Pavilion in 1835, and is also associated with the designs for canopied thrones for William IV and Queen Adelaide.[71] The drawings for these thrones survive in the Royal Collection.[72] The thrones were never made, but Roberts refers further to a summary account of the year 1835 in which Jones's name appears in relation to the redecoration of some furniture from the State Apartments at Windsor Castle.[73]

In the absence of much concrete information, Robert Jones's wider career has been the subject of much speculation. He is, for example, thought likely to be one of the artists of 'high talent' described by John Gregory Crace (son of Frederick) in the first of 'Two Lectures on the History of Paperhangings', delivered to the Royal Institute of British Architects in 1839.[74] Crace here is referring to the firm of George and Frederick Eckhardt who established their business in Chelsea in 1786, as paperhanging manufacturers of 'considerable taste and spirit', who produced papers 'of such elegance and beauty, as far surpassed those of all other countries'. He praises the variety of manufacturing methods and the high quality of printing, going on to explain that the designs were 'finished by Artists constantly retained by the Manufacturers, men of considerable talent, among whom were M.M. Boileau, Feuglet, Joinot and Jones'. These same artists are also listed, with others, as working for John Sheringham's paperhanging firm at around the same time. It is noteworthy that Jones is the only British name among a group of artists of French background, and Morley goes so far as to speculate that Jones might have developed his particular 'verve and dash' through exposure to such foreign influences.[75]

The Eckhardts' firm was known for their imitations of Chinese wallpaper and use of gold- and silver-leaf detailing – the latter technique known to the Craces but used extensively by Jones for his Banqueting Room and Saloon wall decorations and, most elaborately, in his Banqueting Room murals. The Eckhardts' firm was bankrupted in 1796, as was that of Sheringham. In the search for the continuation of this Jones's career, one might note the intriguing possibility that he is the 'Mr Jones, ornamentation painter' who worked with the paperhanging manufacturers Fricker & Henderson *c.*1804, painting an Egyptian scheme for Robert Heathcote of Hill Street in London.[76] Heathcote was an intimate friend of the Prince of Wales, who saw the mural in progress on several visits to the house at around the time that he reportedly commissioned an Egyptian decoration for the Marine Pavilion.[77]

The Pavilion's artistic genius Robert Jones must have died some time before 1851, as he is referred to as 'the late Mr. Jones' in Wilmott's *Descriptive Guide to the Palace and Gardens of the Royal Pavilion at Brighton* of that year: 'The decorative work in this room ['The Ladies Retiring Room', i.e. the Red Drawing Room south of the Entrance Hall] is in exactly the same style as in the time of George IV, and was designed by the late Mr. Jones, as were also the decorations of the Banqueting Room and the Saloon.'[78]

THE PAVILION AFTER GEORGE: WILLIAM IV, QUEEN VICTORIA AND THE CIVIC LIFE OF A FORMER ROYAL PALACE

In William IV's short reign (1830–37), he made a few significant changes to the Pavilion estate, and had further ambitious plans for it. Soon after he became King he engaged the architect Joseph Henry Good (1775–1857) to survey the entire estate and add several new buildings (see opposite and figs 0.27 and 0.28). Most of Good's architectural plans for the Pavilion survive in the Royal Pavilion Archives. They comprise around 200 detailed drawings of the estate and individual buildings, both existing areas and planned additions, dating from *c.*1827 to 1836. Some designs were in keeping with Nash's style, and it is likely that Nash had some influence on the proposed new structures, which may also explain the presence of the pre-1830 drawings. Several of these earlier drawings are signed and attributed to a William Nixon (for example,

1.90 *(right)* *No. 5 Drawing Centre Dome Pavilion Brighton* (Joseph Henry Good Plan No. 17), ink and watercolour drawing, attributed to William Nixon Jr, 1827

1.91 *(below)* Music Room and details of roof, Royal Pavilion (Joseph Henry Good Plan No. 18), ink and watercolour drawing, attributed to William Nixon Jr, 1827

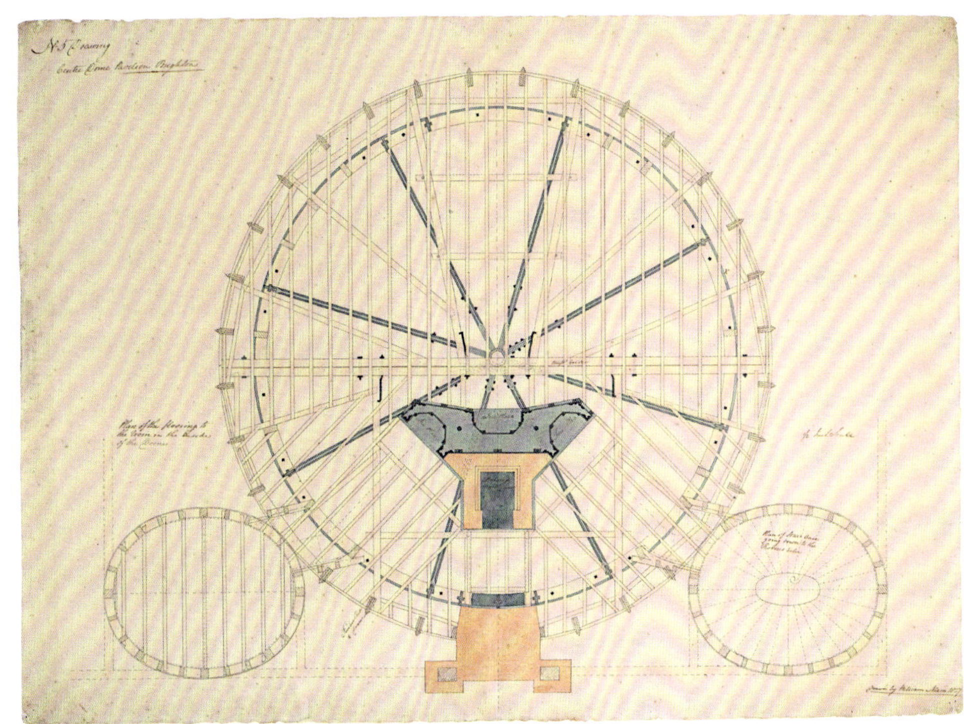

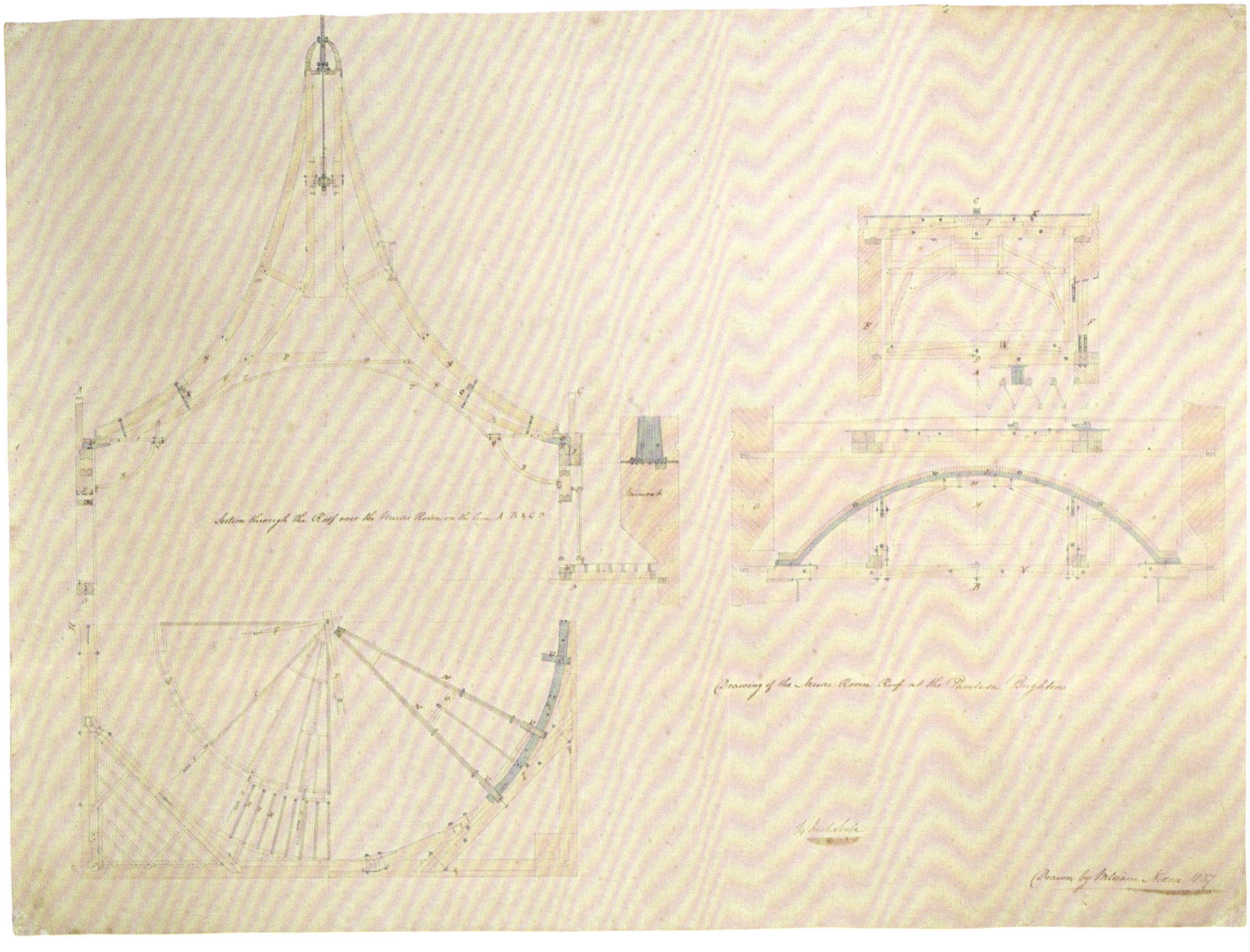

· Nº IV ·
· SECTION · THROVGH · THE · GATEWAY ·
SCALE
FEET

figs 1.90 and 1.91), whose identity is uncertain. He may have been a Clerk of the Works at the Royal Pavilion, or one of two Clerks of Works (Nixon Senior and Junior) connected with John Nash's architectural office. Whatever their origin, in the absence of Nash's original architectural plans for the Pavilion, these are intriguing drawings, despite dating from 1827, more than a decade after the construction of these areas.

Between 1830 and 1832 Good added gateways at the northern and southern entrances to the estate. Of these, the North Gate with its copper-clad dome survives (figs 1.92 and 1.93). His South Gate (figs 1.94 and 1.95), complete with offices and corridors linking it to the main building and servants' dormitories (also designed by Good), was demolished in the 1850s and replaced with a more open municipal entrance, comprising two smaller structures resembling the main porte cochère and North Gate of the Pavilion. This first municipal South Gate can be seen in many late Victorian and Edwardian postcards (figs 1.96). In 1921 it was replaced with the Indian Memorial Gateway, designed by Thomas Tyrwhitt, which is still standing today (fig. 1.97). The Good/Nixon drawings provide us with fascinating detail about many buildings now gone. These include the servants' housing at the southern side of the estate and some subterranean structures, such as a late-eighteenth-century ice-house at the south-west corner of the estate. They are also indicative of William IV's ambitious plans for the Pavilion. Had he lived longer, many more substantial structures might have been added to the estate.

1.92 *(opposite) No. IV Section through the Gateway* (Joseph Henry Good Plan No. 82), ink and watercolour drawing with notes in pencil by Joseph Henry Good, 1832

1.93 *(below)* The North Gate today, seen from the Pavilion Garden. Author's photo

George's extraordinary Pavilion by the sea was nearly lost: his niece, Queen Victoria, having visited only five times between 1837 and 1845[79] and not having shown much interest in or affection for Brighton, sold the entire Pavilion estate to Brighton Town Commissioners in 1850. By then it was in a stripped and devastated state. Victoria had removed almost all the interior decorations in the preceding years, reusing many of the decorative objects, carpets, furniture and fittings for rooms in the new East Wing at Buckingham Palace (figs 1.98 and 1.99), effectively creating a Victorian reincarnation of the Pavilion's chinoiserie interiors.

Immediately after the purchase in 1850 the town commissioners made great efforts to restore part of the interiors to an approximation of their former splendour, as described in Wilmott's new edition of his *Descriptive Guide* (see Chapter 2, pp. 132 and 164). Further redecoration and restoration work was carried out in the principal rooms of the eastern side of the ground floor to designs by John Dibblee Crace (grandson of Frederick) in the 1880s and 1890s,[80] but it was not until 1959 that Clifford Musgrave could state that the period of 'municipal nakedness'[81] of the building was finally coming to an end. Instigated by Musgrave and supported by the Regency Society of Brighton and Hove (founded in 1945), regular furniture exhibitions held in the building from 1946 onwards mitigated this appearance of emptiness, although most of the furniture on display was not original to the building. However, some of the largest and most significant pieces of furniture and ornamentation were returned by Queen Victoria in 1864, after a successful application by the Pavilion's first

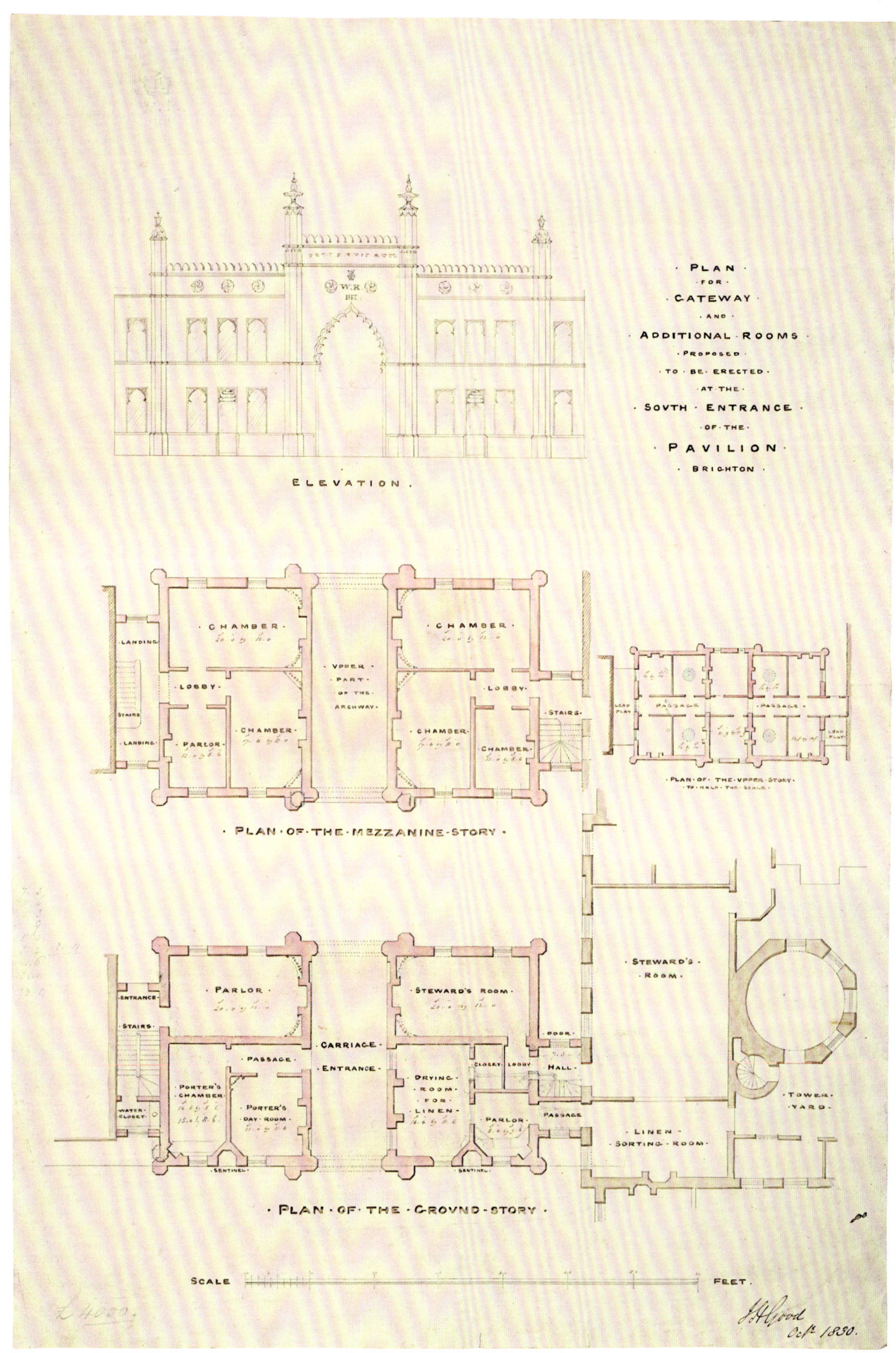
PLAN
FOR
GATEWAY
AND
ADDITIONAL ROOMS
PROPOSED
TO BE ERECTED
AT THE
SOUTH ENTRANCE
OF THE
PAVILION
BRIGHTON
ELEVATION.
PLAN OF THE MEZZANINE STORY
PLAN OF THE UPPER STORY
PLAN OF THE GROUND STORY
CHAMBER
LANDING
LOBBY
STAIRS
PARLOR
UPPER PART OF THE ARCHWAY
PASSAGE
ENTRANCE
CARRIAGE ENTRANCE
STEWARD'S ROOM
PORTER'S CHAMBER
PORTER'S DAY ROOM
WATER CLOSET
DRYING ROOM FOR LINEN
CLOSET
HALL
DOOR
SENTINEL
LINEN SORTING ROOM
TOWER YARD
SCALE
FEET.
£4000.
J.H. Good
Oct. 1830.

1.94 *(opposite) Plan for gateway and additional rooms, proposed to be erected at the south entrance of the Pavilion, Brighton* (Joseph Henry Good Plan No. 28), ink and watercolour drawing with notes in pencil by Joseph Henry Good, 1830

1.95 *(right) The Entrance to the Royal Palace, Brighton* (showing Good's South Gate), lithograph by T. Cooper after Edward Fox, *c.*1835

Director Francis de Val. Thus, most of the chandeliers from the Music Room and Banqueting Room returned, as well as all the red and gold wall canvases from the Music Room and several of Robert Jones's figurative panels from the Banqueting Room. Gaps in the decorative design scheme of the latter were filled by French artist Tony Dury, who created high-quality replacements for Jones's missing chinoiserie panels, which remain, as Beevers puts it, 'an integral part of the Banqueting Room decorations today'.[82]

Despite these efforts to create a colourful interior reminiscent of the building's original brilliance, many areas and decorative surfaces were painted over and covered in several layers of a copal varnish in the Victorian age. John Dinkel quotes a comment made by the then Prince of Wales during a visit in 1896, noting how dingy the Pavilion had become. Dinkel states that 'copious varnishing over the years had not only dimmed the decorations, but actually altered with a browning yellow film the complex harmony of colours, making nonsense of the decorative schemes'. He explains further that the Victorians valued this kind of 'patina of age' so much that in some cases they also tried to imitate it, resulting in more overpainting.[83]

A new momentum in the interior restorations began after the First World War, partly inspired by Queen Mary's interest in the Pavilion and greatly supported by the appointment of Henry D. Roberts as Director of the Royal Pavilion Estate in 1920. The Queen returned several large free-standing objects, not all of them having come from the Pavilion originally, but of particular importance for the design scheme of the Banqueting Room were the eight Spode china and ormolu pedestal lamps (fig. 1.100). These large blue and gold objects form a harmonious relationship with the gilt panel frames and Prussian blue wallpaper in the room. In the 1930s Queen Mary returned japanned doors, gilt and silvered pilasters from the Saloon (figs 3.1 and 3.14) and Chinese wallpaper. These material gifts were matched by Roberts's scholarly interest in the building and his understanding of historically accurate representation. Roberts was the first Director of the Pavilion who examined original manuscripts and archival resources in order to pursue a conscientious restoration of the interiors. In 1939 he published the first book on the Pavilion based on original archival sources.[84]

Roberts made first attempts to remove discoloured varnish and dirt from several surfaces in the building, an effort that would continue throughout most of

the twentieth century. Several directors, artists and conservation specialists carried out the slow but thorough cleaning of the interior surfaces, but much of the most important work can be credited to Roy Bradley, the Pavilion's first full-time artist/restorer, who worked there from 1946 and 1976.

Shortly after her accession to the throne, Her late Majesty Queen Elizabeth II returned a collection of several dozen original objects on a long-term loan basis, including the four free-standing candelabra from the Music Room Gallery (fig. 1.101). These Robert Jones designs, incorporating multicoloured hexagonal Chinese porcelain columns, are of a similar significance to the decorative scheme of this room as the Spode lamps in the Banqueting Room.

From at least Roberts's time as Director the intention behind all restoration and recreation projects was to present the building and its garden as a complete Regency design, as George IV and his designers and architects had intended it. An earlier move in the direction of historic accuracy was made by John Dibblee Crace in 1899. Jessica Rutherford notes that, despite his earlier inventive redecoration of the Banqueting Room Gallery and Music Room Gallery, Crace's primary concern during this later project was 'to restore the room to the original designs with appropriate techniques' and credits him with an awareness of the

1.96 *(above) South Gate Royal Pavilion Brighton*, colourised photographic postcard, 1904

1.97 *(below)* The opening of the India Memorial Gate, photographic postcard, 1921

original colour schemes.[85]

There were two severe setbacks in the restoration of the Music Room in the twentieth century. In 1975 an arson attack caused great damage to the east side of the room. One long canvas panel on the north wall closest to the windows was destroyed and all decoration above the coving badly burnt, while most other surfaces suffered from exposure to heat, smoke and water. The restoration of the room took eleven years, during which major structural repair work to the entire roof structure began. A decade later the newly restored Music Room suffered once again, when a stone ball from one of the minarets surrounding Nash's tent-shaped roof became dislodged in the great storm of 1987 and crashed through the ceiling. A hand-knotted carpet, replicating the original Axminster carpet, had just been laid and had to be sent back to the manufacturer in Killybegs, Ireland, for the damage to be repaired.

Major restoration was carried out on the chamber floor of the Pavilion from the late 1970s until the mid-1990s, including Queen Victoria's private apartments above the Entrance Hall, the Bow Rooms and the South Galleries. Here the recreation of the chrome yellow and blue verditer wallpapers was of particular importance to the understanding of the complete design scheme of the building.

In 2019, a major temporary loan of more than 130 objects – many of them mounted Chinese porcelain – from Her late Majesty Queen Elizabeth II enabled visitors to experience George's vision of the interiors of the Pavilion in near-complete form and as close to their appearance in the 1820s as they had been since the mid-1840s. The exhibition *A Prince's Treasure: From Buckingham Palace to the Royal Pavilion* ran from September 2019 until January 2022 and was organised and curated jointly by the Royal Pavilion and the Royal Collection Trust. Many of the contemporary images of the Pavilion interiors in this

1.98 *(below) The Pavilion Breakfast Room at Buckingham Palace,* watercolour and bodycolour with gum arabic by James Roberts, 1850. RCIN 919918, © Royal Collection Enterprises Limited 2025 | Royal Collection Trust

1.99 *The Yellow Drawing Room at Buckingham Palace*, watercolour and bodycolour over pencil by James Roberts, 1855. RCIN 919924, © Royal Collection Enterprises Limited 2025 | Royal Collection Trust

book show these loans in situ during that period.

The role of the building has changed significantly since its creation, not least due to the move from royal to municipal ownership in 1850. The Pavilion is now a historic building that is predominantly experienced by following a prescribed visitor route in daytime. This route approximates the sequence of rooms a guest in the mid-1820s would have passed through, with the addition of some servants' areas, the King's Apartments and many of the rooms on the chamber floor. Visitors approach the main entrance by the porte cochère (no. 1 on Nash's ground plan in fig. 0.9). Unless the approach is from the India Gate on the south side of the estate, a visitor today walks along the meandering paths or coach lanes of the gardens as laid out by Nash and planted by John Furner from 1813 onwards. In his book on the history and development of the Pavilion gardens, Mike Jones explains that this relatively small park is a typical example of a quintessential Regency garden,

> which can be summarised as a group of trees, shrubs, herbaceous plants, bulbs and annuals mixed together in a relaxed composition. . . . The idea was to create in the garden subtle, accidental effects seen in the countryside. Shrubs and trees were looked at more closely; leaf shapes, texture, seedpods, colour and seasonal changes were celebrated and combined.[86]

He continues that principles of pleasing and harmonious irregularity and informal appearance of architecture fashionable at the time were applied to the Pavilion garden. Nash's bright Bath stone building thus sits in picturesque manner in informal gardens and is framed by various shades of green (figs 0.1 and 0.2), with a subtle increase in colour the closer you get to the entrance. Jones explains the connection between the colouring of the planting and the interior design schemes:

> The Regency colour palette was not subdued or tonal; the colour combinations seen in the garden reflected those inside the Pavilion. Lilac and yellow were seen as harmonious and with an Autumn flowering plant such as *Aster amellus* 'Violet Queen', they were combined in the same flower with its lilac petals and yellow centres. The colours of flowers, used as jewel-like accents, were offset by the surrounding greenery and foliage, unlike later blazing miniature bedding . . .

From 2025, this picturesque framework for George's Romantic vision of a pleasure palace by the sea will receive renewed and much needed attention: Brighton & Hove City Council and Brighton & Hove Museums have received a substantial National Lottery Heritage Fund grant for the restoration of the Regency garden. Plans include the restoration of the Regency planting design, using the original planting plans, as well as new visitor and community facilities, the reinstallation of historic fencing, and improved irrigation and drainage.

1.100 *(opposite)* Spode stone china, glass and ormolu pedestal lamps, designed by Robert Jones, *c.*1818, in the Banqueting Room

1.101 One of the free-standing candelabra, wood and ormolu with Chinese porcelain columns, designed by Robert Jones, *c.*1823, in the Music Room Gallery. Lent by His Majesty King Charles III (RCIN 26105)

Escaping to Other Worlds

Chinoiserie and the Royal Pavilion

Chinoiserie has influenced European interior design, the decorative arts, art, architecture, landscape gardening and fashion since the early seventeenth century. In interior decoration, the chinoiserie style was mainly chosen for informal rooms, and was often associated with female taste and women's spaces.[1] The style went in and out of fashion over the years but was at its height in the late seventeenth century, and again in the mid-eighteenth century. At the time it was referred to as 'the Chinese taste', 'India work', 'Japan work' or occasionally 'China work'. Only later did it become known by the French term chinoiserie.[2] The taste waned in the later eighteenth century, but it continued to be popular in France well into the nineteenth century. Almost always restricted to a wealthy and privileged circle, by the early nineteenth century the style had become primarily a court taste, of which the Pavilion is a prime example, as well as one of the last.

2.1 Mantel clock, designed by Robert Jones and made, or assembled, by Benjamin Lewis Vulliamy, for the north end of the Banqueting Room, gilt bronze, silver, lapis lazuli, *c.*1819, during the exhibition *A Prince's Treasure*, 2019–22. RCIN 30006, © Royal Collection Enterprises Limited 2025 | Royal Collection Trust

Light and airy, unpredictable and surprising, architectural chinoiserie was particularly associated with small or temporary garden structures such as teahouses, pagodas, bridges and pavilions. Examples of more substantial chinoiserie structures are rare, with the Great Pagoda at Kew (completed in spring 1762 and likely inspired by the Porcelain pagoda in Nanking[3]) being a notable exception in Britain.

Chinoiserie is not a reflection of genuine Chinese design, art and aesthetics but an expression of the Western imagination of China, and Asia in general. Few Europeans had contact with or indeed in-depth knowledge of China until the later nineteenth century. Because of its geographical remoteness and relative impenetrability, China became a land of fantasy and myth, often known to Europeans as Cathay. Philosophers, theorists and readers found in China a model of freedom, tolerance and stability based on Confucian wisdom, while artists and designers saw the cultural riches as a vibrant alternative to classicism. As David Porter put it, in seventeenth- and eighteenth-century Europe 'Chinese goods were valued not only as a fashion statement, but simultaneously as enchantingly unfamiliar tokens of a well-established culture'.[4] Lacquer, porcelain, paintings, patterned silk and other artefacts seemed to abide by no rules familiar to Europeans, embodying the whimsical and exciting. When imitating

2.2 *A View of the Wilderness, with the Alhambra, the Pagoda and the Mosque in the Royal Gardens at Kew*, engraving after William Marlow, *c*.1763. RCIN 702947.t, © Royal Collection Enterprises Limited 2025 | Royal Collection Trust

these artefacts, designers decorated them with an imagined land of flowers inhabited by mandarins, fishermen, lovers, children, exotic birds and other creatures. Human figures on decorative surfaces, fabrics or in paintings languidly rest, meditate, drink tea or smoke. Often, they look Indian or Persian rather than Chinese, as is the case with the large figures painted for the Banqueting Room by Robert Jones (figs 2.3, 2.4 and 2.5), which are repeated in three-dimensional form in the figurative design for the clock and thermometer on the mantelpieces in the room (fig. 2.1). The designs and motifs for the chinoiserie style were liberally lifted from many sources and many cultures, including China, Japan, India and Persia, and this eclecticism is particularly prominent in the Pavilion.

Authentic Asian objects, images and textiles directly influenced European designers of chinoiserie objects and interiors, as is evident in the case of John and Frederick Crace and their designs for the Pavilion. These were largely imported via several East India Companies from around 1600. In Europe, the export objects were often embellished, altered and essentially taken out of their original context, making almost every piece of Asian export art a complex, hybrid and multicultural object. Especially in interiors, export ware from Asia was often incorporated into chinoiserie schemes. For example, real bamboo furniture could be found next to imitation bamboo carved from beechwood or mahogany, or recreated in cast iron or brass (as is the case in the Long Gallery, see for example figs 2.6 and 2.7), while Chinese blue-and-white porcelain would sit next to early European porcelain on mantelpieces. This manipulation of objects, motifs and materials was not restricted to European interventions: the Chinese, too, augmented and adjusted the objects offered to European and American

2.3 The largest of Robert Jones's figure paintings, in its original location on the west wall of the Banqueting Room, oil on canvas, *c*.1818–20

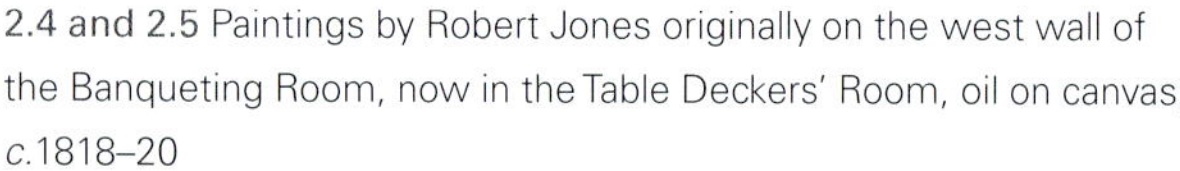

2.4 and 2.5 Paintings by Robert Jones originally on the west wall of the Banqueting Room, now in the Table Deckers' Room, oil on canvas, *c.*1818–20

merchants in the Hongs of Canton (Guangzhou),[5] constructing an image of Chinese culture they believed was appealing to the traders and their clients on the other side of the world. It was a clever, market-driven and calculated form of self-representation. Many objects, such as the mandarin nodding figures (fig. 1.66), sets of images of Chinese life and traditions (fig. 2.8), or certain types of hand-painted wallpaper (fig. 2.9), were in fact made specifically for the Western market.

What underpins most chinoiserie buildings, interiors and designs is a fascination with other cultures, and an enjoyment of leisure and extravagance, paired with ignorance of the finer details and meaning of motifs, symbols, traditions of Asian culture, or indeed their geographical origin. As the curator Emile de Bruijn notes in *Borrowed Landscapes* when discussing a chinoiserie wallpaper that emulated Chinese export silver, 'authenticity was clearly irrelevant here, and playful interaction between the wallpaper and the silver instead emphasised the creative potential of orientalist design, divorced from reality but appealing to the imagination'.[6] Similarly, Greg M. Thomas, in an essay on 'Chinoiserie and Intercultural Dialogue at Brighton Pavilion', notes that 'patrons, designers, and craftsmen of chinoiserie wilfully blurred boundaries: between architecture and decoration; between European and Chinese styles and motifs; between European and Chinese figural attributes, between reality and dream.' He suggests that 'a certain aesthetic inebriation was central to chinoiserie viewing effects, releasing the mind from the rigid rules of classical design, skirting the norms of social behaviour, enabling the kind of free play aesthetic sensation that, according to Porter, was associated with China's supposed sensual overindulgence.'[7] At Brighton's Pavilion, the inebriation of the senses was both literal and metaphorical.

The Pavilion is one of the most visible, emphatic and best-known examples of the chinoiserie taste in Europe, yet it is also a highly unusual witness to a style that, by the time George embraced it fully in Brighton, had gone out of fashion in Britain. The point of time of its creation, its location, and George's individual character, means and tastes, may help explain its singularity. The building is positioned between Enlightenment visions

2.6 and 2.7 Details of the cast iron, brass and mahogany staircase in the Long Gallery

2.8 *(left)* A Chinese export painting in the North Yellow Bow Room, oil on board, *c.*1800

2.9 *(below)* Chinese hand-painted wallpaper, early nineteenth century, in Queen Victoria's Bedroom, restored and rehung in 2020

of 'the East' that manifested themselves in whimsical, light-hearted architectural follies, and the much more industrialised and manufactured 'oriental' style that became dominant in the decorative arts and architecture of the mid-Victorian era. At the time of its creation, the Romantic imagination conjured up feverish visions of 'otherness' and Middle Eastern and Asian culture in poetry and decorative arts, while the British were simultaneously beginning to value, study and establish their own history in the wake of revolution and war in Europe. While George was acutely aware of Britain's post-Napoleonic status as the richest and most powerful country in the world, and wanted his palaces to reflect that, the shadow of the French Revolution still loomed large. Escapism, vanity, pomposity, denial, fascination, and fear of one's own possible fate would all have contributed to George's utopian vision of Regency exoticism in Brighton.

In recent years several authors have discussed the changes in Europeans' view of China, and by extension the Chinese taste in architecture and the decorative arts, at the beginning of the nineteenth century, among them de Bruijn. In *Borrowed Landscapes*, he reminds readers of Edward Said's notion of Western entrepreneurs, scholars and artists as 'gatekeepers' of 'the East', who claimed to admire Asian cultures yet dictated how they should be studied, understood and represented, thus exerting imperialist control over other cultures.[8] He notices that this concept becomes more complex at the end of the eighteenth century into the early nineteenth century and identifies a gradual shift in European attitudes to and perspectives of China. Citing the historian Jürgen Osterhammel, he explains the phenomenon of the 'Eurocentric turn', when China and Chinese culture were increasingly judged by European standards, rather than simply admired.[9] Two failed British diplomatic missions to China (Macartney's in 1792–3 and Amherst's in 1816) contributed to the cooling of the relationship between China and Britain, while at the same time it resulted in a new wave of enticing images of China.

De Bruijn recognises orientalism not just as a mechanism of Western control over 'the East', but as an 'oscillation between attraction and disdain, misunderstanding and inspiration', which creates a creative environment that is one of the most intriguing aspects of the style and results in its 'paradoxical and fundamentally imaginative nature'.[10]

The Pavilion could be considered the most comprehensive, still tangible example of this change in attitude to Chinese culture and an expression of the new-found British confidence that would soon develop into exploitative imperialism on an unprecedented scale. A comment from a guidebook published in 1823 by the Brighton writer Richard Sickelmore, whose work will be discussed later, may serve as an indicative example of this: after describing some of the Chinese and Chinese-inspired features of the Pavilion in a flight of fancy, he makes sure to stress that 'everything here and throughout the Palace is almost entirely the work of British materials and British hands; it combines a whole, in which the high and cultivated taste of a patriot monarch forms a strong feature, as diffusing its rays and illuminating national worth and industry, that merits, and must obtain, the admiration of the world',[11] thereby suggesting that the decorative scheme is an expression of national worth and reflects British manufacturing power and taste. In so doing, Sickelmore, like most other popular writers of the time, largely ignored the original Asian objects, motifs and colours that were present in and inspired the Pavilion's interiors.

PRINTED SOURCES OF INSPIRATION

An important source of inspiration for the chinoiserie, apart from the imported goods, were engravings in illustrated travel or costume books. One of the earliest was Johan Nieuhof's *An Embassy from the East India Company of the United Provinces to the Grand Tartar Cham Emperor of China*, first published in Dutch in 1665 and in an English translation by John Ogilby in 1669. It recorded the Dutch embassy to China in 1655–7 and was the most comprehensive textual and visual European record of Chinese life for almost 100 years. Its 113 plates of illustrations became a major source for chinoiserie. In 1735 Jean-Baptiste du Halde's *A Description of the Empire of China and Chinese-Tartary, together with the Kingdoms of Korea, and Tibet*, based on the reports of Jesuit missionaries and containing many important maps, tables and other illustrations, was published in France, with an English translation appearing in 1741.

William Chambers

In the 1740s, the Swedish-Scottish architect William Chambers made three voyages to East Asia, visiting Canton at least twice, where he studied Chinese designs at first hand.[12] However, like all European merchants he was not allowed to enter inland China. In 1757 he published the illustrated volume *Designs of Chinese Buildings, Furniture, Dresses, Machines, and Utensils . . .*, followed in 1763 by *Plans, Elevations, Sections, and Perspective Views of the Gardens and Buildings at Kew in Surrey*. His designs for Kew included the Great Pagoda, which along with his publications established Chambers's reputation as an authority on Chinese buildings, though it was never meant to be an accurate replica of real Chinese architecture.

Designs of Chinese Buildings was the first serious attempt to record the architecture of China and became extremely influential throughout Europe after *c.*1770. With it Chambers intended to put a stop to 'the extravagancies that daily appear under the name of Chinese'. The engravings, however, accord with classical principles of design and even include European decorative details; and some of the designs appear to be of the author's own devising. Both the Chinese room at Carlton House and some aspects of the interiors of the Pavilion in Brighton owe much to Chambers's illustrations, as his books were known to the Craces and possibly Robert Jones.

Chambers's buildings at Kew, a gift for Princess Augusta, the founder of the gardens and mother of George III, might have sparked her grandson's interest in the Chinese taste. Apart from the Pagoda, the young George would also have seen an 'Alhambra' (built in 1758), a 'Mosque' (1761) and other 'oriental' structures and follies at Kew. This area is referred to by Chambers, as well as in a watercolour from 1763 by William Marlow, as 'the wilderness' (fig. 2.2, p. 118) and was almost certainly George's first exposure to Asian-inspired architecture and design. Of these buildings only the Pagoda survives, probably because it was the most substantial. Its ten roofs were originally covered with 'plates of varnished Iron of different colours'[13] and from

2.10 *(below)* The Red Drawing Room in *c.*1823, after Augustus Charles Pugin, aquatint from John Nash's *The Royal Pavilion at Brighton*, 1826

2.11 *(opposite)* Palm tree column in the Red Drawing Room, designed by Robert Jones, *c.*1821. Photo: Stephen Roberts-Pratt

each of the eight corners of each roof was suspended a dragon 'covered with a kind of thin glass of various colours, which produces a most dazling [*sic*] reflection'.[14] These 80 polychrome, shimmering dragons, probably carved from wood, disappeared in the 1780s, but were likely a direct inspiration for the transparent coloured glazes found on many silvered objects, including carved dragons, in the Pavilion's Music Room and Banqueting Room. The Kew dragons were replaced with replicas in 2018, after many years of meticulous research into their possible design, materials and colours.

Other 'wilderness' buildings, now lost, may also have informed George's later design decisions, for example the 'House of Confucius', a two-storey building in a Chinese style, probably designed by Joseph Goupy. Its interiors are described by Chambers thus: 'Its walls and ceiling are painted with grotesque ornaments, and little historical subjects relating to Confucius, with several transactions of the Christian missions in China.'[15]

Another of these lost ornamental buildings might have inspired a specific motif in the Pavilion: the interior of Chambers's Mosque, an octagonal building flanked by two minarets and topped by a dome, boasted stucco palm trees which, in execution and colouring, are reminiscent of the intricately painted palm trees in Robert Jones's Red Drawing Room. Chambers's description – and the objects themselves – might well have been known to Nash, the Craces and Jones: 'At the eight angles of the room are palm-trees modelled in stucco, painted and varnished with various hues of green, in imitation of nature; which at the top spread and support the dome, represented as forms of reeds, bound together with ribbons of silk.'[16] The whole is set against walls painted in 'rich rose colour' and 'straw colour'. By comparison, an entry in Jones's account books describing the colouring of the palm trees in the Red Drawing Room (figs 2.10 and 2.11) reads 'Painting in imitation of Bamboo 14 trees with their gradations of Color from the ground upwards to their foliage, which is finished with bright Greens and highly Varnished.'[17]

William Alexander's images and the Macartney embassy

Many chinoiserie surfaces in the Pavilion, and the Music Room in particular, were decorated with motifs inspired by images of China created by William Alexander, an artist who, at the age of just 25, was chosen to accompany Lord Macartney's embassy to China (1792–4) as a junior draughtsman. Alexander's carefully observed anthropological images and descriptions were widely disseminated, and they shaped a new image of China through European eyes in the early nineteenth century. His popular images illustrated the accounts of the embassy in print form, including Sir George Staunton's *An Authentic Account of an Embassy from the King of Great Britain to the Emperor of China* (1797), and his own book published in 1805, *The Costume of China* (see Chapter 1,

2.12 *(above)* Frontispiece of William Alexander's *The Costume of China*, 1805 (plate printed in 1804)

2.13 *(opposite above) A Chinese Lady and her Son*, double page from William Alexander's *The Costume of China*, 1805 (plate first printed in 1798)

2.14 *(opposite below)* Design for a wall elevation, probably for the Banqueting Room, or, more likely, the Entrance Hall, watercolour, pen, ink and graphite drawing by Frederick Crace, 1815–22. Cooper Hewitt Smithsonian Design Museum, Acc. No. 1948-40-33

A CHINESE LADY AND HER SON,

attended by a Servant.

The female sex in China, live retired in proportion to their situation in life. The lower orders are not more domesticated than in Europe: but the middle class are not often seen from home, and ladies of rank scarcely ever. Alterations of dress are never made from caprice or fashion: the season of the year, and disposing the various ornaments, making the only difference. Instead of linen, the ladies substitute silk netting; over which is worn an under vest and drawers of taffeta: and, (should the weather require no additional covering,) they have for the external garment, a long robe of silk or satin, richly embroidered. Great care is taken in ornamenting the head: the hair, after being smoothed with oil and closely twisted, is brought to the crown of the head, and fastened with bodkins of gold and silver: across the forehead is a band, from which descends a peak of velvet, decorated with a diamond or pearl, and artificial flowers, are fancifully arranged on each side of the head. Ear-rings, and the string of perfumed beads suspended from the shoulder, likewise make up part of the ornaments of dress. The use of cosmetics is well known among the ladies of China; painting the face both white and red, is in common practice with them: they place a decided red spot on the lower lip, and the eyebrows are brought by art to be very narrow, black, and arched.

Their small shoes are elegantly wrought, and the contour of the ankles are never seen, by reason of the loose bandage round them. Boys, till about seven years of age, frequently have two queues, encouraged to grow from each side of the head. The servant, as is usual with the lower class, wears on the wrist a ring of brass or tutenag.

2.15 *(left)* Detail from *South Gate of the City of Ting-Hai* in William Alexander's *The Costume of China*, 1805 (plate first printed in 1798)

2.16 *(below)* A motif copied from William Alexander's plate, 2.15, in the Music Room murals, designed by Frederick Crace and painted by Henry Lambelet, *c.*1822

pp. 77–88 and figs 2.12, 2.13, 2.15 and 2.18), in which he combined coloured plates with short descriptive texts. Frederick Crace owned a copy of Alexander's book, from which the Craces took numerous motifs and incorporated them into unexecuted designs for walls (for example, fig. 2.14, which relates to 2.13), the paintings on the Music Room walls (for example, figs 2.15 and 2.16) and other decorative surfaces in the building, including lanterns, glass screens and chandeliers (figs 1.71 to 1.75 and 2.17).[18] Elements from Alexander's images can be found in many of the smaller design drawings by the Craces, including in the Pavilion sketchbook and individual rough or more finished sketches (for example, figs 2.18, 2.19 and 2.20). Although Alexander had visited China, it is important to bear in mind that the designs derived from his drawings that we see in the Pavilion still cannot be considered an 'authentic' depiction of Chinese culture and geography. As Elizabeth Hope Chang notes, Alexander's vision of China was a series of types rather than complete landscapes, and the artist himself had to borrow from existing images in print or use second-hand eyewitness accounts of scenes he himself had not witnessed.[19] Alexander was essentially creating picturesque images of China that would appeal to European aesthetics and suit print culture. A second book by Alexander, published in 1814, was indeed titled *Picturesque Representations of the Dress and Manners of the Chinese*, and it comprised a further 50 coloured engravings (fig. 2.21), which were essentially variations of the images in *The Costume of China*.

The aim of the Macartney embassy had been to negotiate better trading conditions in China for the British. Although carefully planned, it turned out to be a diplomatic failure, as did the Amherst mission in 1816. It is perhaps significant that George's bold and grandiose

2.17 Design for a lantern for the old Music Room (demolished *c.*1816), watercolour drawing with an inscription in pencil by John or Frederick Crace, *c.*1803

chinoiserie interiors at Brighton were created in the wake of these two failed missions and were indeed directly informed by images and descriptions created in their context. However, we can only speculate as to whether George was trying to comment on these political and cultural tensions, since he has left not a single line of correspondence on the matter. It is hard to know whether, as Kara Blakley has suggested, George installed objects such as Chinese porcelain pagoda models and other Asian export ware in the Pavilion as 'signifiers of Britain's imperial aspirations', but it is certainly a possibility.[20]

An intriguing comment from another source may corroborate Blakley's interpretation, although it dates from after George's death. In 1833 John Docwra Parry included a lengthy description of the Pavilion in his *Historical and Descriptive Account of the Coast of Sussex*. Parry was one of the first writers to put George's seaside palace into a wider European context, by comparing its eclectic style to other architectural fancies by European rulers:

> And whilst the King of Saxony has his *Japanese Palace*,[21] the Emperor of Austria his *Favorita*,[22] and he of Russia his fanciful palaces of heterogeneous outline, whilst

2.18 *(above) A Sacrifice at a Temple*, double page from William Alexander's *The Costume of China*, 1805 (plate first printed in 1800)

2.19 *(below)* Detail from 2.18

> the Sovereign of England has in addition the noble and regular Gothic pile of Windsor, and the Roman palaces of London, we do not see why, if only for the sake of variety, he should not have his Oriental Marine Pavilion.[23]

Parry continues with his imperialist argument, justifying and hailing the creation of an 'eastern palace' (although it should be noted that the king he refers to was George's successor, William IV):

> The King of England is almost *'de facto' King of India*; and, therefore, may we not say without fanciful exaggeration, that an eastern palace, placed on the shores of that element by the ancient and continual sovereignty of which England wields such a powerful sceptre, presents an idea to the mind, full, interesting, and effective.[24]

2.20 *(above)* A decorative frieze with fantastic creatures, watercolour drawing by John or Frederick Crace copied from William Alexander's plate, 2.18, *c.*1802–4

2.21 *(right) A Chinese Lady of Rank*, plate 43 from William Alexander's *Picturesque Representations of the Dress and Manners of the Chinese*, 1814. Author's collection

Tellingly, this notion is repeated in 1850 by Charles Wilmott in his *Descriptive Guide to the Palace and Gardens of the Royal Pavilion at Brighton*, replacing William IV with Queen Victoria: 'the Soveriegn [*sic*] of England is almost "de facto" Queen of India'.[25]

In 1935, the imperialist notion was discussed once again in print, when Osbert Sitwell and Margaret Barton retrospectively assigned the Pavilion a pioneering role in the development of a 'British Empire Style':

> For, dormant in the building of the Pavilion, lies the possibility of a British Empire Style. India had fired the Prince's aesthetic imagination, and here we see the artistic germ of the dynastic ideal which was to attain to its ultimate and most unforeseen flowering, when, at the end of this new century, his great-niece [Queen Victoria], in her old age, proclaimed herself Empress of India.

The authors even assume that a Chinese visitor would surely 'appreciate the qualities of the building'.[26]

THE FEMALE INFLUENCE ON GEORGE'S TASTE FOR CHINOISERIE

While the 'oriental' buildings dotted around Kew Gardens' 'wilderness' may have been a formative influence on George's taste for Asian-inspired architecture in general, he was also greatly influenced, especially in respect of interior decoration, by female members of his family: in particular his mother, Queen Charlotte, and his sisters Charlotte (the Princess Royal), Elizabeth and Augusta (fig. 2.22). A painting by Johan Zoffany depicts Queen Charlotte in her sitting room in Buckingham House (later Buckingham Palace) in *c.*1764, in the company of her eldest sons George and Frederick, aged two and one (fig. 2.23). The princes are wearing fancy-dress costume: the Prince of Wales is dressed as Odysseus' son Telemachus, while Frederick wears Turkish-inspired attire and a turban. The Queen, too, was known to occasionally wear fashionable dress *à la turque* and attend masquerade balls. The furnishings and decorative objects in the room reflect Charlotte's interest in collecting Asian ceramics, while on the table behind her two Chinese 'nodding' clay figures can be seen, which appear almost identical to those later purchased by George and displayed in the Long Gallery of the Pavilion (visible in fig. 0.7).

Collecting Asian export ware and furnishing rooms in a chinoiserie style were, as Beevers has explained, associated with the female sphere,[27] so Queen Charlotte's tastes were not unusual, but they appear to have made a significant impact not just on her daughters, but also on her eldest son. George would also have been familiar with the substantial collection of blue-and-white porcelain (Chinese and Japanese export ware as well as European imitations) introduced to the English court by Queen Mary II (r. 1689–94) at Hampton Court and Kensington Palace and augmented by Queen Charlotte and her daughters.[28]

Queen Charlotte had several rooms at Windsor Castle and Buckingham House designed in a chinoiserie style or embellished with Chinese and Chinese-inspired elements. Although these interiors do not survive, they are well recorded in Pyne's *Royal Palaces*. In the case of the Queen's State Bedchamber at Windsor Castle, where red constitutes the dominant colour, Pyne notes that 'the new walls [are] judiciously coloured with a tint that does not obtrude itself on the eye; a circumstance that should be attended to in all picture galleries'.[29] The room is significant in having at least four black lacquer cabinets, introducing a chinoiserie element to what was effectively a picture gallery. It is shown in Pyne as it appeared in James Wyatt's design from 1804,[30] making it only slightly later than the first chinoiserie interiors at the Pavilion. However, other chinoiserie interiors predate both the Pavilion and even George's early Chinese Drawing Room at Carlton House. Queen Charlotte's Breakfast Room at Buckingham House was furnished with black and gold painted panelling that had been transferred from the Crimson Drawing Room in 1763.[31] Pyne describes the panels as 'formed of beautiful japan, which has a pleasing effect'.[32] The room was further embellished with some of Charlotte's collection of Asian and European porcelain. The watercolour that informed Pyne's aquatint shows the arrangement of the room in *c.*1817, but the collection of porcelain had been in situ from at least 1783.[33] This room may have been the inspiration for lacquer-panelled rooms at Frogmore House in Windsor Park.

2.22 *(right) The Three Eldest Princesses: Charlotte, Princess Royal, Augusta and Elizabeth*, oil on canvas by Thomas Gainsborough, 1783–4. RCIN 400206, © Royal Collection Enterprises Limited 2025 | Royal Collection Trust

2.23 *(below) Queen Charlotte with her Two Eldest Sons*, oil on canvas by Johan Joseph Zoffany, 1764. RCIN 400146, © Royal Collection Enterprises Limited 2025 | Royal Collection Trust

At Frogmore House, the creativity of female members of the Royal Family resulted in several complete chinoiserie schemes in the early nineteenth century. Frogmore House, named 'Queen's House' by Pyne, had long been associated with female royal occupants, such as Queen Anne and Queen Caroline. In 1792 Queen Charlotte acquired the lease on the seventeenth-century house and instructed James Wyatt to convert it into a neoclassical villa in a picturesque setting. Following these improvements, the house was frequently used for fêtes, concerts and garden parties.[34] The house also became strongly associated with three of the Queen's daughters: Princess Elizabeth, Princess Augusta and Charlotte, Princess Royal.[35]

While the Princess Royal and Princess Augusta had inherited their mother's interest in drawing, engraving and botanical illustration, Princess Elizabeth involved herself particularly in the interior decoration of several royal residences. With some input from the Princess Royal, she is thought to have been the creative force behind three chinoiserie interiors at Frogmore House, two of which she appears to have partly executed herself. In Pyne's *Royal Residences* two of the six aquatints illustrating the house, based on Charles Wild's watercolours, show these chinoiserie interiors: the [Red] Japan Room[36] (fig. 2.24) and the Green Closet (fig. 2.25).[37] A further Black Japan Room and a barely described India Room are not illustrated.

2.24 *(above) Frogmore House: The Japan Room*, watercolour, bodycolour and pencil drawing by Charles Wild, *c.*1819. RCIN 922122, © Royal Collection Enterprises Limited 2025 | Royal Collection Trust

2.25 *(opposite) Frogmore House: The Green Closet*, watercolour, bodycolour and pencil drawing by Charles Wild, *c.*1819. RCIN 922123, © Royal Collection Enterprises Limited 2025 | Royal Collection Trust

As complete interior designs, these rooms are of great significance when seen in the context to the development of the decorative schemes of the Pavilion. Similar to the Pavilion's chinoiserie interiors, they are a post-Rococo manifestation of the chinoiserie fashion and represent the late, more vibrant flowering of what was considered a feminine style.

Elizabeth is credited with painting the panels and some of the furniture in the Japan Room: 'The walls of this apartment were painted, in imitation of rich japan, by her Royal Highness the Princess Elizabeth; the furniture was ornamented by the same tasteful hand.'[38] The room seems to have been further embellished with a combination of Chinese teapots and European imitations of Asian porcelain. Elizabeth also appears to have created the walls of the Black Japan Room, a room in which, according to Pyne, 'an additional interest is excited, in knowing that the taste which the room displays, is all the work of female ingenuity', since the embroidery of the upholstery and soft furnishings was carried out by a school for orphans established under the patronage of Queen Charlotte.[39]

The Japan Room was the central room facing the garden on the ground floor of Frogmore House and is now called the Yellow Drawing Room. What the Pavilion interiors and the japanned rooms at Frogmore House have in common is a radical and assured move away from a classically inspired style, including garlands, medallions, urns and trellis-work, to a bold chinoiserie style created sometime between 1797 and 1807. Jane Roberts refers to the drawing by Henry Wigstead, inscribed 'Frogmore Hall at the Fete 1797', that shows the Red Japan Room almost certainly decorated for a fête in the neoclassical style. A decade later, on 19 September 1807, Princess Elizabeth, who had introduced the classical garlands in 1793, told her friend Lady Cathcart in a letter: 'I am busy putting up my Japan room at Frogmore which place is as dear to me as ever.'[40]

The Green Closet formed the third chinoiserie interior at Frogmore and is described as an 'apartment fitted up with original japan, of a beautiful fabric, on a pure green ground. The cabinets and chairs are of Indian cane'.[41] Some of the other Asian objects seen in Wild's watercolour may have been presents given by the Qianlong Emperor to George III in 1793.[42] Crucially, both the Japan Room and the Green Closet are clearly represented as female spaces in the illustrations: both watercolours show the rooms occupied by seated women; in the case of the Green Closet a single female figure is reading, while two female figures, writing and in conversation, are depicted in the Japan Room. This was perhaps supposed to underline

2.26 *(left)* The Long Gallery after 1819, watercolour drawing by Augustus Charles Pugin, *c.*1823

2.27 *(opposite)* A settee from the Visakhapatnam set of furniture, *c.*1770, in the Long Gallery during the exhibition *A Prince's Treasure*, 2019–22. RCIN 489, Royal Collection Trust / © His Majesty King Charles III 2024

both the creative origins of these specific interiors and the association of chinoiserie interiors with female tastes. None of these interiors at Frogmore survive, but some of these lacquer panels were probably transferred to Princess Elizabeth's marital home, Schloss Homburg in Hessen, Germany, where fragments survive in the 'English wing' of the palace.[43] The exact time for the introduction of the Chinese theme at Frogmore is not known. While it is possible that the first chinoiserie scheme at the Pavilion preceded these rooms at Frogmore, the mutual influence and inspiration among the royal siblings in matters of interior decoration is obvious and may help explain this cluster of chinoiserie interiors at the Georgian court in the early years of the nineteenth century.

2.28 Detail of one of the chairs of the Visakhapatnam set of furniture, *c.*1770, in the Long Gallery during the exhibition *A Prince's Treasure*, 2019–22. RCIN 488 © Royal Collection Enterprises Limited 2025 | Royal Collection Trust

The India Room is given a brief description, of only a few lines by Pyne, as an interior featuring an elaborately carved ivory bed, white satin embroidered upholstery and red velvet cushions, with no reference to a designer or creator.[44] A set of Indian sandalwood settees and chairs, veneered in ivory and originating in Visakhapatnam, was an important feature in the later manifestation of the Pavilion's Long Gallery (fig. 2.26). They originally belonged to Queen Charlotte but were bought by George shortly after her death in 1819, indicating that he shared his mother's taste in 'oriental' objects.[45] The objects purchased at the posthumous sale of her goods in May 1819 are perhaps the most compelling and moving piece of evidence of Queen Charlotte's influence on her son's taste. He bought no fewer than 70 lots, of a total value of just over £2,735. Most of the items were of Asian style or origin, including Chinese fans, Indian furniture and boxes, items such as a 'Mandarin Dress' and 55 yards of Chinese scarlet silk.[46] The sale coincided with the busiest period of redecoration ever carried out in the Pavilion, and many of the purchased items were incorporated there. The set of Visakhapatnam furniture is still in the Royal Collection (Royal Collection Inventory Numbers 487-489) and some of it formed part of the temporary loan exhibition: *A Prince's Treasure* in 2019 (figs 2.27 and 2.28).

The chinoiserie designs of the Japan Rooms at Frogmore House were more close in style to Queen Charlotte's japanned Breakfast Room at Buckingham House than the Pavilion interiors. In the Pavilion's early chinoiserie interiors the Craces avoided large-scale use of japanned wall panelling. However, in the later, post-1815 schemes, the Craces introduced large-scale wall decorations for the new Music Room that give the impression of lacquered surfaces and included some japanned panelling. These decorations appear to echo the 'Japan' cabinets at Frogmore House and earlier chinoiserie interiors at Buckingham House. By comparison, they are monumental, covering almost the entire triple-height wall spaces on three sides of the room. George, in his usual manner, did it on a bigger scale and in a more exuberant style than anyone before him, and magnified decorative elements he had seen in the private, female spaces of other royal residences into a much larger architectural space, designed for public entertainment.

2.29 *A View of the South End of the Prince of Wales's Chinese Drawing-Room*, engraving from Thomas Sheraton's *The Cabinet-Maker and Upholsterer's Drawing-Book*, 1793–5 (repr. 1970)

CARLTON HOUSE: GEORGE'S FIRST CHINOISERIE CREATIONS

Carlton House became George's London residence in 1783, when he turned 21. Until then he had spent most of his time at Kew, Buckingham House or Windsor Castle. Carlton House was in many ways an architectural playground for the young prince, where he experimented with interior design schemes, some of which articulated ideas that he would explore further in the Pavilion. Architects and designers first employed at Carlton House were later called to Brighton, including Holland and John Crace, transferring certain design ideas and styles to his new seaside residence. In some cases, furniture and decorative objects were moved from Carlton House to the Pavilion. Crucially, the building featured the first chinoiserie interiors commissioned by George. These, and the history of the house in general, were researched in detail by Geoffrey de Bellaigue,[47] who also curated an exhibition about the decorations of Carlton House in 1991,[48] and more recently by David Oakey.[49]

In *Royal Residences* Pyne criticises the lack of unity of the architectural design of Carlton House, which is perhaps indicative of George's experimental character and eclectic taste: 'The general effect of the exterior of Carlton-House, combined with the Ionic screen, as viewed from the Pall Mall, although imposing in appearance, does not possess sufficient unity of character to satisfy the eye of taste' (fig. 1.16).[50] However, de Bellaigue identified certain unifying elements (including colour) in George's first large architectural experiment, with noticeable similarities to the later naming of rooms at the Pavilion:

> In some cases the unifying factor was colour. We come across such names as The Yellow Bow Room, The Blue Bow Room and, unbelievable though it may sound, the Flesh-Coloured Room. Apart from colour, unity was also achieved – or intended to be achieved – by the repetition of the same materials. For example, the Prince of Wales planned to have a tapestry room in which the walls were to be hung with Gobelins tapestries and the seats were to be upholstered in the same material.[51]

Further descriptions gleaned from Pyne highlight George's interest in the way a variety of imitative paint surfaces and ornaments could form a contrast to the ground colour of a room.

A Chinese Drawing Room on the lower floor of Carlton House, probably designed in *c.*1788–90 by

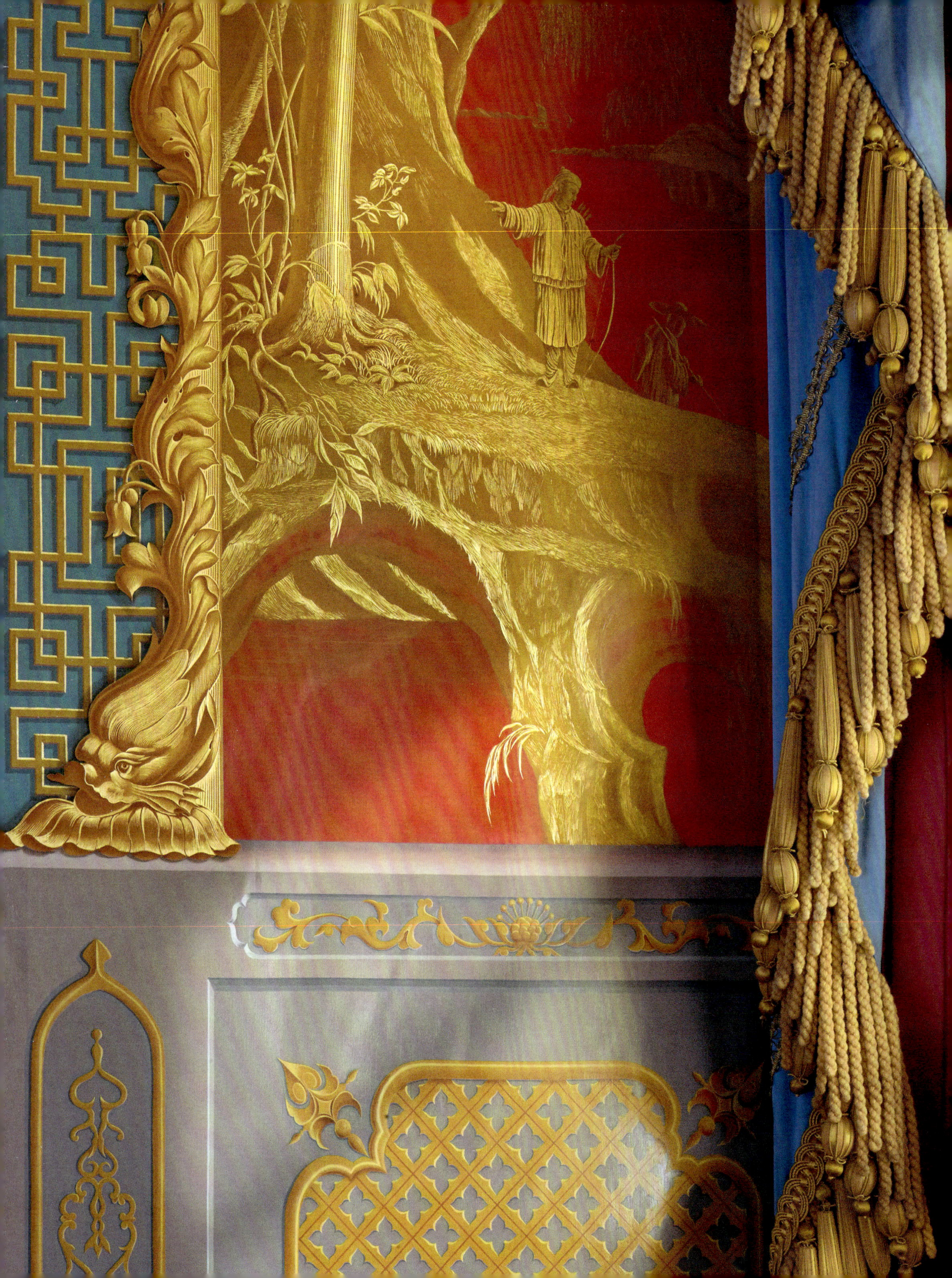

Dominique Daguerre in collaboration with Henry Holland and furnished in an advanced Parisian chinoiserie taste, is regrettably not described in Pyne's *Royal Residences* because by the time Pyne wrote the text the chinoiserie interior had been superseded by other schemes. However, two engravings of the room are included in Thomas Sheraton's *The Cabinet-Maker and Upholsterer's Drawing-Book* from 1793 (fig. 2.29). It is not known when exactly the interior of this room was changed, but it is likely that some of its design elements were reused in a later chinoiserie room, also absent from Pyne. The scheme of this later room, dating from 1805 to 1807 and designed by Walsh Porter, is described in a bill book as predominantly black and carmine, with pagodas painted on a carmine ground on the walls, while the doors were ornamented with figures in gold on a black ground. The ceiling had a ground colour of lilac and green, featuring stars and signs of the Chinese zodiac, with a large painted dragon in the centre. These ceiling decorations were matched by a carpet design in lilac and green, featuring a bamboo trellis pattern, flowers and a harbour scene.[52] Porter added 'four large handsome flying dragons shaded and gilt, to hold lanthorns', supplied by Parker and Perry.[53] Oakey suggests that these bills 'conjure an image closer to the theatrical chinoiserie later seen at Brighton than Holland and Daguerre's version as published in Sheraton ten or so years previously'.[54] Indeed, Porter's Chinese Room featured some elements that were also applied in the Pavilion, notably the combination of carmine ground with gold embellishment (fig. 2.16), centrally placed dragon ornaments on ceilings (figs 1.60 and 1.85), and the rather unusual use of lilac in the bamboo trellis pattern, which can be found at lower level in the Music Room (fig. 2.30), and was also present in the Pavilion in Chinese export wallpaper of the same ground colour (see Chapter 3).

Pyne describes another room with chinoiserie elements at Carlton House, the Rose Satin Drawing Room: 'Situated in the south front of Carlton-House, this elegant room forms the bow which marks the centre of the building. Its embellishments are partly composed of furniture in the Chinese style, although its architecture and other decorations are generally in correspondence with the rest of the apartments.'[55] In this interior, created before 1818, chinoiserie merely consists of additional ornaments: a chimney piece, clocks, mandarin figures and fretwork furniture, all set against an essentially classical interior with a rose-coloured satin as ground colour. This colour may have inspired the pink ground on the walls on the Long Gallery in the Pavilion (figs 0.7, 2.26 to 2.28).

At least three of the Chinese 'nodding' clay figures from Carlton House were later transferred to the Pavilion,[56] as were many other decorative objects,

2.30 *(opposite)* Detail of a corner of the Music Room, showing the combination of carmine, gold and lilac

2.31 *(right)* The Music Room Gallery in *c.*1823, after Augustus Charles Pugin, aquatint from John Nash's *The Royal Pavilion at Brighton*, 1826

including mounted Chinese porcelain as well as chairs and other furniture. The most distinctive of these were the two pier tables, made by Adam Weisweiler and supplied by Daguerre, from the earlier Chinese Drawing Room. These were placed in the Music Room Gallery (formerly known as the Yellow Drawing Room) in 1821, alongside a pair of near-identical copies by Bailey and Sanders (made in 1819), when the room was redecorated. They are clearly visible in the Sheraton engravings and in *Nash's Views* (fig. 2.31) and were returned as part of the *A Prince's Treasure* loan exhibition, along with the French chinoiserie candelabra that also appear in the engravings (fig. 2.32).

Carlton House was in many respects a precursor of the design schemes of the Pavilion, and is described by de Bellaigue as 'a testing ground for the Prince of Wales's essays in chinoiserie, which found their fullest expression in Brighton Pavilion'.[57] Another room in Carlton House that may have informed the Pavilion interiors, the Circular Dining Room, will be discussed in the context of silver in Chapter 3. As well as the chinoiserie interiors at his London residence, the Prince had also planned a 'Chinese Temple' in the garden of Carlton House in 1789, which presumably was never built.[58]

GEORGE IV'S INVOLVEMENT IN DECORATING THE PAVILION

Despite the considerable amount of literature on George as collector and patron of the arts, information about how he communicated with the architects, designers and artists he commissioned remains scarce, and we have next to no written comments from George himself on matters of taste, design and style. After his death, one of his executors, the Duke of Wellington, destroyed many of his private letters, including correspondence with his illegal wife Maria Fitzherbert.[59] Morley suggests that protocol forbade direct exchange between the King and artists and designers, or that communication via letter was often not necessary.[60] The lack of written evidence notwithstanding, E. Maurice Bloch, Keeper of Prints and Drawings at the Cooper Union Museum, New York (now Cooper Hewitt, Smithsonian Design Museum), in the 1940s and 50s, who studied the design drawings for the Pavilion in great detail, was convinced that the 'active and personal interest of the Prince Regent in his marine residence overshadowed and influenced every detail of the work created' – a character trait he likely inherited from his father. Bloch suggests that George was the mastermind of the creation of the Pavilion, 'a kind of Royal impresario about to embark on an operatic production, the staging envisioned over a long period, every detail planned in his fertile mind with relation to the final effect'.[61]

Indeed, the Crace Ledger includes many references to the presence of George during the installation of decorative objects, the hanging of wallpaper and changes to design schemes. A closer look at these site visits paints a vivid picture of George's direct involvement in the design process and his remarkably close observation of the changes being made to the Pavilion. For example, an early entry from the 1802 visit reveals that George was overseeing the hanging of Chinese export wallpaper and other work. Frederick Crace charged for three and three-quarter days 'attending the Prince in hanging the paper in sundry rooms, attending fixing up and cutting out the Birds, &c on the paper in Saloon'.[62] A particularly detailed entry in the Crace Ledger records the regular attendance of George between July 1815 and March 1816, marking the beginning of the major interior and exterior changes of the Pavilion under John Nash:

> DAY WORK in attendance upon HIS ROYAL HIGHNESS
> July Attending His Royal Highness with 8 assistants putting in patterns of sundry works in the Small Drawing Room and Gallery
> 1½ day each and materials
> Aug 7th Attending His Royal Highness with 10 assistants putting in patterns to Small Drawing Room – framework of pannels in Saloon and arranging the India Paper for the different rooms
> 2 days each and materials
> 15th Attending His Royal Highness with 9 assistants putting in patterns to Small Drawing Room, arranging the pictures, India paper &c in Yellow

2.32 *(opposite)* Some of the objects and furniture originally from Carlton House on display in the Music Room Gallery during the exhibition *A Prince's Treasure* (2019–22), including a pier table by Bailey and Sanders after Adam Weisweiler (RCIN 181.2) and two French candelabra (RCIN 4246.3 and 4246.4). © Royal Collection Enterprises Limited 2025 | Royal Collection Trust

Drawing Room; putting in patterns to Entrance Hall and Gallery and arranging Mr Jone's [*sic*] pictures
1½ day each and materials

Sept 16 Attending His Royal Highness with 6 assistants putting in patterns to Yellow Drawing Room, Entrance Hall, Prince Regent's Bedroom &c and arranging the pictures and India Paper
2½ days and materials

Oct 18 Attending His Royal Highness with 8 assistants putting in patterns to Entrance Hall, Saloon and Yellow Drawing Room, making alterations in His Royal Highness's Bed and Anti Rooms
2 days each and materials

Dec 1 To Attending His Royal Highness with 8 assistants in putting in patterns to Yellow Drawing Room, making alteration in the Bedroom, Anti Room and fixing up pictures in Bedroom . . .
20 1 man in attendance by desire of His Royal Highness to keep the skylights and the whole of the house clean and in repair from December 28th to March 30

DESIGNS AND DRAWINGS

Making various designs and working drawings (by order) for the Carver, Skylight maker, Upholsterer, Stove maker &c in the whole 44 drawings including various designs &c by order of His Royal Highness, attending to the execution of the standards, skylights, canopy &c[63]

George also attended the hanging of yet more Chinese wallpaper ('India paper') around the same time: 'Mr Crace and his men attending His Royal Highness in arranging the hanging of the India Paper and birds in Saloon, Prince Regent's Bedroom and other rooms'.[64]

A similar entry is found in 1818, which also alludes to George making drawings of his design ideas and patterns:

Attending at Brighton by His Royal Highness's command from the 23rd December to the 28th in making designs for the finishing of the ornamental painting of the Music Room

To Artist's time assisting in making drawings and patterns

Carriage, Lodging, &c

Preparing designs for His Royal Highness in London and also some large patterns on linen by his desire for the finishing of the Music Room

Paid Artist's time and materials &c assisting for the above

Attending His Royal Highness at Brighton in making drawings and putting in patterns on the wall of the Music Room as intended to be finished . . .

Carriage time and lodging

Attending His Royal Highness in making drawings for the chimneypiece, pagodas and patterns, and putting in sundry D[itt]o in Music Room[65]

A note by John Gregory Crace in the Frederick Crace Book of Designs (fig. 2.33) further illustrates how George would have perused, discussed and chosen ornamental detail and colour schemes for the Pavilion. John Gregory recorded on the flyleaf: 'Scraps from Chinese ornaments drawn by Frederick Crace. This book was often looked on by George IV'.[66] The drawing from the sketchbook shown here (fig. 2.34) was part of a design for the Music Room clerestory windows (fig. 2.35) and relates to a more developed design drawing in the Cooper Hewitt Collection (fig. 2.36). Despite similarities to Crace drawings of the 'Royal Bird Foo Hum', the design was identified by Morley as a 'moth/bird' and as a 'giant moth'.[67]

An entry from 1819/20 in the Crace Ledger reveals how particular George was about details of design schemes. In this occasion, he changed his mind about the exact colour of the latticed borders in the Music Room (from blue to lilac) (fig. 2.30):

Preparing and painting in imitation of bamboo the reeded ceiling at each end of the room and ornamenting the same with blue ribbons and highly varnished

Repainting the ribbons Lilac instead of blue, by order of His Majesty[68]

On another occasion, Frederick Crace charged £49 for removing some 'gold speckling' on several doors because George had not approved of it. The same entry also records the preparation of design drawings for his inspection:

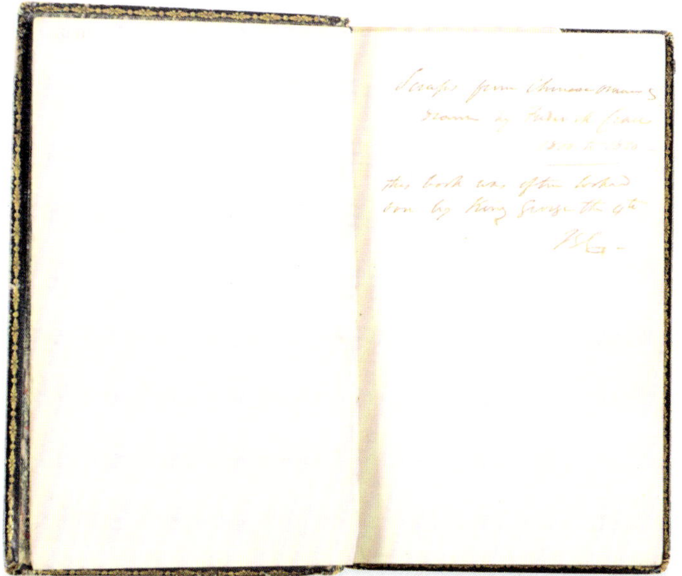

2.33 *(above left)* John Gregory Crace's inscription on the flyleaf of Frederick Crace's Sketchbook with 68 coloured designs from Chinese ornaments, *c.*1800–20

2.34 *(above right)* A drawing that formed part of the design for the Music Room clerestory windows, from Frederick Crace's Sketchbook with 68 coloured designs from Chinese ornaments, *c.*1800–20

> Preparing and fixing up various patterns for the approbation of His Majesty, Artist's and men's time and material . . .
>
> Preparing and gilding in Green Gold the stiles of 7 pair of folding doors and linings, redone in consequence of the Gold speckling not being approved of[69]

Several letters among the Crace papers in the National Art Library, London, give a vivid impression of how George kept his designers on their toes. He frequently ordered the Craces and Jones to meet him urgently in Brighton to inspect and discuss aspects of the decorative schemes. Some of the letters were written on behalf of George by Jean-Baptiste Watier. In one letter, dated 1 January 1818, he expresses his concern about progress and stresses the importance of inspecting and discussing the designs on site: 'The Prince Regent wishes you to come down as soon as you can & to bring with you everything necessary, and also what you have done. The P.R. w'd rather see your progress here. He is fearful that you will not understand him unless he has you on the spot.'[70]

Entries and letters like these prompted Morley to suggest that George was 'always in direct intercourse, on more than equal terms, with his architects and decorators – constantly at their elbows; designing; making technical suggestions; ordering, and no doubt cajoling with his well-known "condescension"; often rejecting, as is seen over and over again in frequent changes of mind and changes of scheme.'[71]

Morley noted that George's interest in fashion and masquerade costumes might have been precursors to a preference for complementary colour schemes, referring to a sketch in his own hand of a Hussar's uniform.[72] Jane Roberts, too, attested to the practical design interests of George, and his focus on fashion and interior design:

> The few drawings that survive from the Prince of Wales's hand are, perhaps characteristically, sketches of designs for furniture, a fountain, and for the decoration of the panels of the New Music Room at Brighton Pavilion in 1818 . . . His interest in design and his own clothes manifested itself in his earliest drawings, in 1780 for a tripod or therme made up for him by a cabinet maker, and the present elaborate Hussar's uniform with a jewelled sword and flowered blue sash which he evidently intended to wear to a masquerade celebrating his twenty-first birthday.[73]

Finally, George's close supervision of any aspect of building work and design projects is also reported in the context of the production of *Nash's Views*. Benjamin

Ferrey, chronicler and biographer of Augustus Welby Northmore Pugin and his father Augustus Charles, records that George revised the proof impressions of the engraved plates for the book personally.[74] According to Ferrey, A.C. Pugin was also once surprised by the King while making the sketches for the work in the Pavilion (possibly in the Music Room Gallery or Banqueting Room Gallery, figs 2.37 and 2.38); the King was clearly intent on inspecting the artist's progress:

> He was engaged in one of the galleries of the Pavilion colouring a view. Deeply intent upon his drawing, he did not observe that someone had entered the apartment, but on looking round, to his surprise, saw the King, who was then advancing to the spot where he was sitting. Pugin had scarcely time to rise when the King, passing by him and not perceiving a stool on which a colour-box was placed, accidentally overthrew it. The King stooped, and instantly picking up the box, gave it to Pugin with an expression of apology.[75]

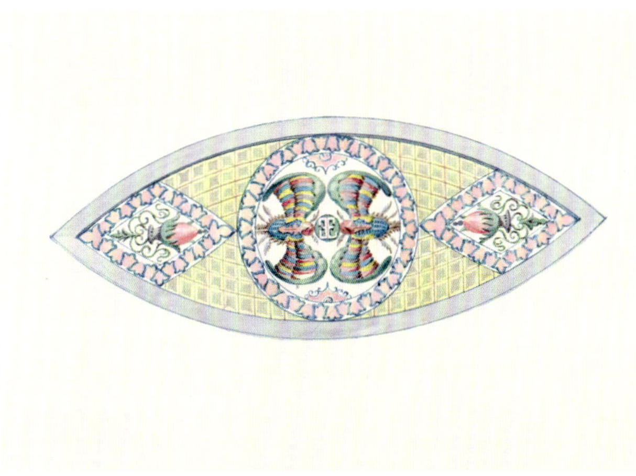

2.35 *(opposite)* View of part of west wall of the Music Room and the clerestory window above the chimneypiece during the exhibition *A Prince's Treasure*, 2019–22

2.36 *(above)* Design for a glass panel window for the coved ceiling in the Music Room, watercolour drawing by Frederick Crace, *c.*1817., Cooper Hewitt Smithsonian Design Museum, Acc. No. 1948-40-89

2.37 *(below)* The Banqueting Room Gallery, watercolour drawing by Augustus Charles Pugin, 1821 or later

Given the range and variety of anecdotes and archival evidence, there can be little doubt that George was interested in every detail of the Pavilion's interior design. He probably provided his designers with ideas, rough sketches and instructions, and regularly inspected and supervised the installation and execution of design schemes on site. What is less clear is how architects, interior designers and suppliers of wallpaper, furniture and other design elements communicated and worked together. Unfortunately but one letter between Nash and the Craces survives, but a letter from Nash to Frederick Crace dated 19 May 1818 suggests that Nash, instructed by George, regularly inspected the design drawings produced by the interior decorators: 'I am directed to inspect the designs you are painting for Brighton. I will thank you to bring all the drawings here at 9 tomorrow morning, particularly of the chimney pieces & such as relates to the architectural or constructive parts of the room.'[76] A letter in the National Art Library from Watier to Frederick Crace dated 7 April 1818 describes a similar exchange between Crace and the furniture makers Bailey and Sanders, suggesting that a system was in place that ensured communication between the various designers and makers involved in creating the decorative scheme of each room: 'Mr Crace will be so good to give his designs and instructions to Mess Bailey & Sanders for the canopies, cornices, glass frames, pannels, pillasters, & serpents connected with the draperies, for the fitting up and decorating the Music Room, at the Pavilion, at Brighton.'[77]

'IT ENCHANTS THE SENSES, AND EXCITES': THE PAVILION'S INTERIORS IN NINETEENTH-CENTURY LITERATURE

Early descriptions of the Pavilion's decorative schemes from people not directly involved in its creation both reflected and influenced the general public's opinions

2.38 *(above)* The Music Room Gallery, watercolour drawing by Augustus Charles Pugin, 1821 or later

2.39 *(opposite)* Design for a passageway with a canopy for the Royal Pavilion (probably for the Glass Passage), ink and watercolour drawing by Frederick Crace, *c.*1817. Cooper Hewitt Smithsonian Design Museum, Acc. No. 1948-40-65

of this unusual building. These popular descriptions are useful for identifying public tastes, and imagining how first-time visitor in the early nineteenth century would have experienced the building and its garden.

A considerable degree of repetition is noticeable in descriptions of the building before municipal ownership, because access to this royal residence was not easy for the general public. Eyewitness descriptions of the interior were therefore freely recycled and embellished until the sale of the Pavilion in 1850, by which time it had been stripped of the Craces' and Jones's decorative schemes. For example, in 1826 Karl Friedrich Schinkel, John Nash's counterpart as perhaps the most celebrated German architect at the time, was keen to see the inside of the Pavilion, but he notes in his journal on 9 June that 'Lord Conyngham had refused the Ambassador's request for permission for us to view the Pavilion in Brighton, as the King does not allow anyone in.'[78] Schinkel finally gained access when the King learned who the prospective visitor was.[79]

Among the key early authors or publishers considered here are Charles Walker, H.R. Attree, Richard Sickelmore and Edward Wedlake Brayley. Brayley included an early overview of the recently finished interiors in *Topographical Sketches of Brighthelmston* from 1825 and, in 1838, provided the first detailed description and a history of the building in the new edition of *Nash's Views*. This was entitled *Illustrations of Her Majesty's Palace at Brighton* and the text can be considered the first complete and stand-alone description of the interiors.[80] A later guidebooks, which add information about early restoration efforts and interpretations under municipal ownership and changing attitudes to chinoiserie style, will also be discussed briefly.

The earliest handbooks and travel guides published after 1800 and aimed at visitors to the fashionable resort, such as Charles Walker's *Brighton and its Environs* and Attree's *Topography of Brighton* (both from 1809) include only brief descriptions of the Pavilion, then still in its neoclassical exterior manifestation. When these were published, the first interior redecoration in a chinoiserie style, begun in *c.*1802, would have been implemented.

2.40 Design for two Chinese-style screen doors with painted glass floral panels, possibly for the Glass Passage, watercolour drawing by John or Frederick Crace, *c.*1802

The building had also been extended in 1801, in the shape of two wings on the east side, referred to as an 'Eating Room' at the north end and a 'Conservatory' (used as a music room) at the south end (see Chapter 1, p. 57). Although the exact appearance of these rooms, removed in *c.*1817 during Nash's transformation, is not recorded, many Crace drawings and account entries, as well as the early guidebooks, suggest that they were decorated in a chinoiserie style. Walker informs the reader that 'the entrance hall . . . is embellished, as are all other rooms, according to the Chinese taste'.[81] He notes distinct changes in colour schemes in different rooms, and describes the 'Glass Passage' leading to the Conservatory as being 'entirely formed of stained glass, on which is painted the insects, flowers, and fruits of the Chinese'.[82] A few Crace drawings in the Cooper Hewitt Collection (for example, fig. 2.39) likely show designs for this glass passage, and several smaller drawings in the Royal Pavilion Archives (for example, fig. 2.40) may relate to this structure.[83] Referring to it as a 'lamp of beauty', Walker tells the reader that this room is 'on particular occasions . . . brilliantly illuminated, and an observer of no very warm fancy may, at these seasons, imagine himself in Fairy Land'.[84] He thus identifies a number of design features of the Pavilion interiors that were carried over and developed into the extended building after 1815: distinct colour schemes, 'oriental' imagery, coloured glass and dramatic lighting.

Many reactions to the Chinese-inspired interior before the 1820s are notably positive, expressing awe and wonder, and rate the exterior less highly by comparison. Attree states that the interior 'never fails to excite the most rapturous astonishment; but the exterior, though it may please for the moment, possesses nothing very strikingly grand to surprise or interest.'[85] This is not surprising, since Nash had not yet given the exterior its Indian-inspired makeover and until 1818 the Pavilion was eclipsed by William Porden's recently finished stables complex. Attree refers to the 'brilliancy' of the interiors in almost all of his brief paragraphs on each of the rooms, thus providing one of the earliest detailed descriptions of the colour layout: the Entrance Hall is 'the colour of . . . warm clay', in the Ante Room the ground colour is identified as 'scarlet', in the Drawing Room 'bright yellow', while the Conservatory is described as 'indescribably brilliant in effect', with a roof 'painted in imitation of tea and rose wood, and supported

by twenty columns of a scarlet colour'.[86] The most detailed information is given of the Rotunda (Saloon): the clouded sky ceiling, suspended dragons and 'lanthorns' are described in effusive detail, as are other ornamental features: 'The cornice and frieze of this elegant apartment are scarlet, blue and yellow, before which hangs a yellow silk net, with tassels and bells, splendid in effect, and perfectly unique' (figs. 2.41 and 2.42).[87]

As in Walker, lighting and illumination are here identified as key aspects of the decorative scheme: 'In the various lanthorns are upwards of thirty organd [*sic*] burners, which diffuse a brilliance more easily conceived than expressed and display the panelled sides of the room, and a beautiful paper of a blue ground, the ornaments of which are white etched with silver.'[88] The emphasis on reflective surfaces is evident, and the description of the blue and silver wallpaper matches a design drawing by Frederick Crace in the Cooper Hewitt Collection, dated 1802 or earlier (fig. 2.43). The anonymous publication *Three Grand Routes from Brighton to London, and Topography of that Fashionable Watering Place* from 1815 copies Attree's text word for word, suggesting that either Attree himself was the author or that the text was plagiarised. In any case, it suggests that the text was still considered a reliable description of the interiors at that point in time.

From 1815 to the late 1820s the local historian, writer and publisher of guidebooks and maps, Richard Sickelmore (Senior) provides detailed descriptions of the evolving decorative schemes. His popular books *An Epitome of Brighton* (1815), *The History of Brighton* (from 1823 to 1827, in at least five editions) and *Descriptive Views of Brighton* (1824) all include accounts in excess of ten pages of the principal rooms of the Pavilion. Sickelmore's books are of particular importance since they record the changing interior schemes during the crucial period of Nash's involvement. That said, his 1815 publication closely follows Attree's descriptions of Holland's building, with additional notes on building work being carried out, for example: 'At present, this Hall, which makes part of the

2.41 *(opposite)* Design for the decoration of the Saloon in the Royal Pavilion, graphite and watercolour drawing by Frederick Crace, *c.*1815 or earlier. Cooper Hewitt Smithsonian Design Museum, Acc. No. 1948-40-25-a,b

2.42 *(below left)* Design for a Chinese-style spherical lantern with tassels, probably for the Saloon, watercolour drawing by John or Frederick Crace, 1815 or earlier

2.43 *(below right)* Design for blue and silver wall decoration for the Royal Pavilion, graphite and watercolour drawing by Frederick Crace, 1802 or earlier. Cooper Hewitt Smithsonian Design Museum, Acc. No. 1948-40-64

late improvements, is in an unfinished state, and plain in appearance.'[89] In a similar vein, Charles Wright, author of *The Brighton Ambulator, Containing Historical and Topographical Delineations of the Town, from the Earliest Period to the Present Time* (1818), which is 'dedicated, by permission, to His Royal Highness the Prince Regent', attests to the 'internal beauties and embellishments of this delightful residence', but adds that owing to the unfinished state of the Banqueting Hall and Music Room 'it is impossible to do justice to the magnificence of the taste and style displayed in the principal apartments'.[90] The book includes an unusual engraved frontispiece by R. Alford (fig. 2.44) showing the east front of the Pavilion in 1818, with Nash's Music and Banqueting Rooms already flanking Holland's building.

The completion, or near completion, of the Pavilion's interiors following Nash's transformation was evidently a catalyst for a great number of authors offering descriptions of the new and newly decorated rooms, beginning with an article in the *Brighton Herald* on 21 January 1821. This was probably written by Sickelmore and forms one of the first detailed published accounts of the interiors, despite their unfinished state. This is evidence of journalists and other members of the public having had occasional access to a building still under construction, and reflects the considerable public interest in the development of the Pavilion. Many contemporaries of Sickelmore refer to him as the definitive source of information and several subsequent guidebooks and newspaper articles copy his text or paraphrase his descriptions: for example, Brayley in *Topographical Sketches of Brighthelmston* (*c.*1825), Whittemore in *Brighton and its Environs* (first edition 1825) and Bruce in *Bruce's History of Brighton* (1828).

In November 1821 the London-based author John Evans acknowledges an 'original account' from the *Brighton Herald* and copies the passages describing the Music Room and Banqueting Room in *An Excursion to Brighton*, a popular guidebook for London travellers.[91] All other rooms are omitted, emphasising the interest in the new Nash extensions to the north and south of the building. An article from January 1822 in the *Brighton*

2.44 *View of the Pavilion taken from Wright's Circulating Library May 1818*, engraving by R. Alford from Charles Wright's *The Brighton Ambulator*, 1818

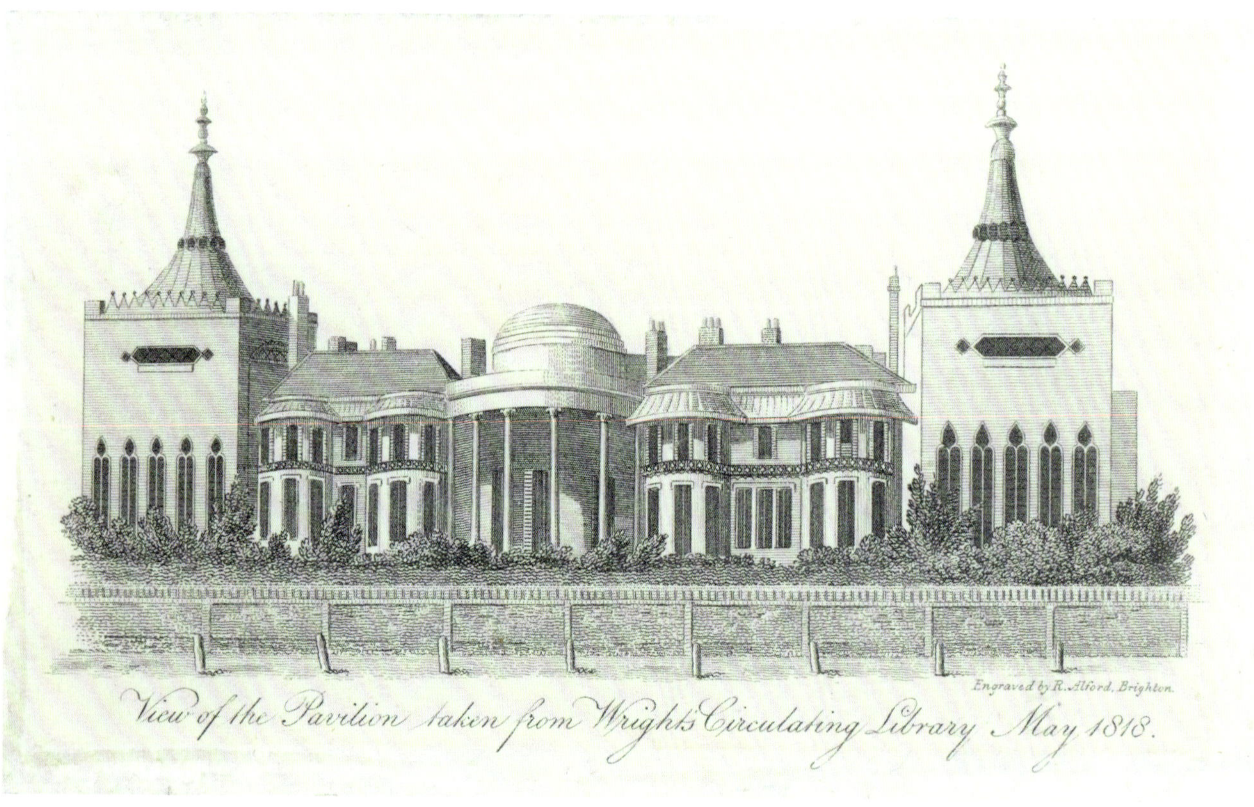

2.45 The Long Gallery before 1820, showing Frederick Crace's 'peach-blossom' wallpaper, watercolour drawing by Augustus Charles Pugin, before 1820

Gazette reports on the elaborate lighting and use of coloured glass in the Pavilion, which included placing gas lights on the roof of the building to illuminate the interiors:

> in no single instance has gas been used within the walls of the palace; exteriorly it is so illuminated, and most brilliantly, when needed, and the stained glass of the Music and Banqueting Rooms, together with that of the hall etc are made to display their rich variety of tints inwards by the blaze of gas without.[92]

The sense of awe and wonder continues to be expressed in the majority of these early publications. Light, lighting, stained glass, lanterns, mirrors and the large chandeliers are considered crucial aspects of the decorative scheme, enhancing the 'magical' effect of the building. Sickelmore states that 'it is scarcely in the power of words to convey an accurate idea of [the Pavilion's] rich and glowing magnificence'.[93] Much attention is given to the design scheme of each individual room, from the tints and shades of wallpaper and carpets to the material and sheen of many decorative objects and furniture, in particular ceramics. However, the number of rooms described is limited to the principal state rooms, and in some cases to the post-1817 Banqueting Room and Music Room only.

In 1823 Sickelmore captures the colours in the principal rooms of the finished Nash buildings as follows. Omitting the Octagon Hall and Entrance Hall ('Vestibule' and 'Hall') he begins by describing the Long Gallery in a string of superlatives as 'one of the most superb apartments that art and fancy can produce and which, for richness in effect, and dazzling brilliance of decoration and design, is not to be equalled, perhaps, in Europe, if [not] the world'.[94] He refers to the ceiling and walls as 'coloured peach-blossom throughout, with niches, figures, &c. and light blue emblazonments in the Chinese fancy'. This is the hand-painted wallpaper by Frederick Crace (figs 2.26 and

2.45), which forms a contrast to the 'yellow marble' and 'light yellow' of the niches.[95] By labelling the wallpaper design as 'in the Chinese fancy', Sickelmore expresses a certain level of understanding of the difference between Chinese and chinoiserie objects. The colouring of the Long Gallery wallpaper may well have been inspired by eighteenth-century polychrome Chinese ceramics, such as famille rose.

Sickelmore compares Nash's Music Room to '*Thousand and One Nights*, and the popular tales of magic, involving the enchanted palaces of Genii', summarises it as 'the beautiful combination and effect of the myriads of glittering objects'.[96] It must be assumed that he is here referring to not just export ware in the form of ceramics and furniture but also fixed ornaments, such as the silvered dragons and snakes around the room (pp. 162–3) and the gilt scallop shells on the ceiling.

He continues with a description of these plaster shells ('gilt with green gold') and the central ornament on the ceiling 'representing, in all its vivid tints, the sunflower' (figs 2.46 and 1.75).[97]

Sickelmore meticulously describes the colouring and surfaces of Crace's wall paintings of the Music Room: 'highly finished, imitative of crimson japan; the subjects introduced are views in China . . . of a bright yellow, heightened in gold . . . frames of gold, with a bordering of blue and yellow fret, heightened in gold'.[98] Here he captures one of the principal effects of this particular Crace design: the imitation of lacquer furniture. He continues with the three-colour scheme of the window draperies (blue, red and yellow) and the Axminster carpet 'of a light blue, with Chinese subjects, in gold colour' and concludes by mentioning the brilliance and the colours of some of the ceramics in the room, for example the pagodas 'resting on [Spode] bases of shining blue' (fig. 2.47).[99]

2.46 *(below)* Detail of the Music Room ceiling

2.47 *(opposite)* The window side of the Music Room during the exhibition *A Prince's Treasure* (2019–22), with Chinese porcelain pagodas (RCIN 1.2, 1.3 and 1.4) and an 'Orleans jar' (RCIN 204.1) in situ.

Sickelmore's paragraph about the central chandelier in the Banqueting Room (fig. 2.49) is as dazzling and elaborate as the object itself and was copied in many later guidebooks:

> The lilies, when illuminated, dart their copious and vivid rays through the multiplied and sparkling tints, and influence connected objects to the semblance of rubies, pearls, glittering brilliants, and shining gold – creating, if the figure may be allowed, in mid-air, a diamond blaze. Its effect is magical: it enchants the senses, and excites, as it were, a feeling of spell-bound admiration in all within its radiance and circle.[100]

In the Banqueting Room, Sickelmore frequently likens surfaces to mother-of-pearl or actual pearls and, crucially, interprets the 'silvery hue' of the background of Robert Jones's figurative chinoiserie wall paintings (figs 2.3, 2.4 and 2.5) as 'a contrast to the splendid furniture, and brilliant colours of the paintings which it surrounds',[101] thus identifying the important role of silver as a colour in the Pavilion (see also Chapter 3, pp. 207–224). The overall 'grand and successful aim' of the Banqueting Room, he concludes, is a 'splendour of light and colour, with a natural and effective disposition of shade'.[102]

After having covered the Long Gallery, the Banqueting Room and the Music Room in such elaborate detail, Sickelmore devotes only about 150 words to the rest of building, mentioning the Saloon, the Music Room Gallery (the 'Yellow Room'), the Banqueting Room Gallery and other rooms only briefly, praising instead the 'close alliance' of the rooms, considering them 'several links of the radiant chain' which resolve themselves 'into a species of glowing perfection as a whole'.[103] While his writing style may seem a little too emphatic at times, it is evident that Sickelmore understood an important principle of the interior design of the Pavilion: the building ought to be considered a complete work of art, not simply a sequence of rooms with varying interiors. This important aspect of the Pavilion, and the significance of silver in this context, will be discussed further in Chapter 3.

In *Brighthelmston* (1825) Brayley copies Sickelmore almost word for word, praising 'this unique, but superbly ornamented structure' and describing the dazzling effect of the interior, created by combining vibrant colour schemes, glossy surfaces and the extensive use of chandeliers, skylights and mirrors.

2.48 The Banqueting Room central chandelier

Whittemore's *Brighton and its Environs* (1825) is significant because it includes two early images of the interior of the Pavilion, rare in small guidebooks: the Banqueting Room and the Music Gallery (figs 2.49 and 2.50). They are reproduced as small hand-coloured steel engravings, based loosely on images from *Nash's Views*.[104] The colouring of the pair shown here is unreliable and was probably executed by someone who had not seen the interiors.

A few early descriptions of the Pavilion were written by foreign visitors who had not been George's guests. Of particular interest, given that chinoiserie was strongly associated with continental interiors, is the publication of a French visitor's travel account. Published in 1834 in both Paris and London, this account by Comte Auguste de La Garde of his travels to England in 1827 provides an invaluable example of how a French citizen experienced the Pavilion. Like Schinkel, he needed written permission from the Lord Chamberlain to enter the building. While the architecture is described as 'bizarre', the Comte is delighted by the 'striking' interior, commenting on the amount of gilding, the bright colours and especially the tones and patterns of the wallpaper. He seems genuinely deceived by this 'Chinese' fantasy, created with the help of lavish decorative schemes and colours:

> The exterior of the Pavilion had struck me as bizarre; the interior was so unexpectedly different as to be equally striking. As might be expected, [the saloon], the banqueting hall, the music room, the gallery were all resplendent in gilt and bright colours, with rich hangings of every kind; but the astonishing feature – in the residence of a European monarch – was a meticulous imitation of the style and luxury of China! No detail had been overlooked: the strange colours and patterns of the wallpaper; the shapes of the lacquered furniture made from cypress- or laurel-wood, delicately scented; console tables, curiously carved; a profusion of porcelain, of vases in jasper or ivory . . . everything, down to the very carpets on the floor, reproduces with scrupulous exactitude a residence of the Emperor of China.[105]

By contrast, the notes Schinkel made on his visit to the Pavilion in June 1826 are unmistakably written from the perspective of an architect and designer. His diary entries are peppered with quickly drawn yet accurate sketches of technical and structural detail, such as the bannisters of the grand staircases in the Long Gallery or a steam outlet system in the kitchen. Crucially, he focuses on colour and surface finish as the main features in his notes on the rooms on the ground floor:

1) State Banqueting Room. Wall-covering of shimmering silver material (painted), various groups of Chinese figures. Dome culminating in a banana-tree, the chandelier also of the same tree. Candelabra of Indian porcelain, vases and banana forms. Various stained glass in the lunette. Long banqueting tables.
2) Gallery [Banqueting Room Gallery], white and gold, palm trees.
3) Domed hall [Saloon]. In the ceiling a painted gold-leaf dragon. Crimson and yellow wall-covering[106] (French taste), but embossed with elegant silver frieze. – Tables with inlaid work, sumptuous chairs in gold.
4) Gallery [Music Room Gallery], white and gold, palm trees.
5) Great state room [Music Room]. Organ. The walls lacquered in crimson, with Chinese landscapes painted in gold, the dome imitation of mother-of-pearl. The four corners of the ceiling lacquered wood and scaled like a gallery. Magnificent fireplace of

2.49 *The Pavilion No. 1. The Royal Banqueting Room*, coloured engraving by E. Brain from J. Whittemore's *Brighton and its Environs*, 1827 [1825]

white marble. Dragons everywhere. 8 towers forming candelabra of porcelain, genuine.[107]

Schinkel also adds a note to a sketch of the grand staircase and its runner, which is the only recorded direct description of its colour and design: '*a.* grey, granite-like cloth, *b.* red cloth striped, *c.* screwed down bronze plate'.[108] He thereby provides a rare visitor's description of a hardwearing and practical floor covering called drugget, which was probably made of undyed natural wool fibres.

Schinkel's description is a brief but reliable eyewitness account of the recently completed Nash/Crace/Jones schemes that gives a good indication of the dominate colours in each room and of the elaborate interplay between a variety of decorative surface finishes, ornamental features and materials. His descriptions are immediate (he appears to be under some time pressure while in the building) and it must be noted that he did not experience the building when in use for entertaining, meaning that several elements, such as festive lighting and illumination, were in all likelihood not in place during his visit.

Extremely positive and at times ecstatic reactions to the Pavilion's interior continue to be the norm in guidebooks and historical accounts of Brighton throughout the period of royal occupation. John Bruce's *History of Brighton* (1828) is notable for its superlative phrases, but adds little to Sickelmore's account. A few years later, in 1833, John Docwra Parry published the most detailed account of the Pavilion's interior to date, as part of his *Historical and Descriptive Account of the Coast of Sussex*. The number of rooms covered increases

2.50 *The Pavilion No. 2. The Music Gallery*, coloured engraving by E. Brain from J. Whittemore's *Brighton and its Environs*, 1827 [1825]

significantly and now even the kitchen and the Red Drawing Room are included. Parry attempts to interpret the iconography of some of the designs and alludes to the playfulness of the colour scheme, which, surprisingly, he considers restrained in style:

> The Pavilion is enriched with the most magnificent ornaments and the gayest and most splendid colours; yet all is in keeping and well relieved. There is positively nothing glaring or gaudy, and the person who would quarrel with its richness might as reasonably do so with flowers of the parterre – the lively carnation or painted tulip.[109]

New guides were published following the opening of the London to Brighton railway line in 1841, but they need to be interpreted very carefully, since Queen Victoria began removing some furnishings, ornaments and decorative objects as early as 1846. By 1850, the year of the sale of the Pavilion estate to the town of Brighton, the building had been stripped of most of its contents, fixtures and fittings. Charles Wilmott's new edition of his *Descriptive Guide to the Palace and Gardens of the Royal Pavilion at Brighton* (1851) is the first guidebook that focuses solely on the Pavilion and records its appearance following the sale and the valiant effort to recreate the interiors as quickly as possible, so as to be able to open the building to the public: 'In three brief months, the dingy, dilapidated ruin of the town's purchase has been transformed into "a thing of beauty"'.[110] While the interiors described here are predominantly those of the restoration efforts, they still throw light on what was considered worth restoring or copying, or how compromises were found in recreating a costly decorative scheme.

Generally speaking, the tone appears to harshen during Queen Victoria's reign, particularly after the sale of the Pavilion in 1850. Some descriptions, as for example those by Charles Fleet in his *Illustrated Hand-book of Brighton* (1847), are reserved and matter-of-fact, resorting in some cases to providing the reader with only the dimensions of the rooms. In 1853 George Measom voices highly critical opinions in *The Official Illustrated Guide to the Brighton and South Coast Railways*, calling the Pavilion 'that bizarre and unintelligible pile of buildings . . . as anomalous and insipid in idea, as ridiculous, too, in absurdity, as the Kremlin in Moscow'.[111] The interior fares no better: 'splendid as it was in the palmy days of George IV, [it now] only too closely corresponds in wretchedness of taste with the exterior'.[112]

Others are critical of some but not all aspects of the decorative scheme. In *Page's Handbook* (1875) the author remarks that 'the colours are fresh and well selected, the subjects well chosen to portray Chinese life and customs; though the workmanship is not always faultless'.[113] In his comprehensive *History of Brighthelmston* from 1862, John Ackerson Erredge has stronger views and criticises the 'reckless extravagance' displayed and the lack of nobility, and considers a detailed description of the interior unnecessary:

> with the exception of the Chinese Gallery, and the suite of rooms which forms the east front, there was not, while it remained Royal property, a room that would content any commoner of substance . . . vile in taste and of meagre proportions; wholly devoid of the grandeur and nobleness which should attach itself to Royalty.[114]

The increase in negative responses in the later nineteenth century might reflect Victoria's perceived dislike of the Pavilion or the decline in popularity of chinoiserie style in general, as well as an uncertainty about the Pavilion's future after it had entered municipal ownership.

Even during George's lifetime excessive use of Chinese- and Mughal-inspired features in architecture and ornament were ridiculed, as expressed in the satirical travelogue *The English Spy*, published by Charles Molloy Westmacott in 1825 under the pseudonym Bernard Blackmantle. In it a traveller (incidentally, on his way to Brighton by stagecoach) makes the following general observations on a decorative style that he considers too eclectic, with 'oriental' features ill-applied:

> On both sides of the road may be seen a variety of incongruous edifices, called villas and cottage ornées, peeping up in all the pride of a retired linen-draper, or the consequential authority of a man in office, in as many varied styles of architecture as of dispositions in the different proprietors, and all exhibiting (in their possessors' opinion) claims to the purest and most refined taste. For example, the basement story is in

the Chinese or Venetian style, the first floor in that of the florid Gothic, with tiles and a pediment à-la-Nash, at the Bank; a doorway with inclined jambs, and a hieroglyphic à-la-Greek . . . The parterre in front (green as the jaundiced eye of their less fortunate brother tradesmen) is enriched with some dozens of vermilion-coloured flower-pots mounted on a japanned verdigris frame . . .[115]

This mixture of styles clearly does not signify sophistication, and Blackmantle concludes with another ironic exclamation: 'Happy country! Where every man can consult his own taste, and build according to his own fancy, amalgamating in one structure all the known orders and varieties, Persian, Egyptian, Athenian, and European.'[116]

Examining these early sources shows that in the nineteenth century the Pavilion evoked strong reactions – both negative and positive. Almost all focus on its 'oriental' motifs, colouring, lighting and rich ornamentation.

Even in the twentieth century, writers were still puzzled by the Pavilion's place in the context of Asian-inspired architecture in Europe. In 1935, perhaps influencing Musgrave's later writings, Osbert Sitwell and Margaret Barton describe it as 'the most peculiar mirage that ever floated above our northern seas', possessing the 'dreamlike quality which often is found to infuse poetry',[117] while in 1977 Oliver Impey comments on the fusion – or confusion – of styles, architects and designers of the building, as well as the surprising contrast between exterior and interior:

> Brighton is even odder [than Sezincote, a house in Gloucestershire designed in a neo-Mughal style by Samuel Pepys Cockerell in 1805]: not the product of a single-minded client, nor the work of one sole architect. . . . The style was Hindoo, and was certainly partly based on Sezincote, which the Prince Regent visited in 1807. Outside, it is Hindoo, or partly so: inside it is Chinese – the Prince had changed his taste by 1815.[118]

However, Impey appears to rate the interior a success, precisely because of its unflinching scale and execution. He calls it 'one of the most thorough of all chinoiserie interiors', both the pinnacle and the swansong of chinoiserie, concluding that 'it all ended in 1822 . . . Chinoiserie could go no further, and the Regent's example was not much followed'.[119] Indeed, in 1840 Henry William Arrowsmith published a substantial *House Decorator and Painter's Guide* but makes no mention of Chinese or Oriental style or ornament at all, despite proclaiming to 'investigate the rise, progress, and decline of the various styles of decoration, as used by the architects of the present period'. The styles covered by Arrowsmith are 'Greek, Roman, Arabesque, Pompeian, Gothic, Cinque Cento, François Premier, Elizabethan, and the more modern French'.[120] Associated neither with native British tradition nor with classical authority, the chinoiserie style fell out of fashion in the 1840s, its decline in popularity likely accelerated by the Opium War fought between China and Great Britain from 1839 to 1842. But, as we have seen, the Pavilion had a Victorian afterlife, a reincarnation of sorts, in the decorations of the principal rooms and corridors of the East Wing of Buckingham Palace. From the mid-nineteenth century Japanese designs and motifs, often combined or confused with Chinese elements, became hugely influential on European and American art and fashion, and this taste has since found new expressions and remains a consistently popular theme.[121]

2.51 *(previous)* High-level decorations shown on the window side of the Music Room

CHAPTER 3

'A Splendour of Light and Colour'

Colour, senses and sensuality in the Royal Pavilion

In 1823 Richard Sickelmore described one of the state rooms in the Pavilion as a 'splendour of light and colour'.[1] As Chapter 2 has shown, many early visitors emphasised the exuberance of the colour schemes, which formed a contrast to the bright but monochrome exterior of the building. The Pavilion's interior design schemes were directly influenced by the fascination China held for Europe generally and by imported Asian artefacts, materials and images. George's English decorators echoed the range of vivid colours seen in paintings, wallpapers, ceramics, lacquer furniture and silks (see Chapter 1, pp. 72–83). The colours of the interior were full of subtleties, some of them unfortunately lost or diminished over the last 200 years. Visitors to the Pavilion in the 1820s would have experienced a gradual intensification of not just colour, but also light, sound, smells and textures as they moved through the building.

Another influence on the decorative scheme was the sharp increase in synthetic and commercially manufactured pigments, which suited George's personal tastes and adventurous spirit. He embraced the use of new pigments and elaborate decorative surface treatments and decorations, partly because of his interest in innovative new ideas and materials, and also because highly saturated and contrasting colour schemes were key features and indeed signifiers of the chinoiserie style in interior decoration, and of Chinese export ware. In his essay *Chromophobia*, contemporary artist David Batchelor explains that the historical suspicion of colour in the West stemmed from the fear of not being able to control it, and the association with 'otherness'. Colour was regarded 'the property of some "foreign" body – usually the feminine, the oriental, the primitive, in the infantile, the vulgar, the queer or the pathological . . . It is other to the higher values of Western culture.'[2] This notion of intensely coloured objects, images, and fabrics being 'other' or 'foreign' was considered both a negative and positive aspect of chinoiserie: the style was often mocked and associated with a lack of taste, but, as Emile de Bruijn notes in *Borrowed Landscapes*, it also meant that certain 'Chinese and Japanese objects and goods were highly valued by Westerners for their lustrous sheen, saturated colours and sophisticated decoration...' In any case, 'their original meaning was lost in translation, their "signal" distorted'.[3]

Despite persistent critical or cautious attitudes to colour in some quarters, there was also an increased general interest in all aspects of colour during the Regency period, ranging from the publication of philosophical

3.1 A panel in one of the doors in the Saloon, designed by Robert Jones, in imitation of Chinese lacquer, *c.*1820

CHROMATICS

or,

An Essay

on

THE ANALOGY AND HARMONY

of

COLOURS.

London:

PRINTED FOR THE AUTHOR,

BY A. J. VALPY, TOOKES COURT, CHANCERY LANE;

AND SOLD BY

MR. NEWMAN, SOHO SQUARE.

1817.

6

EXAMPLE IV.

§ 12. And thirdly, from the union of blue and yellow, proceeds medially the secondary GREEN.

EXAMPLE V.

§ 13. It follows, of course, that the SECONDARY COLOURS are capable of the same variety of union as their prima-

7

ries, and with like relation to their fundamentals: accordingly from the pairing of the secondaries purple and green proceeds the tertiary OLIVE, on the dark extreme.

EXAMPLE VI.

§ 14. From that of green and orange, on the light extreme, proceeds the tertiary drab, or CITRINE.*

EXAMPLE VII.

* See Appendix, Note V.

3.2 and 3.3 Title page and double page from George Field's *Chromatics*, with hand-coloured diagrams showing colour mixtures, 1817. Author's collection

treatises on the theory of colour and artists' drawing manuals to research into the durability of pigments, in which the British colour theorist and chemist George Field (*c.*1777–1854) was a pioneering figure. During his long and successful career, he provided many artists with high-quality pigments and paints and published several books on colour, combining theory with chemistry and even spirituality. Field had been experimenting with colour manufacture since 1804 and invented several tools for producing pigments and dyes. Over the years, he ran pigment factories in Bristol, London and Syon Hill Park. From 1808 he began supplying pigments to artists, artists' suppliers and printers. In 1817, coinciding with the most radical transformation of the Pavilion, he published his first book on colour, *Chromatics; or, An Essay on the Analogy and Harmony of Colours* (figs 3.2 and 3.3).[4]

In his work, Field was responding to the need for good-quality artists' materials, but also to the need for scientifically sound and reliable published information on colour and pigments in the early nineteenth century. His pigment marketed as Field's Extract of Vermilion appears to have been particularly popular, having been practically commissioned by the portraitist Sir Thomas Lawrence, who was 'anxious for a supply of [red], which differed in hue from any other Vermilion'.[5] Lawrence's use of vermilion red is a feature of many of his works, and he enjoyed the patronage of George III as well as George IV. The latter commissioned many official portraits of himself (fig. 1.77) and others from the artist, such as the full-length portraits for the Waterloo Chamber at Windsor Castle. It is highly likely that the Craces and Robert Jones were aware of Field's pigments and their quality and brilliance, and of his book *Chromatics*, perhaps even through direct

3.4 *(opposite)* Red lacquer effects in the north-east corner of the Music Room

correspondence with him. The elaborate use of brilliant reds in the Royal Pavilion to achieve the lacquer-like effects of many of the wall decorations (for example, figs 3.4, 3.5 and 2.16) supports this theory.

Concurrently, several new synthetic pigments had been invented in the eighteenth and early nineteenth century, even before the 'revolution' in colour production in the mid-nineteenth century and the resulting unbridled polychromy of Victorian architecture, fashion, art and interiors.[6] Several pigments used in the Pavilion have been identified, such as carmine and vermilion reds (figs 3.4, 3.5 and 3.6), Prussian blue (fig. 3.7), blue verditer (figs 3.8 to 3.11), chrome yellow (figs 3.12 and 3.13) and Turner's Patent Yellow. Most of them are of particularly high quality and high saturation, and are frequently described in the Crace Ledger as rich, varied and expensive. In many respects, the early nineteenth century, and specifically the Pavilion interiors, can be considered a precursor to later nineteenth-century movements and directions in colour and interior decoration.

The colours of the Pavilion cannot be discussed without considering the impact of lighting, mirrors and surface finishes. Reflective surfaces are of great importance in the design schemes of the building. It has expansive areas of gilding and silvering, sometimes in combination, and treated using various techniques – matt, burnished, glazed and sanded – to reflect light in different ways. Many silvered objects have transparent coloured glazes. On walls, paintwork was often polished or highly varnished, a technique most obvious in the Music Room (see, for example, figs 3.4, 3.5 and 3.6). Varnish and paint were used to create 'japanned' furniture, doors and panels in imitation of Chinese lacquer in different colours. One of the best surviving examples of this is Robert Jones's set of doors at the south end of the Saloon (figs 3.1 and 3.14).

This chapter looks at the use of colour and transparent glazes as mood setters and unifying elements in the Pavilion, by setting the colour schemes in a historical context and carefully examining the chromatic layout of the interiors.

3.5 *(overleaf)* Detail of the Music Room wall paintings, showing the lacquer-like effect

3.6 *(above)* Fragment of original wallpaper from the Red Drawing Room, oil paint on paper laid on canvas, designed by Robert Jones, *c.*1820–21

3.7 *(left)* Fragment of original wallpaper from the Banqueting Room, block-printed on a Prussian blue ground in a darker shade of blue and embellished with silver leaf, designed by Robert Jones, *c.*1817–20

3.8 *(above)* The South Gallery in *c.*1822 with blue verditer wallpaper, after Augustus Charles Pugin, aquatint from John Nash's *The Royal Pavilion at Brighton*, 1826

3.9 *(right)* A fragment of English block-printed bamboo trellis paper from the upper floor of the Pavilion, with blue verditer pigment in distemper, *c.*1815

3.10 *(opposite)* View of the South Gallery today, looking south

3.11 *(right)* Detail of blue verditer wall decorations in the South Gallery today

3.12 *(above)* English hand-printed wallpaper from the Yellow Bow Room, block printed in chrome yellow distemper on hand-made paper, designed by Robert Jones, 1821

3.13 *(below)* The South Yellow Bow Room today with chrome yellow reproduction wallpaper

3.14 *(opposite)* Doors in the Saloon, designed by Robert Jones, in imitation of Chinese lacquer, *c.*1820

'THE POWERS OF BALANCING, HARMONISING AND UNITING': ATTITUDES TO COLOUR IN INTERIOR DESIGN IN THE EARLY NINETEENTH CENTURY

Colour studies and the use of colour in the eighteenth century were heavily informed by Enlightenment ideas and the desire for objective and scientifically verifiable explanations of colour concepts. The search for a representative visual system of colour order and colour interaction led to a multitude of diagrams and geometric representations of colour, with the aim of forming a useful tool or source of reference for many disciplines within the fine arts and beyond. In 1704 Isaac Newton published *Opticks*, in which, after decades of research, he proposed that white light was composed of the seven colours of the spectrum visible to humans. Newton visualised his colour system as a circle divided unevenly into the seven colours. Publications on colour in the eighteenth and early nineteenth century frequently referred to Newton, but many of them were general books on painting

techniques and pigments, including house-painters' handbooks. Some of those relevant to the Pavilion will be discussed below.

While scientific interest in colour was considerable in the early and mid-eighteenth century, *colore* still played a subordinate role in fine art theory in contrast to *disegno*. Neoclassical ideas of beauty did not yet embrace the experimental and exuberant use of colour. This was expressed poignantly in 1764 by Johann Joachim Winckelmann in *Geschichte der Kunst des Alterthums (History of the Art of the Ancients)*, in which he assigns the essence of beauty to pure white tints, here seen in relation to sculpture, while colour should merely act as a tool in assisting beauty:

> Colour contributes to beauty, but it does not constitute beauty in itself; rather it heightens beauty and its forms. Since white is the colour which reflects the greatest number of light rays, and thus becomes the most easily recognised, a beautiful body will appear more beautiful the whiter it is . . .[7]

His allusions to Newton's concept of white light are likely deliberate. However, today Winckelmann's equation of white and white skin colour as manifestations of the highest form of beauty display racist undertones that reflect the times he lived in, but he also shaped ideas of classical white beauty in artistic discourse that were as inaccurate and inappropriate then as they are now.

These purist and chaste beauty ideals changed dramatically in the later eighteenth century, reflecting new ideas about beauty, individuality and sensibility. Colour was beginning to take the lead in the creation of 'the Beautiful', or 'the Picturesque', culminating in an application of the concepts of colour contrast, and the use of more saturated colours and colour schemes, especially in fashion and interior decoration. The Romantic Movement focused on new ideas about beauty in art, and writings about colour (including George Field's) often discussed the harmony of compositions and the effect of colour on mood. Some, such as Johann Wolfgang von Goethe (1749–1832), criticised Newton's findings, and even assigned moral values to certain colours. Others, such as the landscape designer Humphry Repton (see Chapter 1, pp. 60–69), interpreted Newton in new ways. In *Observations on the Theory and Practice of Landscape Gardening* (1803) he quotes an entire treatise on colour theory, and his book *Fragments on the Theory and Practice of Landscape Gardening* (1816) includes an engraved plate depicting rainbow colours he observed during his experiments with prisms, as well as a 'Diagram to explain the Harmony of Colours' (fig. 3.15).

COLOUR LITERATURE IN GEORGE IV'S TIME

A large number of books on colour were published between 1805 and the 1820s, coinciding with the implementation and finalisation of the Chinese-inspired interiors of the Pavilion. The majority of these dealt with painting in watercolour and oil, and many were aimed at amateur artists. Even scientific and theoretical writings, when they considered the painter's craft and material colour, were predominantly concerned with painting on a small scale. Far fewer publications dealt specifically with architectural colour, the durability of pigments and finishes in interior design, or the application of colour theory to architectural spaces. The comparatively small number of guidebooks specifically aimed at house-painters and decorators makes it likely that artists, manufacturers and designers involved with the Pavilion did refer to this specific pool of literature.

One of the most influential early publications that aimed to apply colour theory to interior decoration was David Ramsay Hay's *The Laws of Harmonious Colouring, Adapted to House Painting*, first published in 1828. In later editions the subtitle was changed to *Adapted to Interior Decorations, Manufactures, and other Useful Purposes*. Hay was a Scottish interior decorator who, later in life, enjoyed royal patronage, receiving a Royal Warrant from Queen Victoria in the early 1840s, followed by several high-profile commissions, including the interior decoration of the Palace of Holyroodhouse and the National Gallery of Scotland. *Laws of Harmonious Colouring* is a seminal work in the field of architectural colour because it presents a fully developed sense of the importance of colour perception, individual taste and aesthetic principles in relation to interior decoration. Hay begins with a chapter

3.15 'Diagram to explain the Harmony of Colours', hand-coloured engraving from Humphry Repton's *Fragments of the Theory and Practice of Landscape Gardening*, 1816

A
B
C
RED
Violet
Orange
Blue, or cold neutral tints
for Sky & distances
Diagram
to explain the
Harmony of Colours
Orange or warm tint
for the foregrounds
BLUE
YELLOW
Green
Morning, after the Sun is risen.
Morning twilight, before Sun rise.
Relative
Proportions
45 Red
27 Orange
48 Yellow
60 Green
60 Blue
40 Indigo
80 Violet
360 parts
according to S.r
I.s Newton's scale
of Quantity
London: Published by J. Taylor, Feb. 1. 1816

on harmony and contrast, explaining the significance of a complete design scheme of a building: 'In arranging the colours for an apartment, whether a few or a great variety are to be employed, the effect of the whole, as well as the several component parts, will depend on the skilful arrangement, as pointed out by the accidental or contrasting colours.'[8] Alluding to the complexities interior designers are faced with, he notes that, with regard to colouring, 'the House-painter's styles must not only be as various as the uses of the apartments which he decorates, but must vary according to the different tastes of his employers'. Hay concludes that further elements that inform a house-painter's choice of colours are 'not only the style of architecture, the situation, whether in town or country, but the very rays by which each apartment is lighted, whether they proceed directly from the sun, or are merely reflected from the northern sky'.[9]

To Hay, architectural colour and colour schemes must reflect and respond to the function of the building and each individual room, the owner's personal taste, the building's geographical location and its orientation with regard to light. He also highlights the complexities of colour schemes created by the great number and variety of surfaces, materials and objects that form the design scheme, and identifies unity, balance and harmony as guiding principles in interior decoration: 'The house-painter has often another very serious difficulty to encounter: A variety of highly and variously coloured furniture is shown him, to which the colouring of the different parts of a room must be suited. It is here that his powers of balancing, harmonising, and uniting, are called forth . . .'[10]

With his generous references to other researchers and historical sources Hay is exemplary of a generation of authors who had applied new ideas about colour to the now fully established genre of interior decoration. His friend, the Scottish painter David Roberts (1796–1864), referred to him as 'the first intellectual housepainter'.[11]

Eighteenth- and nineteenth-century house-painters' manuals

In eighteenth-century philosophical treatises on beauty and art, colour in architecture was seldom discussed at length, but Edmund Burke included a chapter on 'Light in Building' and one on 'Colour considered as productive of the sublime' in *Philosophical Enquiry Into the Origin of Our Ideas of the Sublime and Beautiful*. In both he advocates darkness and gloom and advises against gaudiness induced by colour: 'the cloudy sky is more grand than the blue; and night is more sublime and solemn than day',[12] before applying the same concept to historical painting and to the interior of buildings, suggesting a dark palette and little ornament or surface shine as desirable for a sublime effect: 'in buildings, when the highest degree of the sublime is intended, the materials and ornaments ought neither be white, nor green, nor yellow, nor blue, nor a pale red, nor violet, nor spotted, but of sad and luscious colours, as black, or brown, or deep purple, and the like. Much of gilding, mosaics, painting or statues, contribute but little to the sublime.'[13] Burke advises caution against 'anything light and riant; as nothing so effectually deadens the whole taste of the sublime,'[14] leaving one to wonder how his beauty ideals fared against the light and whiteness of Rococo and Neo-classical interiors as well as playful chinoiserie schemes of the mid-eighteenth century.

Several colour manuals were published in the eighteenth century, one of the most influential being Robert Dossie's *Handmaid to the Arts* (first published in 1758, revised and enlarged 1796, with further editions up until 1829). The enduring demand for Dossie's *Handmaid* might have been influenced by the increased promotion of the arts in Britain from the mid-eighteenth century onwards. As Leslie Carlyle points out, the first edition appeared just four years after the founding of the Society for the Encouragement of the Arts, Manufactures and Commerce, and was dedicated to the newly formed society, expressing the desire and need to publish and disseminate information on the arts in Britain.[15] In the foreword Dossie stresses the importance of his publication for 'the national improvement of skill and taste in the execution of works in design . . . but likewise of the commercial advantages resulting from it'.[16] Instructive and technical books on painting, artists' materials and design are here assigned high cultural and eventually economic value for society, far beyond their basic purpose of the education of artists and designers. Practical handbooks like Dossie's *Handmaid* were rarely concerned with colour theory beyond basic principles of colour mixing, but they do provide an invaluable source of information on what materials and pigments were available and fashionable and how these materials were prepared and applied. It is likely that the

Craces and Robert Jones used the 1796 revised edition of Dossie's *Handmaid*. Ian Bristow considers the start of the nineteenth century as the time when a 'profound change in English architectural literature took place' and links this to the 'advent of a series of copy books in which colour was discussed as an integral part of a scheme, rather than its provision simply being assumed'.[17]

The 1820s brought a cluster of new publications on architectural paint, which recorded house-painting techniques and materials in the early nineteenth century. In 1828 T.H. Vanherman's *The Painter's Cabinet, and Colourman's Repository* appeared, with a revised and renamed edition, *Every Man his Own House-painter and Colourman*, published just a year later. In 1827, Nathaniel Whittock published *The Decorative Painters' and Glaziers' Guide*, which Bristow considers, alongside Vanherman's *House-Painter*, the most important publication on architectural paint in the 1820s.[18] Whittock focused on the variety of uses of colour in interior design and put particular emphasis on paint effects and surface finishes, such as marbling, lacquering or wood graining. The full-page illustrations in Whittock's book emulate surface finishes, rather than picturing complete decorative schemes. Although the manual was published a few years after the Pavilion was finished, it is a typical example of the kind of book the Craces or Robert Jones would have consulted, since woodgraining, lacquering, marbling and stencilling are prominent techniques in the Pavilion.

Incidentally, Whittock was an author who understood and was able to convey the difference between additive and subtractive colour, as well avoiding confusion of colour names with pigment names. His heightened awareness of these matters arguably stemmed from the author also writing about coloured glass, transparent glazes and the use and effect of light in architecture and interior decoration. However, despite advocating imitative surfaces in interior design, he makes critical comments about the 'Chinese style':

> An attempt was made some years ago to introduce the Chinese style of decoration into general use; but the civilized mind revolts at the sprawling dragons, squat houses, and a perpetual recurrence of ornaments like nothing in nature, or, if like anything, making a preference of the most ugly and loathsome, as the toad lizard. If the Chinese style is ever to be used with effect, it must be in summer apartments, devoted to public amusement.[19]

Critical attitudes and scepticism towards the Chinese taste were not uncommon in the Georgian period. Even William Chambers, who had travelled to China and designed the dragon-embellished Great Pagoda at Kew (see Chapter 2, pp. 122-126 and fig. 2.2 on p. 118), displayed an ambiguous attitude to chinoiserie designs. In his *Designs of Chinese Buildings* he makes a case for more authenticity in Chinese-inspired designs and bemoans the 'extravagancies that daily appear under the name of Chinese, though most of them are mere inventions, the rest copies from the lame representations found on porcelain and paper-hangings'.[20] While he praised the achievements of Chinese design and ornament, he does not associate them with greatness, beauty or intricacy. His comments on authentic Chinese buildings are curiously condescending:

> The buildings of the Chinese are neither remarkable for magnitude or richness of materials: yet there is a singularity in their manner, a justness in their proportion, a simplicity, and sometimes even beauty, in their form, which recommend them to our notice. I look upon them as toys in architecture: and as toys are sometimes, on account of their oddity, prettiness, or neatness of workmanship, admitted into the cabinets of the curious, so may Chinese buildings be sometimes allowed a place among compositions of a nobler kind.[21]

He does, however, note the characteristic use of primary colours and highly polished surface finishes of Chinese buildings: 'These doors are neatly made of wood; have several characters and figures on them, and are sometimes richly varnished, in red, blue, yellow, and other colours,'[22] and furthermore recognises the deliberate use of contrasting forms, colours and shapes in Chinese design. In the chapter on gardens, he notes:

> The Chinese artists, knowing how powerfully contrast operates on the mind, constantly practise sudden transitions, and a striking opposition of forms, colours, and shades. Thus they conduct you . . . to dark and

> gloomy colours they oppose such as are brilliant, distributing . . . the different masses of light and shade, in such a manner as to render the composition at once distinct in it's [*sic*] parts, and striking in the whole.[23]

These comments reveal Chambers's understanding of colour contrast resulting in increased brilliance, which is also expressed in his *Treatise on the Decorative Part of Civil Architecture* (originally published as *A Treatise on Civil Architecture* in 1759), in which he recommends keeping the number of colours on any one piece of ornament to a minimum. He states, for example, that 'there should never be above two, or at the utmost three different sorts of colours in the same chimney-piece, all brilliant and harmonizing with each other'.[24] Significantly, the first Joseph Gwilt edition of this book, published in 1824, was dedicated to George IV, with Gwilt acknowledging the King's remarkable contribution to 'the architectural embellishment of the Metropolis [London] and the foundation of a National Gallery of ancient and modern art'.[25]

Illustrated books on interior decoration and fashion

The creation of the Pavilion's chinoiserie interiors coincided with the publication of a wealth of books and popular magazines on fashionable interiors. Of particular importance in this context is Rudolph Ackermann, who embraced new techniques in colour printing and became the leading publisher of colour plates in Britain, and in 1826 printed John Nash's *The Royal Pavilion at Brighton*. From the late 1790s onwards, Ackermann published many illustrated books on design, fashion, travel and topography, as well as painters' and decorators' manuals. Between 1809 and 1829 he published the monthly journal *The Repository of Arts, Literature, Commerce, Manufactures, Fashions, and Politics* (in 1829 it was renamed *Repository of Fashion*), which included hand-coloured plates. The early issues are remarkable for their 'Allegorical Wood-Cut' plates, onto which samples of fabrics for use in dressmaking, soft furnishing or upholstery. This made the colour, texture and design of these fabrics tangible for the reader. Some issues also included samples of embossed paper for use in interior decoration. The accompanying text informed the reader about where to purchase the material.

The fashion plates, fabric swatches and descriptions constitute a lively image of fashionable colours and designs in the Regency. The 'Allegorical Wood-Cut' from the February 1811 issue featured a sample of a 'rich furniture chintz for drawing-rooms, boudoirs and

3.16 *(left)* An illustration featuring Egyptian-inspired furniture and decorations, engraving from Thomas Hope's *Household Furniture and Interior Decoration*, 1807

3.17 *(right)* The tent-shaped roof of the Octagon Hall

sleeping rooms', with a multicoloured flower-pattern design on a pale cream ground. This fabric was designed by Abraham Allen of Pall Mall for one of the bedrooms at Carlton House and is not dissimilar to the flower pattern on the Brussels weave carpets on the chamber floor of the Pavilion. Carlton House itself featured regularly in Ackermann's *Repository* and, significantly, the journal was dedicated throughout its run to George.

Hope for colourful houses

In 1807 the Dutch-born designer and collector Thomas Hope (1769–1831) published *Household Furniture and Interior Decoration*, based on his own designs, which were mostly inspired by classical aesthetics. It is highly probable that George and his designers would have owned or consulted a publication of this significance. The book is notable in this context for several reasons: firstly, Hope's designs frequently embedded 'exotic' (in his case Egyptian) elements in his overtly neoclassical style (fig. 3.16), thus creating an eclectic style similar to that in some rooms of Carlton House and the Pavilion. Egyptian elements were present in the Pavilion even before Nash's transformation in the form of an 'Egyptian Gallery' connecting the Saloon to the Banqueting Room in Holland's layout of the building (probably forming part of what is now the Music Room Gallery). It is described only briefly in early accounts, for example in Attree's 1809 *Topography of Brighton*, as 'fifty-six feet in length, and twenty in width, the walls of which are covered with historical paper'.[26] Later, Egyptian elements were included in the green, yellow and gold King's Apartments on the ground floor, created from 1819 by Robert Jones and described by Morley as 'Chinese, Indian, even hints of Egyptian and Gothick . . . blended into perfect harmony of form and decoration'.[27]

Secondly, Hope's book introduced the term 'interior decoration' in printed sources, and thirdly, the book discusses the effect of design schemes on the sensual experience of an interior and stresses the significance of each individual object in the larger context of an interior design scheme. The architectural historian David Watkin suggested that Hope, like Sir John Soane, was familiar with Nicolas Le Camus de Mézières's *Le Génie de l'architecture; ou, l'analogie de cet art avec nos sensations* (The Genius of Architecture; or, The Analogy of that Art with Our Sensations) published in 1780.[28] De Mézières provided a detailed and room-by-room description of a generic grand French building, and elaborated on the individual character

3.18 *(above)* The Entrance Hall, watercolour and pencil drawing by Augustus Charles Pugin, *c.*1821 or later

3.19 *(right)* The Entrance Hall today, looking east towards the Long Gallery

of each room and how rooms relate to each other: 'Each room must have its own particular character. The analogy, the relation of proportion, decides our sensations; each room makes us want the next; and this agitation engages our minds and holds them in suspense.'[29] The sequential exploration and sensual experience of a building described here is reminiscent of the design and the colour experience of the Pavilion. Hope deliberately illustrated his book with uncoloured outline engravings in order to make it affordable for craftsmen and designers, sacrificing the depiction of 'the harmonious blending, or the gay opposition of the various colours'.[30]

Signs of this essentially Romantic attitude to interior decoration were apparent as early as 1793, when the American-British-German scientist Count Rumford discussed the principles of colour harmony in *Conjectures Respecting the Principles of the Harmony of Colours*, remarking on the usefulness of these ideas, not only to painters but to 'ladies [who] may choose ribbons for their gowns, or those who furnish rooms, [who] may arrange their colours upon principles of the most perfect harmony and of the purest taste'.[31] An 1827 comment by John Britton on Soane's house in Lincoln's Inn Fields in London (like the Pavilion, designed in the early nineteenth century and known for exuberant colour schemes) also reflects ideas about complete and harmonious design schemes, rooms communicating with each other with regard to colouring and decoration, and interiors having an effect on the

3.20 *(above)* The north end of the Long Gallery looking towards the Music Room in *c.*1819, after Augustus Charles Pugin, aquatint from John Nash's *The Royal Pavilion at Brighton*, 1826

3.21 *(opposite)* The Long Gallery today, looking south towards the Banqueting Room. The large chandelier, designed by the Craces, originally hung in the Saloon

3.22 *(right)* A fragment of the floral wallpaper from the Long Gallery, designed by John or Frederick Crace, hand-painted in blue distemper on a light pink, or 'peach blossom' ground, on hand-made paper, *c.*1815

person experiencing them: 'The respective apartments should either relieve or contrast, or enhance the effect of each other; that the imagination be called into play: and that the whole offer to the eye a masterly arrangement and picturesque combination.'[32] Significantly, John Crace collaborated with Soane on various interior design projects from as early as 1790, including at Lincoln's Inn Fields. Crace and Soane were most likely introduced to each other by Henry Holland.[33]

A SENSUAL COLOUR WALK THROUGH THE ROYAL PAVILION IN THE 1820S

The subtle manipulation of visitors' moods and reactions to the Pavilion was achieved by the gradual introduction and intensification of colour, lighting, ornament, floor coverings, perfume, sounds and reflective surfaces. Highlighting just one of these aspects, the colour schemes of the completed Pavilion in the mid-1820s gives a clear idea of the multi-sensory experience that a visitor to the building would enjoy. None of the design elements were left to chance, and the interiors can rightly be considered a *Gesamtkunstwerk*.

Having meandered through the Pavilion garden with its subtle shades of different greens, interspersed with the intense colours of flowering plants, both indigenous, and newly introduced ones from Asia, visitors in the 1820s would have entered the building via the sparsely decorated Octagon Hall (fig. 3.17), painted in one shade of very pale pink referred to as 'peach blossom' in the Crace Ledger.[34] The next room was the pale green Entrance Hall (figs 3.18 and 3.19), where visitors may have noticed the first two-dimensional dragon motifs on the walls, clerestory windows and lanterns (fig. 1.57). If you had a private audience with the King, you were taken to the Yellow Ante Room to the left (a room that does not survive), with bright yellow walls decorated with small-scale Chinese export paintings, or the Red Drawing Room to the right (figs 2.10), where the wallpaper was of a saturated red, the design of which incorporated spaces for more Chinese export paintings (fig. 3.6). Most guests would proceed into the intriguing and highly decorated Long Gallery (figs 0.7, 2.26 to 2.28, 3.20 and 3.21), where a fully developed chinoiserie interior would give them much to discuss while they waited for their host to arrive. Here the pink wall colour was much more saturated than in the Octagon

3.23 *(below)* The Banqueting Room in *c.*1823, after Augustus Charles Pugin, aquatint from John Nash's *The Royal Pavilion at Brighton*, 1826

3.24 *(opposite)* The Banqueting Room today

Hall and, significantly, the ground colour was no longer uniform or monochrome but embellished with floral decorations in a contrasting blue.

The colouring and decoration of the Long Gallery deserves closer inspection. A fragment of the original wallpaper by the Craces survives (fig. 3.22). The design was possibly influenced by *famille rose* Chinese ceramics or Chinese export wallpaper. In terms of saturation, the pink and blue wallpaper falls between the pale green of the Entrance Hall and the deep blues and reds found in the Banqueting Room and Music Room, indicative of the room's position in the sequence of corresponding interiors. It is also worth noting that, although never referred to as 'peach blossom' by the Craces themselves,[35] the pink on the walls of the Long Gallery was quickly described thus, for example by Sickelmore in *History of Brighton*.[36] The term 'peach blossom' does not refer to a pigment but is a colour name, although in 1828 Vanherman provided a basic recipe for creating it from lake or 'rose-pink' and unspecified white.[37] Its descriptive name from the botanical realm indicates that it was supposed to describe a range of pink tones. In 1826 George Smith commented that it is one of the tints that are particularly suitable for interior house painting.[38] Bristow notes a cluster of references to peach blossom in early nineteenth century English literature and suggests a possible intellectual link with Goethe's early work on colour *Beyträge zur Optik* (1791–2), where peach-blossom colour ('Pfirschblüt') is discussed as a prismatic colour.[39]

The next rooms a visitor would have entered are the Pavilion's culmination of ornament, light, sparkle, saturation and variety of colour. The Banqueting Room (figs 3.23 and 3.24, but see also 2.3, 2.48 and 1.100) and the Music Room

3.25 The Banqueting Room, watercolour drawing by Augustus Charles Pugin, *c.*1823

(figs 3.25 and 3.28, but see also 0.8, 0.15, 0.22, 2.30, 2.35 and 2.47), Nash's two great state rooms at either end of the Long Gallery, are interior spaces of spectacular dimensions, unusual shape, vivid colour schemes and intricate decoration. At once a continuation and intensification of the decorative schemes introduced in the preceding rooms, these interiors formed the climax of the visitor experience, and still do today. Then as now, the change in scale – from single to triple height – and the sensual inspiration when moving into either room would have been astonishing.

In the Banqueting Room, which was almost entirely the work of Robert Jones, guests would have marvelled at a multicoloured, spectacularly lit and partly silvered and gilt interior with complex and illusionistic decorations on every surface and in every space, while walking on a thick hand-knotted Axminster carpet. The dominant colour here is a deep-blue wallpaper (fig. 3.7), but the colours of the room need to be considered in the context of the silvered and gilt surfaces present. The wallpaper was block-printed, on a Prussian blue ground in a darker shade of blue and embellished with silver leaf. Before

3.28 *(overleaf)* The window side of the Music Room in 2020 during the exhibition *A Prince's Treasure*, with Chinese porcelain pagodas (RCIN 1.2, 1.1, 1.3 and 1.4) and the 'Orleans jars' (RCIN 204.1 and 204.3) in situ. © Royal Collection Enterprises Limited 2025 | Royal Collection Trust

3.26 *(above)* Proposed design for the west wall of the Music Room, watercolour and graphite drawing by Frederick Crace, *c.*1817. Cooper Hewitt, The Smithsonian Design Museum, Acc. No. 1948-40-13

3.27 *(below)* Design for the north wall of the Music Room, gouache drawing by Frederick Crace, *c.*1818–19. Cooper Hewitt, The Smithsonian Design Museum, Acc. No. 1948-40-10

the silver leaf tarnished it must have formed a stunning contrast to the saturated blue. A rich, deep colour, Prussian blue was used for both opaque and transparent blue finishes all over the Pavilion. The pigment was first made at the beginning of the eighteenth century in Germany and is regarded as the first 'modern' colour. It was first commercially produced in England in 1724.

Entering the Music Room at the north end of the Long Gallery would have felt like walking into a red-and-gold lacquer cabinet, with wall paintings on canvas providing expansive panoramic views of Chinese landscapes peppered with pagodas, flora and fauna, many of the motifs copied William Alexander's images of China (see pp. 30, 77–88 and 126–131). Designed predominantly by Frederick Crace (initially with his father John), and painted by the artist Henry Lambelet, the lacquer effect of the Music Room murals was achieved by applying a transparent carmine oil glaze over an opaque vermilion ground (figs 2.30 and 3.5).

3.29 Design for the west wall of the Music Room, watercolour, gouache and graphite drawing by Frederick Crace, *c.* 1817, with the overlay lifted. Cooper Hewitt, The Smithsonian Design Museum, Acc. No. 1948-40-9-a,b

Robert Jones used the same sequence of layers for his Red Drawing Room wall decorations (figs 2.10, 2.11 and 3.6).

The saturated red walls of the Music Room are complemented with strong blues and yellows in the draperies and a predominantly blue and yellow Axminster carpet. Secondary tints such as lavender, large-scale gilding, complex lighting (partly through painted clerestory windows) and tall multicoloured ornaments in the form of Chinese porcelain pagodas, torchères incorporating Chinese ceramic vases and elaborate candleholders made from Arita vases, would have added to the dazzling effect. It is a room that immediately draws you in and plays with your senses, through its sheer scale and intensity of colour. Decorative motifs such as dragons, bells and snakes appear in both two- and three-dimensional form in a visual dialogue across the architectural space. The tall porcelain pagodas would have drawn your eyes upwards to the magnificent ceiling. There, more than 24,000 plaster scallop shells, covered in gold leaf of different colours and subtly diminishing in size towards the centre of the dome, seem to echo the movement of couples waltzing below (figs 1.75, 2.46 and 3.28). Nine waterlily-shaped chandeliers, made by William Perry & Co. in 1820, appear to float

3.30 the Yellow Drawing Room, later known as the Music Room Gallery, *c.*1818-1820, watercolour and pencil drawing by Augustus Charles Pugin

in mid-air. Tiny baubles of frosted glass on their edges resemble dew drops, and gilt dragons cling to the outside of the large central chandelier as if they had just landed on them. Several unexecuted designs by Frederick Crace for walls in the Music Room reveal that he experimented with the motifs and colour schemes. In some, large figure groups and even large single mythological creatures appear on the walls in a less saturated palette (fig. 3.26). Frederick Crace clearly offered these drawings to George as options. In the more developed, more saturated designs for the Music Room, he included chromatic alternatives for George to choose from. For example, in the drawing for the north wall from *c.*1818–19, he shows several colour options for the simulated bamboo coving (fig. 3.27). In another drawing, for the west wall, Crace even added a Humphry Repton style overlay that could be lifted to show a slightly different colour scheme and the effects of lighting for a portion of the clerestory frieze (fig. 3.29).

The two galleries leading from the Music and Banqueting Rooms, were, in accordance with their altered purpose and position in the layout of the building after Nash's transformation, no longer brilliantly blue (fig. 2.23, pp. 31–32) or yellow (fig. 3.30) but painted 'flake white' in combination with sophisticated gilding and a slightly less exuberant use of colour (figs 2.37, 2.38 and 3.31). The more subdued colour schemes formed a necessary contrast to the adjoining Banqueting Room, Music Room and Saloon, offering a sensory relief after so much visual stimulation, but they also made the numerous smaller pieces of mounted Chinese and Japanese porcelain shine brighter and more intensely against a less chromatic background.

In 1838 Brayley commented on the history of the colour schemes of the two galleries, explaining that the Banqueting Room Gallery 'was originally called the Blue Drawing Room, from the general tone of its decorations . . . but it is now called the Green Drawing Room, from the prevalent hue of its draperies, which are of richly woven

3.31 *(overleaf)* The Music Room Gallery in 2020

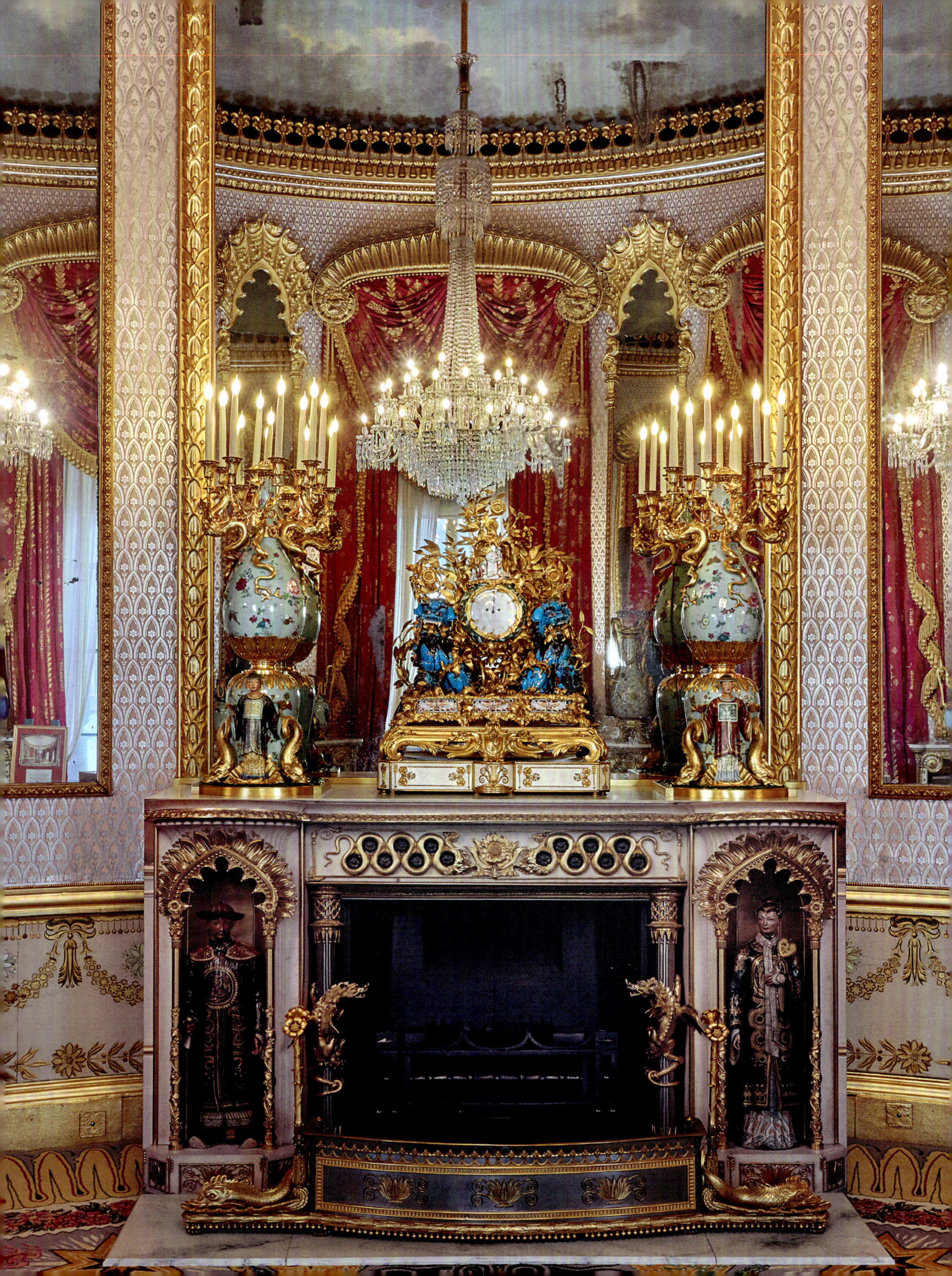

silks, of a pale green colour, tastefully wrought with groups of fruit and flowers.'[40] He did not provide much detail about the pre-1820 yellow incarnation of the Music Room Gallery, but commented on the two Saloon schemes illustrated, stating that the existing Jones design of white, gold, silver and crimson from 1823 was 'conceived and executed in a style of far superior taste and costliness than have been previously exhibited',[41] referring here to one of the earlier Crace designs (fig. 1.60, p. 77).[42]

The Saloon, in its last, more regal incarnation by Robert Jones (figs 0.18 and 3.32), also fits into the concept of interiors that were designed with a sequential experience in mind. After 1817 it needed to form a balancing link between the intensely coloured and ornamented Banqueting and Music rooms and the more subdued and calming galleries. It is grand and sumptuous, yet elegant and refined, with a gold, silver, off-white and red scheme, lifted by a brightly coloured Axminster carpet with a light ground colour, and contrasting red and gold silk hangings, draperies and upholstery. The Saloon can be regarded the harmonising centre of the building, combining motifs, colours and themes of the other rooms on the ground floor, such as the sunflower, the combination of red and gold, and, as I will explain later in this chapter, the pairing of silver and gold.

3.32 *(opposite)* The west side of the Saloon in 2020 during the exhibition *A Prince's Treasure*, with the complete garniture of the chimneypiece in situ. The chimneypiece itself is a photographic reproduction of the original. © Royal Collection Enterprises Limited 2025 | Royal Collection Trust

3.33 *(above)* Fragment of Chinese wallpaper with areas of silver on a blue ground, *c.*1800 or earlier, paper that was probably hung in George's private apartments on the chamber floor in *c.*1804

With the erection of Nash's state rooms at either end of the building, the balance of the interior had shifted dramatically. George's designers responded by changing the colour scheme of the rooms in acknowledgement of the function of each room and how a guest would have progressed through the building. This deliberately planned visitor route is reflected in the numbering of the ground floor principal rooms in the ground plan from Nash's *Views* (fig. 0.9), where numbers 1 to 10 mark the sequence of the porte cochère, Octagon Hall, Entrance Hall, Long Gallery, Banqueting Room, Banqueting Room Gallery, Saloon, Music Room Gallery, Music Room and Red Drawing Room. All other rooms are marked by letters, indicating they belong to the different grouping of private or servants' rooms.

On the chamber floor, consisting of comparatively small and low-ceilinged private apartments and rooms not intended to be seen by occasional guests, the chinoiserie style continued with the same confidence. Extensive woodgraining and highly saturated colour schemes seen on the ground floor are not repeated but are presented in variations. The Craces' pink and blue wallpaper from the Long Gallery continues up the staircases (figs 1.76, 2.6 and 3.20), thus forming a chromatic link to the galleries on the upper floor. The rooms on the upper floor feature a luminous blue in the galleries (figs 3.8 to 3.11), from where a visitor ascending the North Staircase would wander into the suite of Bow Rooms on the east side, where intense yellows dominate (figs 3.12 and 3.13). The sky blue of the galleries was created with blue verditer, also known as mountain blue, copper blue or lime blue, an artificial blue first produced in the seventeenth century. Like Prussian blue, it formed a good synthetic alternative to more expensive blues such as ultramarine or azurite.

The Bow Room wall colour scheme was created using the new pigment chrome yellow for the block-printed wallpaper. Chrome yellow, or lead chromate, had been discovered in 1797 by the French chemist Louis Nicolas Vauquelin (1763–1829) and was first made available commercially in Britain by the German Dr Eric Bollman (1769–1821) between 1814 and 1820.[43] Bristow suggests that it 'must be regarded as the pigment for which the 18th century had been waiting'.[44] Its merit lay not just in its brilliance and stability, but in its usefulness in producing a range of greens when mixed with Prussian blue. It is likely that the green used for the walls of the Entrance Hall (figs 3.18 and 3.19) and the block-printed wallpaper in the King's Apartments were created in this manner. Apart from the excitement about a newly available vibrant pigment, George might also have liked the symbolic associations of yellow with the Emperor of China, or the heraldic yellow of the House of Hanover.

Notably absent from the upper floor were highly saturated reds in the style of the Music Room walls. This supports the thesis that the Pavilion interior is almost certainly a manifestation of the ideas about unified interior design schemes formulated by de Mézières, Hope, Hay and others. While each room has an individual decorative scheme, informed by its purpose, location and use, all rooms in the building were also seen in connection to each other, with colours and decorative features distributed accordingly. It is, for example, highly likely that Crace's pink and pale blue design for the Music Room with its figurative panels (fig. 3.26) was abandoned in favour of the existing one because the colour scheme would have been too similar to that of the adjoining Long Gallery, and the motifs too close to Jones's figurative panels in the Banqueting Room. Early nineteenth-century principles of colour composition, contrast and harmony are here applied to the interiors of an entire building.

THE LANGUAGE OF COLOUR AND LIGHT

The language used by the Craces in their accounts to describe the colours and finishes applied in the Pavilion between 1802 and 1823 has been investigated by Janet Brough in her article 'The Significance of Sheen: Surface Finish as an Important Aspect of Early Nineteenth Century Interiors'. She notes that frequent references to the application of multiple layers of varnish or paint, enriching, heightening and 'high polishing' (the Crace Ledger refers to 'varnishing' and 'highly varnished' 228 times) suggest 'a preoccupation with variety and with surface effect: there are many references to different treatments over one area',[45] for example 'richly polished' elements adjacent to 'flatted' areas. Such variations in surface finish in close proximity, Brough argues, 'would reflect the light in different ways, and the decorator [Crace] appears to take for granted that the choice of language is understood and the resulting effect the one desired'.[46]

It is notable that the Craces repeatedly use the term 'proper colours' in the Crace Ledger. This most certainly indicated high-quality pigments and rich colours, as opposed to the cheaper and less saturated 'common colours' that were mostly associated with hallways, servants' areas, flooring and matt finishes. Patrick Baty observes that common colours such as stone, white, pearl, cream chocolate, oak or lead, were derived from cheaper earth pigments, and were therefore more stable and less likely to fade.[47] The stress on 'proper' colours therefore reflects the overwhelming presence of highly saturated and polished paint surfaces in the Pavilion, something that until the later eighteenth century was almost exclusively associated with panelled walls and woodwork.[48] Bristow notes that 'proper colours' are also often associated with painted clouded ceilings in late eighteenth- and early nineteenth-century interiors. Here, 'proper' refers to the illusionary effect of the decoration, another dominant feature in the Pavilion.[49]

The Crace Ledger refers to 'proper colours' fifteen times, while in two cases colours are described as 'expensive'. Interestingly, in both cases actual pigments are named, which is rarely the case in Pavilion account books. In the day account from the fourth quarter of 1802, the Craces charged £77 19s for a variety of work carried out and time spent at the Pavilion, including an astonishing £28 16s for 'materials used consisting of fine colors for the Patterns of Rose wood Vermillion purple brown yellow Lake Best Lake Pattent [*sic*] yellow and other expensive colors'.[50] Similarly, in January 1818 Frederick Crace charged £54 for 'Artist's time assisting D[itt]o and materials used from the 6th January to the 24th. Carmine, Lake, Vermillion, Crome, Yellow and other expensive colours'.[51] The fact that the high price of the

3.34 Design for a wall decoration probably for the Conservatory, watercolour, ink, graphite drawing by John or Frederick Crace, 1815 or earlier. Cooper Hewitt, The Smithsonian Design Museum, Acc. No. 1948-40-63

pigments is alluded to suggests that the Craces may have prepared some of their own paints using dry pigments supplied by the so-called colourmen. Frustratingly, there is no reference in any of the Crace papers to specific pigment suppliers.

The frequency of colour names listed in the Crace Ledger shows an even distribution of the primaries yellow (127), blue (154) and red (159). Green is mentioned 68 times and pink 66 times, while purple, lilac and scarlet feature 16, 16 and 15 times respectively, while other colours occur less frequently. Of the 'common colours' it is notable that while white is mentioned 111 times, other achromatic colours feature noticeably less: black 39 times, grey 37 times and brown 11 times. As mentioned above, pigments are rarely specified, but there are seven references to Chinese red and Chinese vermilion, five mentions of 'verdegrease/verdigrease', two of 'chrome/crome yellow', one of patent yellow, four of carmine and nine of flake white.

CHINESE WALLPAPER: CONNECTING INSIDE WITH OUTSIDE

Another visually and conceptually important element of the Pavilion was the use of Chinese wallpaper. The quantities of these papers once present in the Pavilion is astonishing and deserves further research. We know that so-called 'India paper' (in reference to the East India Companies which imported it) was first used in the early chinoiserie schemes by John and Frederick Crace in 1802, which included the one with silver motifs that hung in the Saloon (see Chapter 2, pp. 152–153 and fig. 2.43) and silvered Chinese export paper in an earlier bedroom of the Prince of Wales's on the chamber floor (fig. 3.33). A particularly stunning panoramic example in the 'Conservatory' (demolished in 1817) was described in 1809 by Attree in *The Topography of Brighton*: '[The Conservatory] is fifty-five feet long, thirty feet wide, and twenty feet high. . . . The sides are covered with a Chinese historical paper, superb in appearance, and indescribably brilliant in effect.'[52] A Crace drawing in the Cooper Hewitt Collection (fig. 3.34) probably shows a wall in the Conservatory and may show this historical paper, although the dating of the drawing is uncertain.

The Pavilion account books and inventories have many intriguing entries relating to Chinese wallpaper, and it is likely that the earliest entry in the Crace Ledger (from the second half of 1802) records the paper for the Saloon and the bedroom: £2 5s 'expended for 12 pieces of Fine India Paper', along with no fewer than 'Seventy pieces of China consisting of Jarrs [*sic*], Beakers, fine Japan dishes' and '4 Paintings on glass'.[53] The papers were supplied by the paper hangers Robson and Hale of Piccadilly, London, who, in October 1821, also charged for 'A full Sett of India Paper on purple ground by Command of His Majesty'. There are also numerous entries in Pavilion ledgers and account books of Chinese paper being repaired, varnished, cleaned or simply 'arranged' on the wall, the latter term referring to the hanging of the non-repeat patterns in the correct sequence. As discussed in Chapter 2, George appears to have been especially keen to be involved with the hanging and arranging of Chinese wallpaper, as recorded in the Crace Ledger. It should also be noted that, as is the case with many other types of Chinese export objects, imitations of Chinese wallpaper were also created by English paperhanging manufacturers, who sometimes used silver embellishments. Combining original Chinese papers with European imitations was also common.

Chinese wallpapers were probably produced by Chinese workshops in Canton (Guangzhou), near the western trading ports along the waterfront, and then imported to Europe, often as 'private trade' by officers of East India Company ships. Predominantly hand-painted in ink and distemper-like colours, they were produced

3.35 *(opposite)* Queen Victoria's Bedroom in 2020, with a painted reproduction wallpaper, prior to the rehang of the original Chinese paper

3.36 *(below left)* and 3.37 *(below right)* Details of the figurative Chinese wallpaper in the Adelaide Corridor on the chamber floor, *c.*1790, hung in this space in either 1815 or 1821

3.38 Chinese wallpaper fragment with a green ground colour, from an unknown location in the Royal Pavilion, *c.*1800

solely for export and became increasingly popular in Western chinoiserie interiors in the seventeenth and eighteenth centuries. They were a cheaper alternative to silk wall coverings or lacquer panels, but were still luxury items. The sheets were usually numbered and hung in a sequence, often with the addition of cut-out birds, flowers and figures, either to disguise blemishes or cover edges. The majority of these papers were hung in bedrooms and drawing rooms and are mostly associated with 'feminine' spaces and taste (see also Chapter 2, pp. 132–138). Many of the patterns show Chinese flowers, trees, birds, insects and stylised gardens or landscape scenes, with some botanical elements identifiable. These usually had a dominant vibrant ground colour, as in case of the recently cleaned and restored yellow-ground paper in Queen Victoria's Bedroom in the Pavilion (fig. 2.9, see also contents page). More expensive varieties included architectural motifs and Chinese figures at work or play. Wallpapers of both kind survive in the Pavilion, with the paper in the Adelaide Corridor on the chamber floor an example of the latter (figs 3.36 and 3.37). It dates from around 1790 but was probably hung there in either 1815 or 1821. It depicts several Chinese festivals and traditions, including a dragon boat race and a lantern parade, and is the only wallpaper in the Pavilion still hanging in its original position.

In *c.*1820 most rooms and some connecting passages on the west side of the chamber floor were hung with Chinese wallpapers. Yellow, lilac and green ground colours are recorded, and many large fragments of these papers survive in the Royal Pavilion archives. The predominantly organic pigments used for the ground colour, such as gamboge yellow in the case of the paper in Queen Victoria's Bedroom, have largely faded, making it difficult to imagine the full visual impact of comparatively small rooms entirely covered in them, but it must have been a fascinating immersive chromatic experience. It is, for example, difficult to identify what is described as a 'lilac' in the account books, but is almost certainly what now appears as a light-grey background colour (fig. 3.40).

Around the time Chinese wallpapers were in high fashion in European interiors, many plants and seeds were being imported from Asia, especially China. In the very early 1800s, newly arrived Chinese plants were being successfully propagated at Kew. By 1813 the Royal Gardener at Kew, William Townsend Aiton, recorded a total of 120 species that had recently been introduced from China. In the same year Aiton planted the garden at Carlton House for the Prince Regent. Two years later the Brighton gardener John Furner met Nash and Aiton in London to discuss the new planting of the Pavilion gardens, which included many of the newly imported and propagated Chinese plants. In his book *Set for a King* (2005) Mike Jones describes the challenges of transporting live plants over such distances, and shows that certain of these exotic varieties are represented in the Chinese wallpapers.[54] Many of them could be found in the Pavilion Garden in the early nineteenth century, for example the hydrangea, now common in British gardens, but first brought to Kew in 1789. Other examples are autumn-flowering chrysanthemums (1795), the tiger lily (*Lilium lancifolium* or *L. tigrinum*, bulbs of which were planted in Brighton in 1811), the tree peony (*Paeonia suffruticosa*, 1787) and several types of camellia (mid- to late eighteenth century); also present was the Chinese lantern (*Physalis alkekengi*), which had been known in Britain since the sixteenth century.

It is easy to imagine guests in the 1820s marvelling at the wallpaper or walking through rooms that emulated Chinese courtyards, then later trying to spot the same flowers in the garden. It is yet another example of the multi-sensory experience of the Pavilion and the playful repetition of motifs, colours and themes.

'BOLDLY CARVED, SILVERED AND TINTED': THE HARMONISING USE OF SILVER IN THE ROYAL PAVILION

There is a further element of the overall design scheme of the Pavilion interiors which is as unusual as it is difficult to identify and restore: the use of silver on decorative finishes. Decorative silver objects and silver fabrics and textiles were common in seventeenth-, eighteenth- and nineteenth-century European interiors, and play

3.40 *(opposite)* Chinese wallpaper fragment with a light-grey ground colour, possibly originally described as 'lilac', from an unknown location in the Pavilion, *c.*1800

3.41 *(overleaf)* Carved wooden silvered and glazed bells at high level in the Banqueting Room, decorated by Robert Jones, *c.*1817

3.42 *(opposite)* Silvered and gilt cornices in the Saloon

an important role in both Chinese export ware[55] and George's personal tastes and collecting habits. While ostentatious displays of silverware and silver gilt were common in aristocratic and royal households, silver used as a colour in interior decoration is noticeably rare in Britain. The use of silver on architectural surfaces in the Pavilion was unusually extensive, inventive and varied.

Silver is not a colour in the Newtonian sense. It is a precious metal that, in interior decoration, can be either imitated by using paint (often white mixed with silver powder, or later with aluminium), or used directly as silver leaf applied to an adhesive ground (from now on referred to as 'silvering' to avoid confusion with gold-leaf gilding).

Most silver used in Britain for making or silvering precious objects is an alloy consisting of 92.5 per cent silver and 7.5 per cent copper. Silver may contain other materials such as nickel and zinc, and the percentage of silver in the alloy may be lower. Silver tarnishes over time, which is a gradual process caused by a reaction with sulphur compounds in the atmosphere. The metal turns first pink, then brown and eventually grey or black, making it difficult to identify as silver. Very old, tarnished silver might reveal itself through a very slight reflective shimmer. Tarnish can be removed via various methods (manual or chemical cleaning), but this results in surface loss. The removal of tarnish on silver leaf is therefore almost impossible, because of its thinness. Tarnishing can be prevented or delayed by certain surface treatments, for example a lacquer coat, but removal of lacquer coats is very difficult and will normally result in abrasion.

3.43 Original tarnished silver (right) and replacement platinum leaf (left) in the Saloon during restoration in 2018

Silver is found and documented in the Pavilion in various locations and on many ornamental features and materials (wood, paper, plaster, canvas and individual decorative objects) through several design phases. It was used by both the Craces and Robert Jones, with Jones displaying the more inventive and wider use. The application techniques in the building also vary, making the Pavilion a rare example of an extensive range of the use of silver in interior decoration.

As noted in Chapter 2, Richard Sickelmore interpreted the silvered background of Jones's figurative chinoiserie wall paintings in the Banqueting Room (figs 2.3, 2.4 and 2.5) as 'a contrast to the splendid furniture, and brilliant colours of the paintings which it surrounds'.[56] This identifies one possible key function of the use of silver as a colour in the Pavilion. The reflectivity of gold and silver on mouldings and wall decorations enhanced the effects of light throughout the rooms. This was particularly effective and necessary in low-light conditions after dark, when candles and oil-lit chandeliers disseminated a warm, flickering light.

References to silvering in historic paint manuals

House-painting and decorating manuals of the eighteenth and nineteenth centuries that touch on silvering all discuss the problem of tarnishing, which destroys the reflective quality of silver. This was probably the main reason for the restrained use of silver in interiors, especially in Britain. In the 1796 edition of Dossie's *Handmaid to the Arts* (first published 1758), the author significantly extends the section on 'silvering, bronzing and Japanning, lacquering and staining'[57] and explains the limited use of silver in interior decoration. This is the edition that was most probably used by the Pavilion's interior designers:

> [Silvering] is nevertheless but seldom used, notwithstanding the effect would be very beautiful and proper in many cases; and there is an extreme good reason for such a neglect of it. The reason is its tarnishing in a very short time, and acquiring frequently, besides the general depravity of the whiteness, such spots of various colours as render it very unsightly; and this tarnish and specking is not only the constant result of time, but will be often produced instantly by any extraordinary moisture in the air, or dampness, as well as by the fumes and effluvia of many bodies which may happen to approach it.[58]

Ian Bristow does not list silver as a colour in *Interior House-Painting*, but does discuss gilding and silvering as a technique. He discusses the significance of silvering and gilding and refers to their intrinsic 'capacity to lend grandeur and sparkle to architecture'.[59] He acknowledges the rarity of silvered interiors, singling out Chippendale's use of silver on carved timber borders in the Yellow Damask Sitting Room at Harewood House, Yorkshire, in 1775, and in the cornices in the early chinoiserie scheme in the Pavilion's Saloon. He also mentions silver elements in Carlton House, as described in Pyne's *Royal Residences*.[60]

Bristow further discusses the changing attitudes to the integration of gilding into eighteenth- and nineteenth-century interiors, referring to David Ramsay Hay's interpretation of gilding as a contribution to colour harmony, using either gold or gold colour, in certain colour schemes. According to Hay, gilding lends a particular gaiety and cheerfulness to a room, which should be avoided in the 'more substantial and sombre atmosphere of the dining room'.[61] Bristow concludes: 'No doubt silvering was often seen as especially appropriate for more feminine interiors, as too, perhaps, was the painted imitation of mother-of-pearl described by Vanherman.'[62]

Significantly, Bristow emphasises that 'it was also possible, when occasion demanded, to embellish the work further by means of transparent glazes',[63] with reference to an early-seventeenth-century example of a green glaze over silver on screen decorations at the Tudor chapel at the lost Greenwich Palace, and a possible use of the same technique on James Wyatt's staircase at Frogmore House in the mid-1790s. He continues his list of examples with two important pieces from the Pavilion, the carved snakes and dragons on the east side of the Music Room (figs 0.22, 3.45 and 3.28), and a silvered dragon that once hung on the ceiling of the Entrance Hall in 1815.[64]

Excessive use of gilding appears to have been against aesthetic ideas of taste and elegance in the late eighteenth century, especially in Britain. Both Burke and Chambers stressed the importance of select and moderate use of gold leaf in interiors. Bristow explains that 'party gilding', where only certain parts of an ornamental feature are gilded, and variations in gold leaf colour became fashionable in this period because of the awareness of the potency of gold. He refers to Chambers's notes on the necessity of careful use and distribution of gold in interiors: 'It requires a great deal of judgement to distribute the gilding properly . . . in general, it is to be observed, that, wherever the gilding tends, in the least, to confuse the Design, or make the outline of any part indistinct, it is ill employed.'[65] The question is whether similar notions would and did apply to silvering, and whether George, the Craces and Jones considered ideas of taste that would have been associated with a previous generation.

Specific use of silver in the Pavilion

The Crace Ledger records the first use of silver in as early as 1802, on the very first page: 45 ft (13.7 metres) of 'Silver cut on filletts and mouldings of cornice and high varnished' were applied in the Saloon.[66] 1802 marks the year the Craces were first involved with the decoration of the Pavilion, introducing the first chinoiserie interiors. By comparison, gilding does not appear to have been such an important feature of the early decorative schemes of the Pavilion. As Brough notes, the sharp increase in silvering during and after Nash's transformation can be explained by the grander scale and style of the new state rooms. The greater ceiling height of the new rooms and large chandeliers demanded more reflective surfaces to capture more light and create a dazzling overall effect. It is difficult to properly assess silver finishes in the Pavilion, since almost all have suffered from damage, discoloration and tarnishing through soot and smoke, and loss of protective layers through overcleaning. Later in the nineteenth century varnishes and bronze paint were applied to many surfaces in the Pavilion, which changed the overall impression of the interior with regard to brightness and the variety of the colour scheme in general.

These changes make research difficult, but it is possible to establish that silver was used in at least three ways in the Pavilion: firstly as part of a multi-layered silvering and glazing technique in combination with transparent colours on carved wooden ornaments, as for example on the limewood dragons and snakes in the Music Room, the bells at clerestory level, and the large dragon and phoenixes that appear to be holding the Banqueting Room chandeliers (figs 1.85, 2.48 and 3.24). Secondly, an oil-based size is applied to architectural ornaments of plaster or wood, such as cornices, friezes, door or window frames or pilasters. This is particularly prominent in the Saloon scheme of 1822–3, where Jones created a daring combination of gilding and silvering, using both water-gilding (burnished and matt) and oil-gilding techniques in proximity (fig. 3.42). Thirdly, silver is applied as silver leaf on either paper or canvas, in a technique similar to stencilling on wallpaper designs or wall paintings (figs 2.3 to 2.5, 3.7 and 3.43). Wallpaper designs including silver leaf from the final chinoiserie scheme are all associated with Jones but, as will be seen, the Craces had also incorporated silver paint or silver leaf in wall panels for an earlier design scheme of the Saloon.

As mentioned above, the Craces applied silver leaf to the cornices of the Saloon as early as 1802. It was used there in combination with 'Rose wood and Grey satin wood imitated and high varnished'[67] and a wallpaper (likely Chinese, but possibly an example of an English imitation) with silver leaf or silver paint decorations (see also Chapter 2, p. 153). This is the paper described by Attree in 1809 as 'a beautiful paper of a blue ground, the ornaments of which are white etched with silver, interspersed with birds of the richest plumage, and which literally appear animated, and fascinate the beholder, to the most enchanting advantage'.[68] Sadly, no fragments of this wallpaper survive, but a drawing in the Cooper Hewitt Collection illustrates the shimmering appearance of the wall panels (fig. 2.43). By Christmas 1816, this wallpaper had been replaced with Chinese wallpaper supplied by Robson and Hale, on a grey/cream ground, perhaps wrongly described in the Crace Ledger as a 'green ground' paper.[69] This is the paper seen in an aquatint from Nash's *Views*, albeit with inaccurate colouring (fig. 1.60).

Silver in the Banqueting Room

Silver is a conspicuous element in the colour scheme of the Banqueting Room, on both three-dimensional ornaments and wall surfaces. The carved silver bells high up around the room (fig. 3.41) would have formed a glistening border at clerestory level, drawing attention to the unusual shape of the ceiling and its decorations. The insides of the bells were painted with a transparent carmine red glaze. Each of these bells had a decorative crystal clapper, which would catch the light created by the oil chandeliers and candles in the room, with the red glaze inside giving the impression of flickering light. The technique of coloured glazes over silver was applied with much greater variety of colour on the more elaborate carved objects in the room, notably the dragon and phoenixes holding the chandeliers. The central dragon (fig. 1.85) is described in detail in the 1828 Royal Pavilion Inventory, and several references are made to its silver elements:

> A very superb Lustre of matchless design and workmanship, upheld to the center of the dome by a flying dragon boldly carved, silvered and tinted: The body of this Lustre has a rich open work border of Metal, gilt with edges of silvered Bells – Six richly carved silvered and tinted dragons issuing therefrom, each bearing a large painted ground glass lotus for a Lamp with burners: The under part composed of gilt leaves, stems and small painted ground glass Lotuses cut Glass Lotuses, Spangles, Icicles, Stars, Festoons, Tassels &c: A beautiful Jet d'eau of cut glass spangles rising in the Center; the body suspended by six silvered metal chains (ornamented with cut glass drops) to a ground glass dome, enriched with large and small silvered balls, lotuses &c surmounted by a splendid star filled with large tassels, &c of silver balls and cut glass drops.[70]

Silver leaf or silver paint also forms the background to most of Jones's large pictorial chinoiserie paintings in the Banqueting Room. The 1828 Inventory describes the largest of Jones's pictures (which survives in its original location): 'A large center pannel (opposite windows) painted on Canvass in a group of Chinese Figures, bearing a Palanquin, on a white and silvered ground of various pattern (see fig. 2.3).'[71] This silver pattern resembles that of the 'dragon wallpaper' from the Red Drawing Room (fig. 2.11) and other rooms in the Pavilion (fig. 3.12). As with the dragon wallpaper, the inspiration for the silver background appears to have been Chinese imperial robes, but Jones only copied some elements of the pattern and motifs, disregarding the robes' polychromy and finer detail.

The silvered background was frequently interpreted as mother-of-pearl, for example in Whittemore's guidebook from 1825: 'The ground of these masterly paintings is in imitation of inlaid pearl, richly wrought in all the varied forms of oriental mythology.'[72] In 1838 Brayley, too, described the background as 'an imitation of inlaid pearl, richly and ingeniously wrought with all the varied forms of mythology of China', and also notes the exquisite quality and extremely brilliant colouring of the scenes.[73] This recalls Bristow's suggestion that mother-of-pearl, silver, and shimmering surfaces were generally associated with a feminine or effeminate style. Such a style clearly appealed to George and might well have been influenced by female family members, as discussed in Chapter 2.

The silvered surfaces in the Banqueting Room underwent unspecified cleaning at least once after George's reign. The Royal Pavilion 'Memorandoms' (1837–45) state that all gilt work in the Banqueting Room had been cleaned in 1836, at the end of William IV's reign, along with Jones's murals, their borders and the central silvered dragon: 'The Dining Room gilt-work all cleaned and the Paintings on the walls cleaned & the borders of d[itt]o re-varnished/The Ceiling & the Draggon cleaned & touched up with paint'.[74] This suggests that many of the silvered surfaces in the Pavilion had already tarnished by that point.

In the mid twentieth century, the conservator William Frost probably mechanically removed, by scraping, the layers of darkened insoluble varnish on silvered surfaces – a procedure that would have removed evidence of original

3.44 *(opposite)* Silver leaves on the ceiling of the south Saloon apse. The slightly tarnished one (fourth from left) is the one discovered in 2005

coloured glazes. Repairs in aluminium to original objects such as the central dragon and the bells in the Banqueting Room suggest that he was at least aware of a silver-coloured finish applied to these objects. A single claw-shaped wooden object that probably became detached from a dragon ornament similar to the high-level dragons in the Music Room is possibly the only original silvered and glazed surface remaining in the Pavilion. The claw was taken to the National Gallery Scientific Department in 2013 for pigment analysis, where the green was identified as verdigris.

The clock made by Benjamin Lewis Vulliamy (1780–1854) and probably designed by Jones (fig. 2.1), which was originally displayed on the north mantelpiece in the Banqueting Room, is a particularly good example of how individual decorative objects often reflected the colour schemes, motifs and variety of surface finishes of an entire room in the Pavilion. The clock combines silvered and gilt surfaces and intense blues in the form of inlaid lapis lazuli, corresponding to the Prussian blue wallpaper and Spode porcelain in the room, while the seated Chinese figures are reminiscent of Jones's figurative chinoiserie wall panels. The iridescent effect of the multicoloured enamelled peacock resembles the silvered and coloured dragon and phoenix birds of the chandeliers:

> A superb Clock by Vulliamy with silvered face in a silvered circular case, mounted in richly chased mat foliage, representing Eagles, and surmounted by Japanned metal peacock: hexagonal base, enriched with lapis lazuli in front and overlaid with a key ornament, and supported by richly painted metal male & female Chinese Figures seated on an oblong ormolu plinth with lapis lazuli.[75]

The colouring of silvered surfaces might also have been inspired by Chinese enamelware and similar glossy and multicoloured surfaces found in export ware. In her essay '"Luscious Colors and Glossy Paint": The Taste for China and the Consumption of Color in 18th-Century England', Vanessa Alayrac-Fielding quotes from Erasmus Darwin's long poem *The Botanical Garden* (written in 1789, first published in 1791 and republished in 1825), where the decoration of Asian porcelain is described with a coincidental reference to 'huge dragons with metallic hues':

> First CHINA's sons, with early art elate,
> Form'd the gay tea-pot, and the pictured plate;
> Saw with illumin'd brow and dazzled eyes
> In the red stove vitrescent colours rise;
> Speck'd her tall beakers with enamel'd stars,
> Her monster-josses, and gigantic jars;
> Smear'd her huge dragons with metallic hues,
> With golden purples, and cobaltic blues;
> Bade on wide hills her porcelain castles glare,
> And glazed Pagodas tremble in the air.[76]

Alayrac-Fielding explains that the term 'smear'd' was not a negative term, but describes a specific technique of enamelling, while the 'metallic' hues were a specific type of Chinese decoration where iridescent colour were created by precipitating gold and tin to create a red glaze, or alkaline salts to produce blueish purples.[77] The glazed Pavilion dragons, bells and other ornaments might be a rare large-scale manifestation of European artists and designers trying to emulate the colours and surface finish of this particular type of export ware. It is testimony to the superior skills and creative minds of George's designers that these colours and surface finishes were transferred to very large objects and a variety of materials in the Pavilion.

Silver in the Saloon

In Jones's design scheme for the Saloon (completed 1823), silver is used most lavishly and creatively. It is found at low and high level on the wallpaper, cornices, capitals and apse ceilings, and on wooden pilasters around the room. Silver leaf is applied to a variety of materials, such as stuccoed plaster, paper, metal and wood, frequently in combination with gilding and contrasting with wall hangings, draperies and upholstered furniture in 'His Majesty's Geranium and gold colour satin decorated with silk gimp'.[78]

The Royal Pavilion Requisitions Book first refers to silvering carried out in the Saloon by Jones on two occasions in or before January 1823: 'Preparing, painting and gilding in Oil Gold, and Silvering in various part the Cornice partly etched &c'[79] and 'Painting and Silvering

3.45 *(opposite)* One of the 'very large Dragons in various colours and varnished, for the support of drapery to window' in the Music Room, restored after the 1975 fire

on Paper the Styles or ground of the walls to a rich design of Leaf and flower'.[80] This is echoed in the Royal Pavilion Abstract of Accounts entry from 5 January 1823: 'Preparing painting and gilding in Oil Gold and Silvering in various parts the Cornice partly &ched [*sic*] &c Paint'g and silvering on Paper the Styles or ground of the Walls to a rich design of leaf & flower'.[81] In the Robert Jones Accounts this work, which relates mostly to the silvered wallpaper (see fig. 3.43), is described in greater detail and dated November 1822:

> Preparing the grounds and Painting and Silvering the Enrichment, which forms the Stiles, or ground Work on the Walls, consisting of Symetric [*sic*] leaves, and flowers in Silver, arranged to fit the different dimensions of various situations, and relieved by shadowing on a fine ground of Pearl white the whole of the Ornament &c secured.[82]

The silvered wallpaper corresponded to the eight silvered and gilt pilasters (visible in fig. 3.47), which are described in the 1828 Inventory: '8 Pilasters in the recesses, carved, gilt and decorated with palm trees, snakes &c, in white and silver ground; with thin silver and gilt plaster caps'.[83] These pilasters were returned to the Pavilion by George V in 1935 and it appears that they were at some stage partially overpainted.

The ceiling of the Saloon dome was decorated with a painted clouded sky with dragons and other Chinese symbols, but in the north and south apse Jones applied more silver leaf in the shape of nine stylised palm leaves arranged in a star pattern. One of the original leaves from the south apse was discovered and restored in 2005 and the rest of the south apse ceiling recreated by the Pavilion's conservation team to Jones's design (fig. 3.44).[84]

Jones also refers to silver in combination with enamel and imitation of enamel when recording the design for the 'grand Oriental chimney . . . with all the ornamental detail of its enrichments in Or Molu and Silver', with the decorative figures in the recesses 'wrought with Silver and Gold &c. &c. and highly Polished and secured from Change'.[85] To 'secure from change' refers to a coating that would have prevented or delayed tarnishing. An intriguing combination of blue and silver is mentioned in relation to the windows: 'Gilding the Stiles and Mouldings, with all the Mouldings of the Sash frames, which are enriched with an imitation of dark Blue Enamel on Silver, the Whole secured and highly Varnished &c.'[86] This is reminiscent of the blue and silver wallpaper in the Banqueting Room, but the attention to colour detail and surface finish is also evidence of the superior design work found in the Pavilion generally.

Silver in other locations in the Pavilion

Other reflective materials were in common use throughout the building and applied by both Jones and the Craces. Silvered carved ornaments, glazed with a variety of colours, were also found in the Music Room. The best example of the visual impact of coloured silver can be seen in the dragon and serpents on the west wall by the windows, created by Frederick Crace in *c.*1820: 'Painting on Silver 4 very large Dragons in various colours and varnished, for the support of drapery to window . . . 1 large double Serpent in various colours, and as above'.[87] The 1975 fire (see p. 111) destroyed some parts and surfaces of the dragons and serpents. While this loss is regrettable, the replacements and repairs make it possible to see how fresh and intense the silver and glazed elements of the decorations would have appeared shortly after the completion of the interior (fig. 3.45).

The various account books and inventories of the Pavilion reveal the presence of many more silvered surfaces from 1802 onwards, with a noticeable increase after 1814. In 1815 the Crace Ledger records silvering in the 'New Gallery' (Long Gallery): 'Repainting and silvering in part the 16 standards in consequence of alterations made by Fricker & Henderson at Brighton'.[88] Furthermore, silvered dragon ornaments appear in a room referred to as the Small Drawing Room (unidentified, but possibly part of the North or South Drawing Rooms flanking the Saloon). Here, in typical Crace fashion, silver is used in combination with the primary colours red, yellow and blue: 'Painting a canopy over glass – red, yellow and blue ornaments, bells gilt and blue scroll, and 2 large columns supporting D[itt]o red with Dragons, silvered scaled and varnished'.[89] In the same room the Craces also silvered and varnished the feet of two screen stands.[90] There are further references to the silvering of ornaments carried out by the Craces in almost every room in 1816, including an intriguing entry for '3 Bats for draperies silvered and varnished green and purple'[91] in the Yellow Room (now the Music Room Gallery), 'bells silvered and varnished green' in the Entrance Hall, and '1 large Dragon silvered and painted in proper colors', also for the Entrance Hall.[92]

An entry in the Robson and Hale Accounts from 1820 may indicate that the blue verditer European wallpaper in the North and South Galleries (figs 3.8 to 3.11) was embellished with silvered Chinese export wallpaper: '6 Dozen Chinese Silver border flower on blue' at £12 12s.[93] Regrettably, this ornamental detail is not referenced anywhere else, but it supports the argument that silver was employed as unifying tone throughout the Pavilion.

In 1822 Bailey and Sanders charged £11 6s for making or furnishing a 'blue and silver bed' in the New North Buildings, which is briefly mentioned in the Royal Pavilion Abstract of Accounts: 'To making furniture for Bedstead with the Lining & Trim'g of the Blue and Silver Bed.'[94] A more detailed entry in the Brighton: Accompts rel. to the Pavilion: 1821–4 describes the blue and silver scheme of the bed, with white satin mentioned in relation to other furnishings in the room: 'To cleaning and repairing His Majesty's silver fringe; To making a furniture [?] for a large bedstead of His Majesty's blue striped silk and decorated with coverings and trimmings of the blue and silver bed.'[95]

Taking the surviving silvered surfaces and objects and the high number of references in primary manuscript sources relating to the Pavilion into consideration, it becomes clear that silver was used much more widely in the building than previously thought.

Historic predecessors of silvering in interior decorations

Silvering does not appear to have been very popular in eighteenth-century British interiors and examples of its use are rare, which makes the Pavilion an important case in the history of silver in European arts, architecture and fashion prior to the 1820s. Reasons for the rarity of historic silvered interiors in Britain may include the country's insularity, the cautious tone with regard to silvering in English language decorators' manuals, and the greater danger of damp damage and deterioration, as well as a significantly more restrained manifestation of the Baroque and Rococo styles compared to in mainland Europe. By comparison, France, Denmark and particularly Germany embraced silvering in many important royal and aristocratic interiors throughout the eighteenth century, despite the unstable nature of the material.

Apart from silver or silvered objects such as table ware or such as chandeliers, silver was most commonly found in the form of silvered picture and mirror frames, as well as silvered furniture. In some cases, furniture was made of solid silver, expressing power and wealth on an unprecedented scale. For example the 'Sun King' Louis XIV (r. 1643–1715) commissioned the extravagant *Grande argenterie*, a suite of silver furnishings for his apartments and the Galerie des Glaces (Hall of Mirrors) at Versailles. While the objects have not survived, descriptions of the state apartments reveal the stunning visual effects of the silver, particularly in combination with candlelight and large numbers of mirrors.

The English court, too, had a taste for silver or silvered furniture. George III had inherited at least three suites of silver tables, mirrors and stands, made for William III in the late seventeenth century. Roberts notes that another set of silver or silvered furniture was acquired by Frederick, Prince of Wales, in the 1740s, but that by 1764 a considerable amount of silver furniture was to be melted down. It is unclear whether this actually happened, since four silver tables and other silver furnishings were recorded in an account from February 1805 of a fête at Windsor Castle, and these are later included in a watercolour by Charles Wild of the Queen's ballroom (RCIN 922101) from 1817.[96]

In terms of interior design schemes, silvered cornices, wall ornaments and mouldings have, for example, been identified in the Rococo addition to Elector of Brandenburg Frederick III's Baroque palace in Berlin, Schloss Charlottenburg, built from 1699 for his wife, Sophie Charlotte. The main building includes several chinoiserie interiors and significant collections of Chinese and Japanese porcelain, as might be expected in a building of that period designed for a woman. In the New Wing (Neuer Flügel), added in 1740–47 for Frederick the Great, the King's Library and other rooms facing the gardens include elaborate silvering on cornices, doorframes and other woodwork, although not in a chinoiserie context. Lavishly decorated silver interiors are also found in the Neue Palais, a large three-winged Baroque palace, which was added by Frederick to his Sanssouci Palace estate in

3.46 *The Circular Room, Carlton House*, watercolour and bodycolour over etched lines by Charles Wild, *c.*1817. RCIN 922177 © Royal Collection Enterprises Limited 2025 | Royal Collection Trust

Brandenburg between 1763 and 1769.

The most significant example of eighteenth-century silvered interiors in Europe is the Amalienburg, a hunting lodge in the grounds of Nymphenburg Palace in Munich, designed by François de Cuvilliés, with interiors by stuccoist Johann Baptist Zimmermann, woodcarver Joachim Dietrich and painter Joseph Pasqualin Moretti. It was built between 1734 and 1739 by the Holy Roman Emperor Charles VII for his wife Maria Amalia and combines highly finished silvered surfaces in almost every room with an elaborate use of mirrors. Some chinoiserie elements are present in the building, although not in the silvered rooms: the Pheasant Room, or 'Indian Cabinet,' is hung with imitation Chinese wallpaper, while the kitchen is decorated with blue-and-white Dutch tiles with Chinese scenery. In typical Rococo style, the ground colours in the silvered rooms, allocated and named by Cuvilliés on architectural drawings, are a *fond de citron* (a pale lemon yellow), a light blue, and *couleur de paille* (a straw colour) and white (*à fond blanc et les ornements argentés*).[97]

The Amalienburg is important in this context because it is the only known surviving building in Europe with a predominantly silver interior. The colour scheme and the large-scale use of silver and mirrors can here be interpreted as reflecting the use and function of the building: the interiors create a cool and bright atmosphere, an association with water or even ice in certain rooms, after the heat of an afternoon's hunting. Similar to the Pavilion, the Amalienburg falls into the category of playful buildings or pleasure palaces (*maison de plaisance* or *Lustschloss*), often associated with less formal and more experimental designs, and placed at some distance from the main palace. Other smaller structures in the gardens of Nymphenburg Palace boast chinoiserie interiors, notably the Pagodenburg and the Badenburg.[98] Friederike Wappenschmidt notes that, as is the case with the Pavilion interiors, the colours and decorations of the Amalienburg were not gimmicky, but represented a 'carefully selected and designed allegorical language and colour symbolism', a highly sensualised interior that aimed to evoke certain moods and sensations.[99]

A late Rococo example of silvered interiors from the Würzburg Residence in Bavaria is particularly relevant in comparison to the coloured glazes over silver found in the Pavilion. The Green Lacquered Room in the northern imperial apartments in the Residence appears to reflect a design idea similar to the Craces' in the Music Room, namely to imitate the effect of lacquer furniture on the walls of an entire room. The particular tonal quality and surface shimmer is achieved here by a very thin layer of green lacquer over a ground of silver leaf, the whole applied to wooden panels and doors.

Silver played a significant part in chinoiserie interiors, but almost exclusively in the form of Chinese export silverware, mounting for porcelain export ware, or chinoiserie designs on European silverware, as surveys by Alan James Marlowe and H.A. Crosby Forbes[100] and James Lomax[101] confirm. The use of silver in surface finishes and as an element in wallpaper designs is rare, not reliably recorded and possibly unidentified in many cases. Lacquer, or 'japanned', cabinets were occasionally mounted on silvered stands and incorporated silver elements in the figurative decoration on the panels, but these are rarer than gilt, black or red varieties.

In chinoiserie interiors silver also played a role in the form of reverse glass or mirror paintings. These popular export paintings usually depicted Chinese motifs similar to those found on export wallpaper, painted on to the glass and thus thrown into sharp relief against the mirror's silvered background.[102] It is highly likely that Chinese glass paintings were one of Jones's inspirations for his Banqueting Room panels, where figure groups are set against a silvered background.

Silver interiors contemporary with the Pavilion

Whereas silvered interiors and silvered ornamental objects enjoyed considerable popularity in eighteenth and early-nineteenth century interiors in continental Europe, they are extremely rare and seldom recorded in Britain. The most direct line of influence on the use of silver in the Pavilion comes from George himself. This is evident in his well-documented love of silverware and highly reflective surfaces and his obsession with gilding. At least one room in Carlton House, the Dining Room, was decorated in a colour scheme that incorporated a considerable amount of silvering. Like most rooms in Carlton House, it underwent several transformations, but the design scheme as it appears in the 1817 drawing and print illustrates a conversion carried out between 1805 and *c.*1808 under James Wyatt, Richard Westmacott, Dominique Jean and other artists (fig. 3.46). In Ackermann's *Microcosm of London* in 1808 it is described enthusiastically:

> The new circular dining-room, when completed, will unquestionably be one of the most splendid apartments in Europe: the walls are entirely covered with silver, on which are painted Etruscan ornaments in relief, with vine-leaves, trellis-work, &c. There are eight fine Ionic columns in *scaglioni*, of red granite; the capitals and bases are silver, as are also the enrichments, moulding, &c. of the architrave, frieze, and cornice: the latter is surmounted by an ornament that is somewhat Turkish in its character, and which, if it does not belong to the Ionic order, nevertheless adds to the splendour of the room.[103]

In *Royal Residences*, Pyne records the colour scheme as a combination of orange, pale blue, red, black, green and silver, with the detailed description revealing the abundance of silver in the design scheme:

> A rotunda of the Ionic order, the parts selected from the purest specimen of ancient Greece. The entablature is fully enriched, and supported by scagliola columns

3.47 *(overleaf)* The Saloon in 2020, with light falling through the windows and the exhibition loans for *A Prince's Treasure* in situ

> in imitation of red porphyry, with statuary plinths and silvered capitals: the principal ornaments of the cornice and architraves also silvered, relieved by a ground of light lavender tint. . . . From the soffit of each recess is suspended a Roman tent drapery of light blue silk, ornamented with silver, with which silk the walls are partly covered, creating a sort of tent-like character; and these are relieved by sub-curtains of white taffeta. Each door is inserted in an arched recess: the architraves, archivolts, and cornices are superbly carved and silvered, the doors are painted in arabesque and bronze on silvered ground . . . the pier-glasses also reflect each other, and produce the appearance of repetition in endless continuity, which gives a magical effect and splendour of the apartment. . . . the plinths, shutters, and such walls that are not covered by draperies, are painted in arabesque upon a silvered ground. . . . The furniture consists of settees, supported at the corners with bronze chimera, and covered with light blue silk, the fringes and lace of which are composed of silver threads and other materials of dazzling brightness.[104]

The scheme as it appeared in 1817 shows some similarities to Jones's design scheme for the Pavilion's Saloon, such as the sky ceiling, the general layout and columnisation of the room, the combination of reflective metal surfaces on one object or in close proximity (bronze, silver, gold) and, most importantly, silvered cornices and capitals.

Considering these obvious similarities, the Circular Room is likely to have been a direct inspiration for Jones's work at the Pavilion in the early 1820s. It is also possible that George instructed Jones to make decorative references to the room, since the redecoration of the Saloon at Brighton occurred shortly before the demolition of Carlton House in 1827.

There are very few other examples of early nineteenth-century silvered interiors. One of these is the block-printed chinoiserie wallpaper in shades of grey on a satin ground, designed by the Dublin paper-stainer Robert Dyas and hung in 1807 at Castle Coole, County Fermanagh. The motifs comprise a dense pattern of flowers, birds and Chinese pavilions, which seems to have been modelled on engraved or embossed Chinese export silver.[105] Another can be found in the library at Moggerhanger House in Bedfordshire, which has several tangible connections with the Pavilion. Sir John Soane remodelled the existing house between 1790 and 1812, during which time John Crace designed some of the interiors, while Humphry Repton was responsible for landscaping the parkland. Peter Inskip explains that the room's decorative scheme, designed by William Watson in or just after 1812, was an exception within the house, as it did not feature the uniform grey and buff pattern of the rest of the interior. Instead, 'green, used on architraves and dado, was allied with grained doors, windows and skirtings, and the walls covered with a simple, but rare, wallpaper with floral motifs in silver leaf (now tarnished and black), edged with verditer green painted borders.'[106] The similarities with the use of silver in the Pavilion are fascinating: a silver stencilled motif on a pale ground, silver in combination with green, and the presence of large surfaces of woodgraining. It is not known who designed or manufactured the wallpaper.

Another important contemporary example of a silvered interior has even stronger links with George and the Pavilion. In the Chinese Drawing Room and the adjoining vestibule at Temple Newsam in Leeds, silver is used in a playful way and on a scale that shows similarities to the silvering in the Pavilion Saloon.[107] It is present on cornices, frames, ceiling moulding and a ceiling rose, although not on wallpaper. The silver decorations at Temple Newsam are slightly later (1827–8) than those in the Pavilion, but there is a direct connection between the two interiors that might explain the similarities to the use of silver: George, when Prince of Wales, gave several rolls of Chinese export wallpaper to Lady Irwin of Temple Newsam on the occasion of his first visit in 1806. The wallpaper was used years later by Lady Irwin's daughter, Lady Hertford, with whom George was said to have had an affair. She began redecorating the Chinese Drawing Room in 1822, incorporating the wallpaper given to her mother, and adding the silver element to the room.[108]

It is highly likely that Lady Hertford was inspired by either the recent silvered decorations at the Pavilion (even if they had only been reported to her) or by earlier silver elements in the Circular Room at Carlton House. John Cornforth believes the source of inspiration was the latter, because the Circular Room was described in Ackermann's popular *Microcosm of London*, but the personal connection between Lady Hertford and George seems just as strong an argument.

When considering these few surviving examples of silvered interiors in Britain in the early nineteenth century, it is obvious that this was a refined and expensive taste. In view of the short reflective and shimmering lifespan of unvarnished silvered surfaces, it was perhaps one that was only applied to interiors that were frequently redecorated or considered temporary. George's excitable and impulsive nature might further explain the lavish use of silvering in the Pavilion. His love of gilding was well known, and he is generally associated with excess rather than restraint in interior design (and everything else), so it is not surprising that he would have embraced the idea of an imaginative use of silver, either in combination with gold or glazed with transparent colours for an iridescent effect. His rapidly changing tastes and reckless spending habits suggest that it was in keeping with his personality to experiment with silver, despite its known tendency to tarnish quickly. It appears likely that both the Craces and Robert Jones were influenced by elements of silvering present in Chinese export ware, for example silverware, silvered wallpaper, leather hangings or reverse glass paintings, as well as silvered European Rococo interiors. The combination of gilding and silvering in proximity and on a large scale appears to be characteristic of Jones's style and reflects his particularly imaginative artistic mind. The variety and high number of silvered surfaces and objects in the Pavilion suggest that silver was a conspicuous and unifying element in the interior design schemes of the building. The fact that silver was used by both Jones and the Craces over a long period of time also suggests that they were responding to George's specific instructions and tastes.

The final decorative scheme of the Pavilion reflected the use and function of the building, and colours were deliberately chosen in relation to how and in what order the room of the building would be experienced by a visitor. The building was designed as a party and pleasure palace and frequently used for lavish dinners, balls, concerts and other entertainment. It was therefore in George's interest to create a sumptuous and glittering look in his seaside residence, with the ultimate aim – to echo Sickelmore's words – of impressing his guests, of enchanting their senses and exciting them.[109] However, although richly coloured and highly ornamented, the interiors were not designed simply to overwhelm visitors. Instead, much attention was paid to the creation of a luxurious, sensual and comfortable environment. This is obvious, for example, in the carefully chosen material for the handrails of the North and South Staircases (fig. 2.7). Here, mahogany in imitation of bamboo was used, which was warmer to the touch than the cast iron and bronze that formed the main body of the staircases. Underfoot, a Regency lady wearing thin-soled kidskin shoes would have felt the difference between hard drugget in the entrance area and the softer Brussels weave carpet in the Long Gallery, before sinking into the thick pile of the hand-knotted Axminster carpets in the Banqueting Room, Music Room and Saloon. In that centre room, natural light would illuminate the shimmering decorations during the day and pick out the bright colours of Asian porcelain, gilt bronze mounts and silvered wall decorations (fig. 3.47), while after dark the flickering light of candles and oil chandeliers would be reflected by the silvered and gilt surfaces and the red and gold silk of the soft furnishings. The repetition of motifs and colours, not just in one room but throughout the entire building, including the garden, added a further element of wonder and surprise, encouraging visitors, then and now, to enjoy the Pavilion with all their senses.

The Royal Bird

Conclusion

'Surreal and Fantastical'

Mood and materials in a Regency pleasure pavilion

The Royal Pavilion is a beautifully executed architectural oddity, seemingly out of time and out of place even at the moment of its creation. It was unusual in Europe in its unflinching and joyful embrace of 'oriental' features, and in unapologetically displaying an excess of decoration and colour. While opulence and splendour would have been expected in a palace, George always referred to his Brighton residence as a pavilion. This would suggest something more lightweight and modest, which it is clearly not. The Pavilion has certain aspects and features that are unique. Yet, as I hope this book has shown, it did not stand on its own, either physically or metaphorically. In its bewildering, fragile and meandering beauty, the Pavilion, its garden, and the other buildings on the estate are an architectural expression of the aesthetics of the Romantic and the picturesque. A building of great intricacy and with a complicated history, it sprang from the mind and desires of an excitable and extremely privileged man who would become King of England, but it is also a reflection of the political, cultural and material circumstances of its time.

Some tantalising questions remain unanswered: what were George's reasons for creating a building so extreme and all-encompassing in its eclectic 'oriental' appearance, at a time when the chinoiserie style had gone out of fashion – at least in Britain? Was it ever intended to be a building with a political purpose, or were George's design decisions purely driven by aesthetics? It is tempting to interpret the move away from neoclassicism as a reaction to anti-French sentiments during and after the Napoleonic wars, but, as this book has shown, the reasons may be more complex. George was likely influenced and inspired by the 'oriental' structures he had seen at Kew in his early childhood, and by the taste, collecting habits and creative occupations of his mother and sisters. Yet however much George may have wanted to disguise his Francophilia with chinoiserie, there is still an overarching Frenchness to the later Pavilion interiors, and he freely and irreverently combined this with Egyptian and Indian elements.

In developing a building and garden so complete and visionary as the Pavilion, other factors come into play, notably location and opportunity. The appearance of the Pavilion has much to do with Brighton, and George's royal wealth and privilege. He not only had the desire, but also the means to create a comparatively small yet opulent pleasure palace away from the London court, exceptional and extreme in style. The social life and location of Brighton probably encouraged him to pursue more daring, playful and experimental designs, which reflected the mood of Brighton in general and enhanced the reputation the seaside resort had already acquired.

(opposite) The Royal Bird Foo Hum, watercolour and ink drawing by Frederick Crace for the Royal Pavilion, *c.*1815

The decorative schemes of the Pavilion were here considered a complete work of art, individually in each room, and comprehensively in all the state rooms and other areas decorated in a chinoiserie style. They represent an all-encompassing vision of a Romantic Regency interior that was designed to entertain and dazzle. Colour is one of the defining aspects of the building and its interiors. As Sitwell and Barton noted in 1935, 'The novelty of the chinoiserie style . . . as presented to us at the Pavilion, resides in its exuberance, its massive effects of colour, as opposed to the almost Pompeian delicacy which had attended it in the earlier epoch.'[1]

The multi-sensory approach and the many elements of surprise that form part of the experience of the Pavilion are typical elements of Romanticism and the picturesque. It is a building that focuses on subjective and individual experience, that seeks to stimulate the senses, that encourages indulgence and immersion. It is tempting to wonder whether Chinese colour symbolism, for example the meaning of colours in the Daoist Wuxing doctrine, Chinese dynastic colours, or the colour codes of state rituals, informed the designs of the Pavilion. However, considering the fragmentary knowledge and romanticised image of Asia among Europeans, it is more likely that these influences were superficial, and that George and his designers cherry-picked from the rich panoply of Asian culture, adapting select elements for the purpose of creating a sensual and theatrical interior.

Mood was firmly underpinned by materiality: the complex, self-referencing and carefully designed decorative schemes of the Pavilion were to no small extent led by the availability of imported Asian objects, as well as the invention of new pigments and techniques. The Pavilion may be considered a precursor of the more industrialised polychromatic decorative styles of the later nineteenth century. George's residence by the sea was indeed a romantic vision, perhaps conceived in several dreams. To take the Coleridge and Kubla Khan analogies from the introduction to this book (see pp. 14–15) further, this dreamy 'pleasure dome' on the edge of England is arguably now a fragment of its former self, since many of the original objects that once adorned it are no longer in situ, and many colours and paint effects have been lost to time. Yet, it was a creation of such opulence and intensity that it still shines and enchants today, and it remains one of the most popular historic buildings in Britain.

In 2021, the broadcaster Fatima Manji described her experience of seeing the Pavilion in her book *Hidden Heritage: Rediscovering Britain's Lost Love of the Orient*. Her words recall Musgrave's image of the Pavilion floating in on a magic carpet (see p. 14, Introduction), while alluding to its pleasantly disorientating effect:

> 'On a gusty September day, from a distance, the Pavilion's sand-coloured structure looks as if it might have been superimposed onto a dull sky. From every angle there are domes, towers and minarets, with the effect so giddying that I am unsure where to fix my gaze . . . It is astonishing, surreal and fantastical . . .'[2]

(opposite) The *porte cochère* on the west front of the Royal Pavilion

APPENDIX

Augustus Charles Pugin's Drawings of the Royal Pavilion (*c*.1818–1823)

In the Collection of Brighton & Hove Museums

Brighton & Hove Museums holds a total of 40 original works on paper by Augustus Charles Pugin which capture the Royal Pavilion during and just after its transformation by architect John Nash and interior decorators and designers Frederick Crace and Robert Jones. These drawings are among the most important, charming, and precious objects relating to the Pavilion. They are here for the first time reproduced as a complete set and in colour, incorporating new research.

Pugin was born in Paris in 1768 or 1769 and left post-revolutionary France for England in *c*.1790. An exceptionally skilled draughtsman, he was taken on as assistant by Nash soon after his arrival, an association that lasted until his death in 1832. From 1808 Pugin worked with artist Thomas Rowlandson and publisher Rudolph Ackermann on *The Microcosm of London*.

The works by Pugin shown here formed the basis for the images in Nash's 1826 book, *The Royal Pavilion at Brighton* (also known as *Nash's Views of the Royal Pavilion*), which comprised high-quality coloured aquatints, outline engravings, and some additional lithographs, capturing the complete transformation of the Pavilion after 1815. The drawings here do not completely match Nash's illustrations, but are the largest group of Pugin's drawings that relate to the building. A further eight are in the Royal Library at Windsor, while others – including the fold-out cross-sectional view – are missing.

It is not clear when Pugin started working on the Pavilion drawings, but given his professional relationship with Nash, it is likely he first visited in *c*.1817, when the new Music Room and Banqueting Room had been erected. He then continued to record the progress over the next six years. Only a couple of the drawings are dated, and although some are numbered, this appears to relate to book's layout rather than the sequence of creation. There are two distinct types of drawings, which reflects the purpose of the project: freehand watercolours that capture the general look and colouring of the building, and meticulously executed pencil and/or ink drawings, which were intended for the engravers of the plates. In some cases, Pugin coloured in isolated areas in the detailed drawings, which would have provided the aquatinter and colourists with the correct colour schemes.

The immediacy, accuracy and freshness of these drawings make them the most valuable source of information about the design and overall appearance of the building during George's lifetime.

(above) East front of the Marine Pavilion estate, A.C. Pugin (previously attributed to Thomas Rowlandson), watercolour on paper. This drawing relates to the first plate in *Nash's Views of the Royal Pavilion*, (commonly known as *Nash's Views*) where it is described as 'The Steine Front previous to the Alterations', (before 1815). It is uncertain whether Pugin would have seen the Pavilion at this stage, but not impossible.

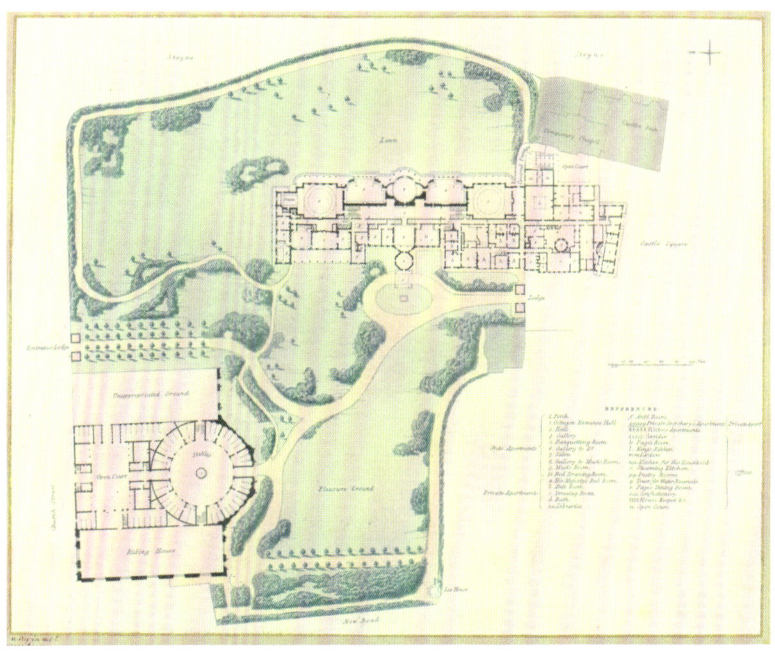

(right) The *Ground Plan* of the Pavilion estate, after A.C. Pugin, hand-coloured aquatint, as published in *Nash's Views* in 1826. *(below)* The Ground Plan, A.C. Pugin, pencil and ink on paper, *c.*1818–23. Like most of Pugin's drawings this is undated, but it is likely that it developed over a longer period. There are additions in different coloured inks (such as sketches and dimensions of some structures) and some text has been rubbed out or overwritten. The list of rooms on the ground floor are more detailed. Whereas Pugin started the numbered sequence of the state apartments and the King's private apartments with the Music Room and then going clockwise, on the print the sequence begins with the porch and follows an anti-clockwise route through the building. There are also significant changes to the allocation of rooms at the southern end. An 'ornamental seat' is drawn in the north-west corner of the estate, but is no longer listed in the references. It is not known whether it was ever built.

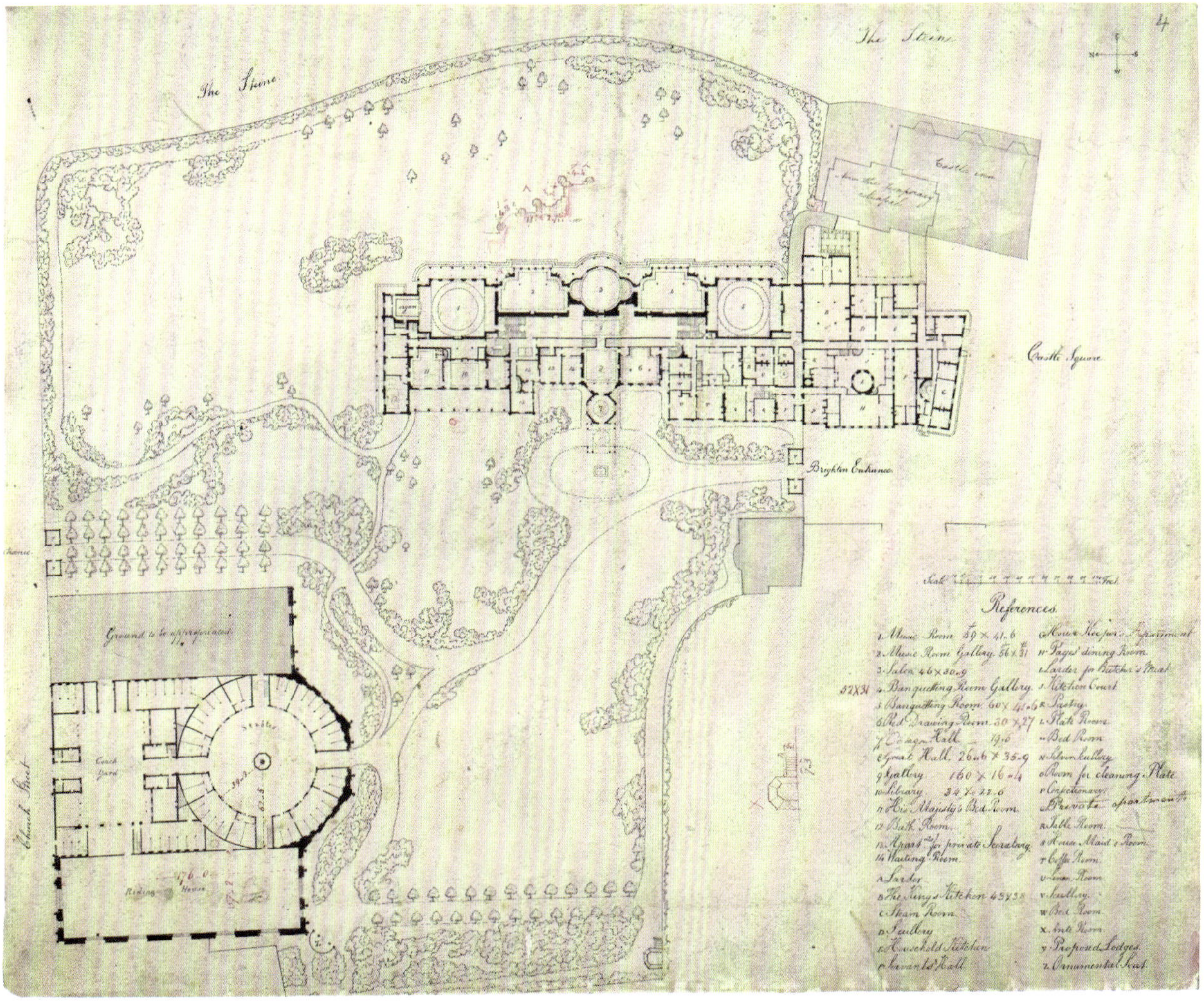

(above) The centre part of the east front of the Pavilion, A.C. Pugin, pencil on paper, *c.*1822. This became the first plate with detail view of the exterior of the Pavilion in *Nash's Views*, and has become one of the most recognisable images of the building. It focuses on Nash's largest onion-shaped dome and other prominent features, such as the soaring minarets and the lacy screen that unifies the east facade.

(above) The east front of the Pavilion, A.C. Pugin, watercolour and pencil on paper, 1823. This is the only drawing in this group inscribed and dated by the artist. It is perhaps the image that best captures the Romantic and picturesque character of the Pavilion after Nash's transformation.

(right) A view of the west front of the Pavilion, A.C. Pugin, watercolour and pencil on paper, *c.*1823 *(below)* A view of the west front of the Pavilion, A.C. Pugin, watercolour and pencil on paper, *c.*1823. These watercolours were probably the preliminary sketches for plate 7 in *Nash's Views*, showing the western side of the Pavilion and much of its newly laid out gardens.

(above) The north end of the west side of the Pavilion, A.C. Pugin, pencil on paper, *c.*1822. *(below)* The north end of the west side of the Pavilion, A.C. Pugin and/or Charles Moore, watercolour and pencil on paper, *c.*1822. These two drawings would form the basis for the plate titled 'The King's Private Apartments' in *Nash's Views*. While the pencil drawing is definitely by Pugin, the watercolour has also been attributed to Charles Moore (b.c.1800), who was one of Pugin's assistants and is credited as the draughtsman for some of the plates in *Nash's Views* (Rogers 1978, p.119). Derek Rogers has suggested that Moore's contribution was to prepare Pugin's watercolours for the engraver.

(left) The *porte cochère* on the west front, A.C. Pugin, pencil, ink and watercolour on paper, *c.*1822. The delightful, small drawing shows the King arriving on horseback at the entrance portico of the Pavilion. The figures, possibly drawn by James Stephanoff, are coloured in.

(below) The north front of the Pavilion, A.C. Pugin, watercolour and pencil on paper, *c.*1822. The work has a section added on the left and is inscribed with 'North End of Pavilion' by Pugin in ink at the top (with some crossing out).

(above) The centre part of the west front, with the *porte cochère* and entrance, A.C. Pugin, watercolour and pencil on paper, *c.*1822. *(below)* The centre part of the west front, with the *porte cochère* and entrance, A.C. Pugin, pencil on. paper, *c.*1822. While the pencil drawing provides architectural detail, the watercolour gives us information about the garden layout and its maintenance. The figure of a gardener (probably added by Stephanoff) can be seen in the latter, trimming the lawn inside the turning circle with a scythe.

The south side of the Stables, A.C. Pugin, pencil on paper, *c.*1820. This shows William Porden's domed stables as seen from the garden. It was the preliminary drawing for the first image of the royal stables in *Nash's Views*, described on the list of plates as 'Perspective View of the Stable Building'.

The interior of the 'Rotunda', A.C. Pugin, pencil on paper, *c.*1820. In the pencil drawing the figures and horses are fully executed. They were probably added by James Stephanoff. It is possible that Pugin used a camera lucida to create this and other views of the Pavilion.

(opposite) The interior of the 'Rotunda', A.C. Pugin, watercolour and pencil on paper, *c.*1820. This pair of drawings of the interior of the magnificent domed stables building, known as the 'Rotunda', gives a good impression of how Pugin worked: the freehand watercolour only includes faint outlines of figures and horses. Note also the shadows cast by the dome structure, which are not shown in the drawing for the outline engraving above.

(right) The Entrance Hall, A.C. Pugin, pencil and some watercolour on paper, *c.*1821 or later. In this drawing Pugin partly colours in some areas as colour references for the aquatinter. For example, only one of the lanterns, one of the clerestory windows, and a small portion of the floor are coloured. A rosewood-veneer piano made for George IV by Thomas Tomkison in 1821 is visible on the right. *(below)* The Red Drawing Room, A.C. Pugin, watercolour and pencil on paper, *c.*1822. This room, to the south of the Entrance Hall, was added by Nash and decorated by Robert Jones in a light-hearted chinoiserie style. This watercolour conveys the chromatic intensity of Jones's red so-called 'dragon wallpaper' but omits the finer details and motifs of the design.

(above) The Banqueting Room Gallery, A.C. Pugin, pencil on paper, 1821 or later. The north-east side of the Banqueting Gallery after Nash's extension eastward. This drawing did not appear as a print in *Nash's Views*. *(below)* The Blue Drawing Room, A.C. Pugin, watercolour and pencil on paper, before 1821. The Blue Drawing Room (also known as the South Drawing Room) was roughly on the site of the house rented by George in the early 1780s. It is now occupied by the Banqueting Room Gallery. This scheme, dominated by the strong blues, in combination with reds and yellows, probably lasted from 1815 to *c.*1820.

The Banqueting Room, A.C. Pugin, pencil and some watercolour on paper, *c.*1820 or later. Like the Music Room, the Banqueting Room was shown in *Nash's Views* as being in use. In this case a banquet is taking place, and the table is laden with food and drink. The King is seated at the centre of the west side of the table, facing the windows. The monochrome figures are probably the work of James Stephanoff. It is unclear who painted the figures in the wall paintings by Robert Jones, but they are remarkably accurate and picked out in colour. At either side of the sheet, Pugin added thin strips of paper to make it wider.

(above) The Banqueting Room Gallery, A.C. Pugin, pencil with some watercolour on paper, 1821 or later. *(below)* The Banqueting Room Gallery, A.C. Pugin, watercolour and pencil on paper, 1821 or later. These two drawings formed the basis for plate no.19 in *Nash's Views*. The more detailed pencil drawing above, intended for the outline engraving, is also partly coloured in, as a guidance for the aquatinter (see also 'The Entrance Hall' and 'The South Galleries').

(left) The Saloon, A.C. Pugin, pencil on paper, *c.*1823. This pencil drawing shows part of the window side and the north apse of the Saloon, with Robert Jones's scheme (completed in 1823) fully executed. This view was not turned into a print for *Nash's Views*

(below) The Saloon in *c.*1817, A.C. Pugin, pencil on paper, before 1818. This is the pencil drawing for plate 29 in *Nash's Views*, an uncoloured image titled 'Salon as it originally was'. It shows the Craces' chinoiserie scheme that preceded Robert Jones's early 1820s scheme seen above. The large, central chandelier is the one that was moved to the Long Gallery in *c.*1820, where it still impresses visitors today with its scale and design.

(above) The Long Gallery before 1820, A.C. Pugin, watercolour and pencil on paper, before 1820. *(right)* The Long Gallery before 1820, A.C. Pugin, pencil on paper, before 1820. In *Nash's Views* this is described 'The Gallery as it was', and probably shows the decorative scheme introduced the Craces in *c.*1815. This included the wall decorations 'on fine linen blue on pink ground', niches in imitation of pink marble, and life-size figures carved from wood and painted by the Craces, clad in real clothes. By 1820 the scheme had been altered, but clearly Nash considered this earlier appearance worth recording.

(above) The Long Gallery after 1819, A.C. Pugin, watercolour and pencil on paper, after 1820. *(right)* The Long Gallery after 1819, A.C. Pugin, pencil on paper, after 1820. By 1820, the Long Gallery had undergone some decorative changes, but some elements of the 1815 scheme remained, including the pink and blue wall decorations. The Craces' large carved figures had been replaced with smaller Chinese export clay figures with nodding heads, and the large chandelier from the Saloon had been moved to the Gallery. George had also introduced a set of Indian ivory veneer furniture bought in 1819 at the sale of his late mother Queen Charlotte's belongings.

(right) The Yellow Drawing Room, A.C. Pugin, pencil on paper, *c.*1818–1820. These exuberant chinoiserie decorations were created by the Craces at the beginning of Nash's transformation, although some design drawings for the room attributed to Robert Jones exist. Between 1815 and 1819, the Craces charged, for example, for 'Preparing and coloring bright yellow the cove with a purple Chinese enrichment' and '243 Chinese drop ornaments in various colours'. Before 1815 the space was probably the Billiard Room, possibly decorated in an Egyptian style. Some ornaments from the yellow scheme were possibly reused in other parts of the building after 1819. *(below)* The Yellow Drawing Room, A.C. Pugin, watercolour and pencil on paper, *c.*1818–1820.

(right) The Music Room Gallery, A.C. Pugin, pencil on paper, 1820 or later. This detailed pencil drawing shows the south-east corner of the Music Room Gallery, with the Adam Weisweiler tables and French chinoiserie candelabra (originally from Carlton House) clearly visible, but it was not included in *Nash's Views*.

(below) The Music Room Gallery, A.C. Pugin, watercolour and pencil on paper, 1820 or later. By 1821 the space formerly occupied by the Yellow Drawing Room had been enlarged as part of Nash's alterations to become the Music Room Gallery (also known as the North Drawing Room). The new decorative scheme by Frederick Crace featured the ceiling coloured in 'light pink', yellow curtains, and wall decorations of 'Chinese trellis in Gold'. Pugin's watercolour gives an impression of this gold-and-yellow scheme.

(above) The Music Room, A.C. Pugin, watercolour and pencil on paper, *c.*1822. *(right)* The Music Room, A.C. Pugin, pencil on paper, *c.*1822. The later Music Room is the most coherent and impressive of the decorative schemes of the Pavilion. Although many other design and colour options were drawn up by Frederick Crace (with some input from Robert Jones) between *c.*1817 and 1820, these two drawings show the room complete, lit and in use during a musical event in *c.*1822. The King can be seen seated on the left, flanked by Lady Conyngham and her daughter. The figures in the detailed pencil drawing were probably added by James Stephanoff.

(above) The King's Bedroom, A.C. Pugin, pencil on paper, *c.*1823. The freehand watercolour of the King's Bedroom is lacking some details that are present both in the pencil drawing and the finished prints in *Nash's Views*, for example the vases on the cabinet on the right.
(below) The King's Bedroom, A.C. Pugin, watercolour and pencil on paper, *c.*1823.

(above) The Library, A.C. Pugin, watercolour and pencil on paper, *c.*1823. *(below)* The Library, A.C. Pugin, pencil on paper, *c.*1823. The images of the King's private apartments were likely among the last Pugin drew of the Pavilion. In this pair (and in the King's Bedroom pair), the painted cloud ceiling and the light falling in from the west-facing windows are only depicted in the freehand watercolour (and the coloured print based on it), while the pencil drawing focuses on architectural and ornamental detail.

(above) The South Galleries, A.C. Pugin, watercolour and pencil on paper, *c.*1822. *(below)* The South Galleries, A.C. Pugin, pencil and some watercolour on paper, *c.*1822. This pair of drawings formed the basis of plate 23 in *Nash's Views*, where it is titled 'Gallery on Chamber Floor'. It is the only view of rooms on the upper floor of the Pavilion. The sky-blue colour of the walls (painted in blue verditer) dominates the scheme. In the second drawing Pugin has picked out some of the patterns and colours, including the polychrome Brussels Weave carpet and some decorative objects. Note how in the mirror we see a perfect reflection of the blue walls and ornaments opposite.

Notes

Introduction – A Vision in a Dream

1. Musgrave 1951, p. 11
2. Ibid.
3. For example, Sitwell and Barton 1944 [1935], p. 183, and Conner 1979, pp. 9–10
4. Polo 1818, p. 251. Also quoted in Conner 1979, p. 9, and partially quoted in Sitwell and Barton 1944 [1935], p. 183, and Musgrave 1951, p. 92
5. Coleridge 1816
6. Quennell 1937, p. 150
7. Musgrave 1946, p. 6
8. Ibid., p. 5

Chapter 1 – Creating a Stately Pleasure Dome

1 For a thorough account of the development of Brighton, see Berry 2005
2 Hazlitt 1826, p. 3
3 For example, Walker 1809, p. 3
4 Sickelmore, 1823, p. 24
5 Huish 1831
6 For a detailed description of Seymour's print, see Baker 2005, p. 131
7 Ibid., p. 139
8 Parissien 2001, pp. 116–65
9 Ibid., p. 143
10 Heard and Jones 2019; see also Lyons 2024
11 Aldrich 2009, pp. 21–9
12 For a detailed account on this sale, see Roberts 2000, pp. 115–37
13 Ibid., p. 119
14 For a detailed overview of Queen Victoria's visits to Brighton, see Conrad 2023
15 Musgrave 1959, p. 14
16 See Morley 1984, pp. 14–16
17 There is some confusion as to whether the tiles were glazed or not. All the literature says they were glazed, but surviving tiles in the Royal Pavilion Archives are unglazed
18 Jones 2005, p. 41
19 Cited in Roberts 1939, pp. 28–9
20 Cited ibid., p. 49 and Musgrave 1959, p. 11. No reference is provided as to the location of this manuscript, which was in the possession of Collett's family in 1935, when Roberts obtained permission to quote from it
21 *Sussex Weekly Advertiser*, 9 July 1787. Also partly quoted in Morley 1959 p. 221. Morley also considers the 1785 date for Collett's diary 'impossibly early' (ibid., p. 252, note 156)
22 Musgrave 1959, pp. 16–17
23 Ibid., p. 17
24 Wigstead 1790, unpaginated. Also quoted in Roberts, 1939, p. 27 and Musgrave 1959, pp. 17–18
25 V&A 2216:37 and 2216:4
26 Musgrave 1951, p. 26
27 Musgrave 1959, p. 18
28 De Bellaigue 1991, p. 190
29 Morley 1984, p. 85
30 See J. Wilton-Ely 1993, pp. 51–71
31 Grant 2005, pp. 5–6
32 [Pasquin] 1796, p. 16
33 Beevers 2020, p. 11 and Beevers 2019, p. 141
34 Repton 1808, vi
35 Quoted in Blake 1911, p. 74
36 The significance of Repton's Red Books in the context of the visual arts was analysed in a doctoral thesis by André Rogger, published in 2007
37 Rogger 2007a, p. 34
38 Morley 1884, pp. 49–50
39 Daniels 1999, p. 193
40 Morley 1984, pp. 36–9
41 Ibid., p. 43
42 Ibid., p. 51 and Daniels 1999, p. 202
43 Daniels 1999, p. 203
44 Quoted in Morley 1984, p. 59, and Daniels 1999, p. 197. The Royal Pavilion Red Book manuscript survives in the Royal Library (RCIN 970493), along with the watercolour drawings and a related letter (RCIN 918069, 918070, 918071, 918072, 918073, 918074, 918075 918076, 918077, 918078, 918079, 918080, 918081, 981082, 981083, 981084 and 981085)
45 Crace Ledger, entry for Christmas 1802 to Midsummer 1803, p. 9
46 Ibid., p. 14
47 Ibid., p. 15
48 Aldrich 1987, p. 5
49 Morley 1984, p. 79; Aldrich 1987, p. 47. The Dighton painting is owned by Crace descendants and there is no image of it in the public domain
50 Lang 1990, pp. 42–50
51 The catalogue is discussed in detail in Aldrich 1987, p. 48. A copy of the catalogue is among the Crace papers at the National Art Library: Crace Family, Interior Decorators
52 For a detailed overview of Nash's involvement in Brighton and his work on other royal residences, see Port 2013
53 Beevers 2020, p. 13
54 *British Luminary and Weekly Intelligencer* 1818, p. 21
55 Cited in Musgrave 1959, p. 77
56 Ibid., p. 78
57 Ibid., p. 79
58 Ibid. For a succinct essay on Pugin's water-colours of the Pavilion, see Rogers 1978
59 Crace Ledger, entry for October to December 1815, p. 71
60 Ibid.

(opposite) The Saloon, as designed by Robert Jones in *c.*1823, after Augustus Charles Pugin, aquatint from John Nash's *The Royal Pavilion at Brighton*, 1826 (detail)

61 Royal Pavilion Abstracts of Accounts, p. 6, transcript p. 48
62 Ibid., p. 8, transcript p. 53
63 Inventory nos FA100888, FA100889 and FA100890
64 Cooper Hewitt Collection, inventory nos 1948-40-20, 1948-40-73, 1948-40-74 and 1948-40-75
65 RCIN 26118
66 Morley 1984, p. 79
67 Smith 1826, p. 164
68 For Jones's bill see The Duke of Northumberland's Estates Archives, Alnwick Castle, cat. Ref. S.Y.U.III.8.d(5). Clare E. Baxter's thesis 'The Transformation of Northumberland House' (1999) gives a detailed account of the work, including Robert Jones's involvement
69 *Northampton Mercury* 1822, p. 3
70 De Bellaigue 1993, p. 178
71 Roberts 2007, pp. 43–54
72 RCIN 918739, 918740, 918741,918742, 918743 and 918744
73 Roberts 2007, pp. 48–9
74 Reprinted as 'The Crace Papers', Two Lectures on the History of Paperhangings, delivered to the Royal Institute of British Architects on 4th and 18th February, 1839 (no place, reprint 1939, with foreword and comments by A.V. Sugden and E.A. Entwistle)
75 Morley 1984, p. 79
76 *The Times*, Friday 7 June 1805; p. 3 (issue 6353, col. A (online article no. CS50473159)
77 Morley 1984, p. 105
78 [Wilmott] 1851, p. 14
79 See Conrad 2023. For the changes made to the chamber floor for Victoria's visits, see Conrad 2022
80 For details on this decoration in an Arabic style see Rutherford, in Aldrich 1990, pp. 42–50, and Aldrich 1987, pp. 165–7
81 Musgrave 1984, p. 145
82 Beevers 2020, p. 68
83 Dinkel 1983, p. 134
84 Roberts 1939
85 Rutherford 1990, p. 178
86 Jones 2005, p. 78

Chapter 2 – Escaping to Other Worlds

1 See Porter 2010, pp. 57–77 and Beevers 2008, pp. 13–26
2 It is thought to have been first used in print in 1836, in Chapter 4 of Honoré de Balzac's novel *L'Interdiction*, to describe decoration in a style reminiscent of China
3 See Conner 1979, p. 82
4 Porter 2010, p. 21
5 For an overview, see Conner 2009
6 De Bruijn 2023, pp. 149–50
7 Thomas 2015, pp. 234–44
8 De Bruijn 2023, pp. 12–13
9 Ibid., p. 139
10 Ibid., pp. 14–15
11 Sickelmore 1823, p. 27
12 For a recent overview of Chambers's travels and work, see Conner 2024
13 Chambers 1763, p. 5
14 Ibid.
15 Ibid., p. 4
16 Ibid., p. 6
17 Robert Jones Accounts, entry for 1820, p. 3
18 The Pavilion is not the only chinoiserie interior where Alexander's images were used for decorative purposes. A small Chinese-inspired pavilion in the grounds of Schloss Pillnitz, Dresden, Germany, built in 1804–5, was informed by William Chambers's designs with wall paintings lifted from Alexander's works. See Welich 2003, 2008 and 2010
19 Chang 2010, pp. 44–5
20 Blakley 2018, p. 206
21 The Baroque palace of Schloss Pillnitz, east of Dresden, Germany
22 A palais in the gardens of Augarten, a Baroque palace in Leopoldstadt, Vienna
23 Parry 1833, pp. 115–16
24 Ibid., p. 116
25 Wilmott 1850, p. 9
26 Sitwell and Barton 1944 [1935], p. 183
27 Beevers 2008, p. 21
28 For Queen Mary's collection of blue-and-white porcelain, see Wilson 1972 and Ayers 2016, pp. 104–12
29 Pyne 1819, vol. 1, p. 116, with facing plate
30 Roberts 2001, p. 143
31 Ibid., p. 120
32 Pyne 1819, vol. 2, p. 21, with facing plate
33 Roberts 2001, p. 120
34 Pyne 1819, vol. 1, pp. 1–3
35 The artistic work of Queen Charlotte and her daughters is discussed in detail in Roberts 1987 and Loske 2019
36 Pyne 1819, vol. 1, facing p. 17
37 Ibid., facing p. 21
38 Ibid., p. 18
39 Ibid., p. 19
40 Roberts, 2001, pp. 147–8
41 Pyne 1819, vol. 1, p. 21
42 Roberts 2001, p. 150
43 Ibid., p. 148
44 Pyne 1819, vol. 1, pp. 20–21
45 Roberts 2001, p. 380
46 Royal Archives GEO/ADD/2/87–8
47 De Bellaigue 1967, pp. 518–28
48 De Bellaigue 1991
49 Oakey 2019
50 Pyne 1819, vol. 3, p. 12
51 De Bellaigue 1967, p. 518
52 De Bellaigue 1991, p. 20, quoting from Fricker & Henderson account books
53 Quoted in Oakey 2019, p. 82
54 Oakey 2019, p. 82
55 Pyne 1819, vol. 3, pp. 31–2, with two views
56 See Crace Ledger, entry for 3 December 1802, transcript p. 40: 'Repairing and painting in part the 3 Chinese Figures brought from Carlton House'
57 De Bellaigue 1991, p. 20
58 See Oakey 2019, p. 78, where he quotes the builder John Groves charging for some preliminary work on the structure
59 Aspinall 1938, vol. 1, lvii–lx
60 Morley 1984, p. 25
61 Bloch 1953, p. 130
62 Crace Ledger, entry for 25 August to 24 December 1802, transcript p. 6
63 Ibid., entry for 1815, pp. 77–8
64 Ibid., p. 80
65 Ibid., entry for 1818, p. 91
66 See also Morley 1984, p. 80, where he discusses the sketchbook in the context of the more sophisticated style of Frederick Crace's drawings, compared to his father's 'somewhat old-fashioned use of the Chinese idiom'
67 Morley 1984, p. 178 and p. 209 respectively
68 Crace Ledger, entry for 1820, transcript p. 110
69 Ibid., p. 115
70 Letter from J. Watier to F. Crace, 1 January 1818, Crace Family, Correspondence, *ca.* 1795–*ca.* 1915. 38 items. National Art Library, Special Collections, London, V&A. MSL/1989/6/2
71 Morley 1984, p. 25
72 Ibid., p. 20
73 Roberts 1987, p. 86
74 Ferrey 1861, p. 9
75 Ibid.
76 Cited in Bloch 1953, p. 130. The letter is in the collection of the Cooper Hewitt, Smithsonian Design Museum, New York, inventory number 1948-40-190
77 Letter from J. Watier to F. Crace, 7 April 1818, Crace Family, Correspondence, no individual accession number
78 Schinkel 1993, diary entry Friday 9 June 1826, p. 104
79 For a detailed account of Schinkel's visit and his connections with Nash, see Watkin 2013
80 A near-complete reprint appeared in Ashton 1899, pp. 262–300
81 Walker 1809, p. 3
82 Ibid., p. 4

83 Morley discusses the Glass Passage and possible related drawings, including a couple of faint pencil scrawls on the reverse of Crace drawings that he cautiously attributes to the Prince of Wales, although this is not confirmed. Morley also believed that some panels of the Glass Passage were used in the 1820s scheme of the Long Gallery, in the form of glass screen doors. Morley 1984, pp. 106–11. The north screen has been reinstated, albeit with several twentieth-century interventions and replacements
84 Ibid.
85 Attree 1809, p. 6
86 Ibid., pp. 6–8
87 Ibid., p. 9
88 Ibid., pp. 9–10
89 Sickelmore 1815, p. 38
90 Wright 1818, p. 45
91 Evans 1821, pp. 41–9
92 *Brighton Gazette*, 17 January 1822, cited in Rutherford 1992, p. 31
93 Sickelmore 1823, p. 24
94 Ibid., p. 22. Subsequent editions repeat the text unchanged
95 Ibid., pp. 23–4
96 Sickelmore 1823, p. 24
97 Ibid., p. 25
98 Ibid., pp. 25-6
99 Ibid., pp. 26–7
100 Ibid., p. 28
101 Ibid., pp. 28–9
102 Ibid., p. 30
103 Ibid., p. 31
104 *Nash's Views* was not published until 1826, but individual plates had been in circulation from 1824, sold by John Nash himself. Printing dates can be found on many of the individual aquatints
105 La Garde 1834, pp. 195–7, translation by Eric Underwood from an unpublished typescript in the Royal Pavilion Archives: La Garde and Underwood 1974, ch. VI, 10, unpaginated
106 Described by Schinkel as a 'tapete', which literally means wallpaper, he is here clearly referring to the fabric panels made of 'His Majesty's Geranium and gold colour satin decorated with silk gimp', Brighton: Accompts rel. to the Royal Pavilion: 1821–1824, entry for 5 January 1823
107 Schinkel 1993, pp. 108–9
108 Ibid., p. 107
109 Parry 1833, p. 115
110 Wilmott 1851, p. 9. In the first edition, published just a year earlier, Wilmott simply copies and paraphrases the descriptions from earlier guidebooks, including Sickelmore's
111 Measom 1853, pp. 52–3
112 Ibid., p. 53
113 Page 1875, p. 75
114 Erredge 1862, p. 270
115 Blackmantle 1825, pp. 280–81
116 Ibid., p. 281
117 Sitwell and Barton 1944 [1935], p. 181
118 Impey 1977, pp. 156–7
119 Ibid., p. 173
120 Arrowsmith 1840, p. 1
121 For a good overview on the age of Japonisme and orientalism after 1900, see de Bruijn 2023, pp. 169–241, as well as Cheang 2008

Chapter 3 – 'A Splendour of Light and Colour'

1 Sickelmore 1823, p. 30
2 Batchelor 2000, pp. 22–3
3 De Bruijn 2023, p. 11
4 Loske 2024, p. 258 and Loske 2021, pp. 17–19
5 From Papers of George Field, MS 11, f. 209 para 287; cited in Gage 2001, p. 8
6 For an illuminating account of the dramatic mid-nineteenth century changes in colour production and how these affected the arts and design, see Ribeyrol and Winterbottom 2023
7 Winckelmann 1764, pp. 147–8 (my translation)
8 Hay 1828, pp. 3–4
9 Ibid., p. 11
10 Ibid., p. 12
11 Cited in Gow 1984, pp. 17–22
12 Burke 1757, p. 63
13 Ibid., p. 64
14 Ibid., p. 65
15 Carlyle 2001, pp. 1–2
16 Dossie 1758, vol. 1, p. v; also cited in Carlyle 2001, p. 2
17 Bristow 1996b, p. xvii
18 Ibid., p. xiv
19 Ibid., p. 114
20 Chambers 1757, from the unpaginated introduction, para. 4
21 Ibid., para. 8
22 Ibid., p. 9
23 Ibid., pp. 15–16
24 Chambers 1862 [1759/1824], p. 299. The original 1759 edition reads 'there should never be above two or three sorts of Marbles, at the utmost . . .'
25 Ibid., pp. vii–viii
26 Attree 1809, p. 10
27 Morley 1984, p. 226
28 Watkin 2008, pp. 23–43
29 De Mézières 1992, p. 88; cited in Watkin 2008, p. 23
30 Hope 1807, p. 15; also cited in Watkin 2008, p. 23
31 Rumford 1875, p. 67
32 Britton 1827, cited in Brough 1999, pp. 1–10
33 See Aldrich 2009, pp. 21–9
34 Crace Ledger, entry for 1820, transcript p. 119
35 bid., entry for 1815, p. 60: 'preparing and ornamenting 6 large paintings 28ft x 11ft on fine linen blue on pink ground for sides of Gallery'
36 Sickelmore 1823, p. 24
37 Vanherman 1828, p. 3, cited in Bristow 1996a, p. 169
38 Smith 1826, p. 161
39 Bristow 1996 a, p. 169
40 Brayley 1838, p. 11
41 Ibid., p. 10
42 For a detailed account of the complex history of the Saloon, see Morley 1984, pp. 84–103
43 Harley 2001, pp. 100–102
44 Bristow 1996a, p. 37
45 Brough 1999, pp. 2–3
46 Ibid., p. 3
47 Baty 1992, pp. 56–7
48 Ibid.
49 Bristow 1996b, p. 163
50 Crace Ledger, entry for 5 October to 23 December 1802, transcript p. 6
51 Ibid., entry for 1818, p. 94. This entry probably relates to decorations in the Music Room
52 Attree 1809, p. 8
53 Crace Ledger, Midsummer to Christmas 1802, transcript p. 32
54 Jones 2005, pp. 49–55
55 For an overview of silver as Asian export ware, see Lomax 2008, pp. 39–54
56 Sickelmore 1823, pp. 28–9
57 Dossie 1796, vol. 1, p. 305
58 Ibid.
59 Bristow 1996a, p. 127
60 Ibid., p. 131. Bristow mistakenly assigns this to the year 1804. See endnote 66
61 Bristow, 1996b, p. 215–16
62 Ibid.
63 Ibid., p. 127
64 Ibid., p. 131
65 Ibid, p. 151, quoting from Chambers's original 1759 edition, p. 84
66 Crace Ledger, Midsummer to Christmas 1802, transcript p. 1. This is the entry Bristow refers to as an example of early silvering in the Pavilion
67 Crace Ledger, entry for midsummer to Christmas 1802, transcript p. 1
68 Attree 1809, pp. 9–10
69 '1 very fine set of India Paper, green ground colored flowers, birds &c containing 24 sheets', Crace Ledger, entry for 1815, transcript p. 80

70 Royal Pavilion Inventory, *c.*1828, p. 7
71 Ibid., p. 3
72 Whittemore 1827, pp. 32–3
73 Brayley 1838, p. 13
74 Royal Pavilion Memorandoms 1837, transcript p. 2
75 Royal Pavilion Inventory, *c.*1828, p. 8. The clock was removed by Queen Victoria and delivered to Windsor Castle in January 1847 and remains in the Royal Collection (RCIN 30006)
76 Alayrac-Fielding 2013, p. 87
77 Ibid.
78 Brighton: Accompts rel. to the Royal Pavilion: 1821–1824, entry for 5 January 1823
79 'Etched' used in several Royal Pavilion accounts means that the gold or silver leaf is applied in the form of fine lines, or 'hatched'
80 Royal Pavilion Requisitions Book, *c.*1820–1825, transcript p. 35
81 Royal Pavilion Abstract of Accounts, 5 January 1823, transcript p. 156
82 Robert Jones Accounts, entry for quarter ending 5 January 1823, p. 11
83 Royal Pavilion Inventory, *c.*1828, p. 20
84 The silver, glazed a pale golden colour, was worn and tarnished, but, surprisingly, intact.' Grant 2005, p. 5
85 Robert Jones Accounts, entry for 27 June 1823, p. 19
86 Ibid., entry for quarter ending 5 January 1823, p. 11
87 Crace Ledger, entry for 1820, transcript p. 117
88 Ibid., entry for 1815, p. 74
89 Ibid., p. 75
90 Ibid.
91 Ibid.
92 Ibid., p. 76. This dragon, originally mounted in central position on the ceiling, survives in the Pavilion, but is not in situ and has been heavily overpainted
93 Robson and Hale Accounts, entry for 5 April 1822, LCII/24/XC000499
94 Royal Pavilion Abstract of Accounts, entry for 5 January 1822, p. 13
95 Brighton: Accompts rel. to the Royal Pavilion: 1821–1824, entry for 5 January 1822
96 Roberts 2001, pp. 251–3 (RCIN 922101)
97 Cited in Wappenschmidt 1990, pp. 97–106
98 Some information on the silvered furniture can be found in Langer and Hojer 2000, while 'oriental' features at Nymphenburg Palace are discussed in Kiby 1990. In 2018 I contributed an essay on the sensual experience of the Amalienburg to a volume on *François de Cuvilliés*: Loske 2018
99 Wappenschmidt 1990, p. 105 (my translation)
100 Marlowe and Crosby Forbes 1990
101 Lomax 2008
102 For a comprehensive study on the subject, see Ambrosio et al. 2022
103 Ackermann 1808–1810, vol. 1, p. 108
104 Pyne 1819, vol. 3, pp. 24–5. See also de Bellaigue 1991, pp. 214–16
105 See de Bruijn 2023, pp. 149–50
106 Inskip 2004, pp. 235–9
107 Discussed in detail by Wells-Cole 1986, pp. 16–22
108 Wells-Cole 1983, pp. 14–15
109 Sickelmore 1823, p. 28

Conclusion – 'Surreal and Fantastical'

1 Sitwell and Barton 1944 [1935], p. 186
2 Manji 2021, p. 187

Cited works and further reading

PRIMARY SOURCES

BILL BOOK for Works at Northumberland House. The Northumberland Estates. S.Y.U.I.83

BRIGHTON: Accompts [*sic*] rel. to the Royal Pavilion: 1821–4. British Library. Add MS 46149. 5 Apr 1821–5 Jul 1825. In Accompt-Books of Furnishing Expenses, Repairs, etc., for Royal Palaces and Other Establishments and for a Number of Royal Occasions; 1821–42. British Library. Add MSS 46149–50

CRACE FAMILY, Correspondence, *c.*1795–*c.*1915. National Art Library, Special Collections, London, V&A. 86.YY.87

CRACE FAMILY, Documents, *c.*1767–1852. National Art Library, Special Collections, London, V&A. MSL/1989/6/3

CRACE FAMILY, Interior Decorators: Papers, *c.*1740–1919. 735 files. National Art Library, Archive of Art & Design, London, V&A. AAD/1992/3, AAD/2000/15, AAD/2001/6

CRACE, FREDERICK, A sketchbook with 68 coloured designs from Chinese ornaments, *c.*1800–20. The Royal Pavilion Archives. Inv. no. FA103696

CRACE LEDGER, Transcript of copies of ledger entries from the books of Messrs Crace & Sons, during the time spent in the Pavilion 1802–4, 1815–19, and 1820–23. The Royal Pavilion Archives. Inv. no. RPFILES0433

FIELD, GEORGE, Papers [1804–25], The Courtauld Institute of Art, London. GB 1518 CI/GF

GEORGE IV ACCOUNTS 1787–1830, Residences and Properties: Pavilion at Brighton. The Royal Archives, Windsor Castle. 33498–34224

GEORGIAN PAPERS ONLINE, Royal Collection Trust: gpp.rct.uk

ROBERT JONES ACCOUNTS 1821–23. The National Archives: Records of the Lord Chamberlain and other officers of the Royal Household, Lord Chamberlain's Department: Bill Books, Series IV. LC11/31–LC11/42

ROBSON AND HALE ACCOUNTS. Goods delivered and work done by Order from the Lord Chamberlain's Office. January 1818–October 1823. The National Archives: Lord Chamberlain's Department: Bill Books, Series IV. LC11/25 XC0867–LC11/41/XC1029

ROYAL PAVILION ABSTRACT OF ACCOUNTS IN THE LORD CHAMBERLAIN'S DEPARTMENT, *c.*1819–25. The Royal Pavilion Archives. Inv. no. 23007

ROYAL PAVILION INVENTORY, *c.*1828 [*c.*1828–39]. The Royal Pavilion Archives. Inv. no. 23006

ROYAL PAVILION MEMORANDOMS, 1837 [1837–45]. The Royal Pavilion Archives. Inv. no. 23003

ROYAL PAVILION REQUISITIONS BOOK, *c.*1820–25. The Royal Pavilion Archives. Inv. no. 29434

LITERATURE BEFORE 1851

Ackermann 1808–10
ACKERMANN, R[UDOLPH], *The Microcosm of London; or, London in Miniature*, London 1808–10

Ackermann 1809–28
ACKERMANN, R[UDOLPH], *The Repository of Arts, Literature, Commerce, Manufactures, Fashions and Politics*, London 1809–28

Alexander 1805
ALEXANDER, WILLIAM, *The Costume of China. Illustrated in Forty-Eight Engravings*, London 1805

Alexander 1814
ALEXANDER, WILLIAM, *Picturesque Representations of the Dress and Manners of the Chinese: Illustrated in Fifty Coloured Engravings, with Descriptions*, London 1814

Arrowsmith 1840
ARROWSMITH, HENRY, WILLIAM AND A., *The House Decorator and Painter's Guide; Containing a Series of Designs for Decorating Apartments, Suited to the Various Styles of Architecture*, London 1840

Attree 1809
ATTREE, H.R., *Topography of Brighton, and Picture of the Roads from Thence to the Metropolis*, Brighton 1809

Blackmantle 1825
BLACKMANTLE, BERNARD [CHARLES MOLLOY WESTMACOTT], *The English Spy. An Original Work Characteristic, Satirical, and Humorous. Comprising Scenes and Sketches in Every Rank of Society, Being Portraits Drawn from the Life. The Illustrations Designed by Robert Cruikshank*, London 1825

Brayley [*c.*1825]
BRAYLEY, EDWARD WEDLAKE, *Topographical Sketches of Brighthelmston*, London n.d. [*c.*1825]

Brayley 1838
Brayley, Edward Wedlake, *Illustrations of her Majesty's Palace at Brighton: Formerly the Pavilion, Executed by the Command of King George the Fourth, Under the Superintendence of John Nash. To which is Prefixed a History of the Palace*, London 1838

***The British Imperial Calendar*, 1838**
The British Imperial Calendar for the Year of our Lord 1838, Being the First Year of the Reign of Her Present Majesty, Victoria the First, or, General Register of the United Kingdom of Great Britain and Ireland and its Colonies, London 1838
The British Luminary and Weekly Intelligencer, London, 17 October 1818

Bruce 1828
Bruce, John, *Bruce's History of Brighton and Stranger's Guide: Including a Description of the Several Buildings, Churches and Other Places of Worship, Public Offices, Most Esteemed Rides, &c.*, Brighton 1828

Burke 1757
Burke, Edmund, *A Philosophical Enquiry into the Origin of Our Ideas of the Sublime and Beautiful*, London 1757

Chambers 1757
Chambers, William, *Designs of Chinese Buildings, Furniture, Dresses, Machines, and Utensils. Engraved by the Best Hands, From the Originals Drawn in China by Mr. Chambers, Architect, Member of the Imperial Academy of Arts at Florence. To which is Annexed, A Description of their Temples, Houses, Gardens, &c.*, London 1757

Chambers 1763
Chambers, William, *Plans, Elevations, Sections, and Perspective Views of the Gardens and Buildings at Kew in Surry, the Seat of Her Royal Highness the Princess Dowager of Wales*, London 1763

Chambers 1862 [1759/1824]
Chambers, William, *A Treatise on the Decorative Part of Civil Architecture. With Illustrations, Notes, and an Examination of Grecian architecture*, ed. by Joseph Gwilt. Rev. and W.H. Leeds, London: 1862 [1759/1824]

Christie 1819
Christie, James, *A Catalogue of the Genuine Library, Prints, and Books of Prints, of an Illustrious Personage, Lately deceased, Which Will be Sold by Auction, on Wednesday the 9th of June, 1819, and the Following Days, by Mr. Christie, at his Halls in Pall-Mall and at Messrs. Nicol's, Booksellers to His Majesty, Pall Mall [The Curious and Extensive Library of the Late John North, Esq., . . .]*, London 1819

Coleridge 1816
Coleridge, Samuel Taylor, *Christabel; Kubla Khan, A Vision; The Pains of Sleep*, London 1816

Crace 1839
Crace, John Gregory, 'The Crace Papers', *Two Lectures on the History of Paperhangings, Delivered to the Royal Institute of British Architects on 4th and 18th February 1839*, London 1839 [repr. 1939]

Daniell 1795–1807
Daniell, Thomas, *Oriental Scenery. Twenty Four Views in Hindoostan Drawn and Engraved by Thomas Daniell, and with Permission Respectfully Dedicated to the Honourable Court of Directors of the East India Company*, London 1795–1807

De Mézières 1780
De Mézières, Nicolas Le Camus, *Le génie de l'architecture, ou, l'analogie de cet art avec nos sensations*, Paris 1780

Dossie 1758
Dossie, Robert, *The Handmaid to the Arts: In Two Volumes*, London 1758

Dossie 1796
Dossie, Robert, *The Handmaid to the Arts: In Two Volumes. A New Edition, with Considerable Additions and Improvements*, London 1796

Du Halde 1735
Du Halde, Jean-Bapiste, *Description géographique, historique, chronologique, politique, et physique de l'empire de la Chine et de la Tartarie chinoise*, Paris 1735

Du Halde 1738–41
Du Halde, Jean-Bapiste, *A Description of the Empire of China and Chinese-Tartary*, London 1738–1741

Evans 1821
Evans, John, *Recreation for the Young and the Old. An Excursion to Brighton, with an Account of the Royal Pavilion, A Visit to Tunbridge Wells; and A Trip to Southend*, London 1821

Field 1817
Field, George, *Chromatics; or, An Essay on the Analogy and Harmony of Colours*, London 1817

Fleet 1847
Fleet, Charles, *An Illustrated Hand-Book of Brighton*, Brighton 1847

Galt 1816–20
Galt, John, *The Life, Studies, and Works of Benjamin West, Esq., President of the Royal Academy of London Composed from Materials Furnished by Himself*, 2 vols, London 1816–1820

Gilpin 1792
Gilpin, William, *Three Essays: On Picturesque Beauty, on Picturesque Travel and on Sketching Landscape. To Which is Added a Poem, on Landscape Painting*, London 1792

Goethe 1791–2
Goethe, Johann Wolfgang von, *Beyträge zur Optik*, Weimar 1791–2

Goethe 1810
Goethe, Johann Wolfgang von, *Zur Farbenlehre*, Tübingen 1810

Goethe 1840
Goethe, Johann Wolfgang von, *Theory of Colours; Translated with Notes by Charles Lock Eastlake*, London 1840

Halfpenny 1752
HALFPENNY, WILLIAM AND JOHN, *Chinese and Gothic Architecture Properly Ornamented*, London 1752

Halfpenny 1755
HALFPENNY, WILLIAM AND JOHN, *Rural Architecture in the Chinese Taste: Being Designs Entirely New for the Decoration of Gardens, Parks, Forrests, Insides of Houses, &c*, London 1755

Hay 1828
HAY, DAVID RAMSAY, *The Laws of Harmonious Colouring, Adapted to House Painting*, Edinburgh 1828

Hay 1836
HAY, DAVID RAMSAY, *The Laws of Harmonious Colouring, Adapted to Interior Decorations, Manufactures, and Other Useful Purposes*, Edinburgh 1836

Hazlitt 1826
HAZLITT, WILLIAM, *Notes of a Journey Through France and Italy*, London 1826

Hogarth 1753
HOGARTH, WILLIAM, *The Analysis of Beauty, Written with a View of Fixing the Fluctuating Ideas of Taste*, London 1753

Hope 1807
HOPE, THOMAS, *Household Furniture and Interior Decoration, Executed from Designs by Thomas Hope*, London 1807

Huish 1831
HUISH, ROBERT, *Memoirs of George the Fourth*, 2 vols, London 1831

La Garde 1834
LA GARDE, LE COMTE AUGUSTUS DE, *Brighton, scènes détachées d'un voyage en Angleterre*. Paris and London 1834. Unpublished edition and translation ('Brighton: 1827') by Eric Underwood, 1974. Typescript. The Royal Pavilion Archives

Macartney 2004
MACARTNEY, GEORGE, *An Embassy to China: Being the Journal Kept by Lord Macartney during his Embassy to the Emperor Ch'ien-lung*, 1793–1794, ed. Jonathan Spence, London 2004

Nash 1826
NASH, JOHN, *The Royal Pavilion at Brighton* [Nash's Views of the Royal Pavilion], London 1826

Newton 1704
NEWTON, SIR ISAAC, *Opticks: or, A Treatise of the Reflexions, Refractions, Inflexions and Colours of light*, London 1704

Nieuhof 1669
NIEUHOF, JOHAN, *An Embassy from the East India Company of the United Provinces to the Grand Tartar Cham Emperor of China*, London 1669
Northampton Mercury, 5 October 1822

Parry 1833
PARRY, JOHN DOCWRA, *An Historical and Descriptive Account of the Coast of Sussex*, Brighton 1833

[Pasquin] 1796
[PASQUIN, ANTHONY], *The New Brighton Guide, or, Companion for Young Ladies and Gentlemen to All the Watering-places in Great Britain*, London 1796

Pillement *c.*1762
PILLEMENT, JEAN, *The Ladies Amusement; or, Whole Art of Japanning Made Easy*, 2nd ed., London n.d. [*c.*1762]

Polo 1818
POLO, MARCO, *The Travels of Marco Polo, a Venetian in the Thirteenth Century: Being a Description, by that Early Traveller, of Remarkable Places and Things in the Eastern Parts of the World*, trans. William Marsden, ed. Thomas Wright, London 1818

Purchas 1613
PURCHAS, SAMUEL, *Purchas His Pilgrimage. Or Relations of the World and the Religions Observed in All Ages Discouered, from the Creation unto This Present*, London 1613

Pyne 1819
PYNE, WILLIAM HENRY, *The History of the Royal Residences of Windsor Castle, St. James Palace, Carlton House, Kensington Palace, Hampton Court, Buckingham House and Frogmore*, London 1819

Repton 1803
REPTON, HUMPHRY, *Observations on the Theory and Practice of Landscape Gardening*, London 1803

Repton 1808
REPTON, HUMPHRY, *Designs for the Pavillon at Brighton. Humbly inscribed to His Royal Highness the Prince of Wales. Including an Inquiry into the Changes of Architecture, as it Relates to the Palaces and Houses in England*, London 1808

Repton 1816
REPTON, HUMPHRY, *Fragments on the Theory and Practice of Landscape Gardening*, London 1816

Sheraton 1793
SHERATON, THOMAS, *The Cabinet-Maker and Upholsterer's Drawing-Book. In Three Parts*, 2 vols, London 1793

Sickelmore 1815
SICKELMORE, RICHARD, *An Epitome of Brighton, Topographical and Descriptive*, Brighton 1815

Sickelmore 1823
SICKELMORE, RICHARD, *The History of Brighton, From the Earliest Period to the Present Time*, Brighton 1823

Sickelmore 1824
SICKELMORE, RICHARD, *Sickelmore's Descriptive Views of Brighton*, London 1824

Smith 1826
SMITH, GEORGE, *The Cabinet-Maker and Upholsterer's Guide: Being a Complete Drawing Book, in Which Will Be Comprised Treatises on Geometry and Perspective, as Applicable to the Above Branches of Mechanics*, London 1826

Stalker and Parker 1688
Stalker, John and George Parker, *A Treatise of Japaning and Varnishing, Being a Compleat Discovery of Those Arts*, London 1688

Staunton 1797
Staunton, Sir George, *An Authentic Account of an Embassy from the King of Great Britain to the Emperor of China*, London 1797

***Three Grand Routes* c.1815**
[Unknown author], *The Three Grand Routes from Brighton to London, and Topography of that Fashionable Watering Place*, Brighton 1815
[Unknown author], 'The Regent's Pavilion at Brighton', *Morning Chronicle*, London, 11 January 1816

Vanherman 1828
Vanherman, T.H., *The Painter's Cabinet, and Colourman's Repository*, London 1828

Vanherman 1829
Vanherman, T.H., *Every Man his Own House-painter and Colourman*, London 1829

Walker 1809
Walker, Charles, *Brighton and its Environs*, London 1809

Whittemore 1827 [1825]
Whittemore, J., *Brighton and its Environs. A New Historical and Topographical Picture of Brighton and Complete Visitor's Guide* (3rd ed.), Brighton 1827 [1825]

Whittock 1827
Whittock, Nathaniel, *The Decorative Painters' and Glaziers' Guide*, London 1827

Wigstead 1790
Wigstead, Henry, *An Excursion to Brighthelmstone, Made in the Year 1789, Written and Designed by Henry Wigstead*, London 1790

Winckelmann 1764
Winckelmann, Johann Joachim, *Geschichte der Kunst des Alterthums*, vol. 1, Dresden 1764

Wright 1818
Wright, Charles, *The Brighton Ambulator, Containing Historical and Topographical Delineations of the Town, From the Earliest Period to the Present Time*, London 1818

LITERATURE AFTER 1850

Alayrac-Fielding 2013
Alayrac-Fielding, Vanessa, '"Luscious Colors and Glossy Paint": The Taste for China and the Consumption of Color in 18th-century England', in Feeser et al. 2013, pp. 81–97

Aldrich 1987
Aldrich, Megan, 'The Crace Firm of Decorators 1768 to 1899'. Doctoral thesis, University of Toronto 1987

Aldrich 1990
Aldrich, Megan (ed.), *The Craces, Royal Decorators 1768–1899*, Brighton 1990

Aldrich 2009
Aldrich, Megan, 'John Crace and John Soane: A Collaboration in Context', *Traditional Paint News*, vol. 2, no. 4, Edinburgh 2009, pp. 21–9

Aldrich 2021
Aldrich, Megan, 'Architecture and Interiors', in Loske 2021, pp. 185–207

Ambrosio et al. 2022
Ambrosio, Elisa, F. Giese, A. Martimyanova and H.B. Thomsen (eds), *China and the West: Reconsidering Chinese Reverse Glass Painting*, Berlin and Boston 2022

Ashton 1899
Ashton, John, *Florizel's Folly*, London 1899

Aslet and Salmon 2024
Aslet, Clive and Frank Salmon (eds), *Royalty and Architecture: Visions and Ambitions of European Monarchs and Nobility*, Stockholm 2024

Aspinall 1938
Aspinall, A. (ed.), *The Letters of King George IV, 1812–30*, 3 vols, Cambridge 1938

Aspinall 1963–71
Aspinall, A. (ed.), *The Correspondence of George, Prince of Wales, 1770–1812*, 8 vols, London 1963–71

Ayers 2016
Ayers, John, *Chinese and Japanese Works of Art in the Collection of Her Majesty The Queen*, 3 vols, London 2016

Baker 2005
Baker, Kenneth, *George IV, A Life in Caricature*, London 2005

Batchelor 2000
Batchelor, David, *Chromophobia*, London 2000

Batty 2018
Batty, Susi (ed.), *Humphry Repton in Sussex*, Sussex Gardens Trust 2018

Baty 1992
Baty, Patrick, 'Palette of Historic Paints', *Country Life*, London, 20 February 1992, pp. 56–7

Baty 2011
Baty, Patrick, 'Gilt leather'. 4 September 2011, https://patrickbaty.co.uk/2011/09/04/gilt-leather/ ((accessed 12 March 2024)

Baty 2017
Baty, Patrick, *The Anatomy of Colour: The Story of Heritage Paints and Pigments*, London 2017

Baxter 1999
Baxter, Clare E., 'The Transformation of Northumberland House: Interior Decoration and Furniture for the Third Duke of Northumberland by Nicholas Morel and Robert Hughes'. MPhil thesis, University of Dundee 1999

Beevers 2008
Beevers, David (ed.), *Chinese Whispers: Chinoiserie in Britain 1650–1930*, Brighton 2008

Beevers 2019
Beevers, David, 'The Royal Pavilion at Brighton', in Heard and Jones 2019, pp. 139–51

Beevers 2020
Beevers, David, *The Royal Pavilion at Brighton*, Brighton and Peterborough 2020

Berg 2005
Berg, Maxine, *Luxury and Pleasure in Eighteenth-Century Britain*, Oxford 2005

Berry 2005
Berry, Sue, *Georgian Brighton*, Chichester 2005

Bishop 1882 [1875]
Bishop, John George, *The Brighton Pavilion and its Royal Associations*, 4th ed., Brighton 1882 [1875]

Black and Sebag Montefiore 2003
Black, Will and Simon Sebag Montefiore, *The Chinese Palace at Oranienbaum*, Boston and London 2003

Blake 1911
Blake, Mrs Warenne [Alice Elizabeth Knox], *An Irish Beauty of the Regency; Compiled from 'Mes Souvenirs', The unpublished journals of the Hon. Mrs Calvert 1789–1822*, London 1911

Blakley 2018
Blakley, Kara, 'Domesticating Orientalism: Chinoiserie and the Pagodas of the Royal Pavilion, Brighton', *Australian and New Zealand Journal of Art*, vol. 18, no. 2, 2018, pp. 206–23

Bloch 1953
Bloch, E. Maurice, 'Regency Styling, the Prince and the Decorator', *The Connoisseur*, no. 531, June 1953, pp. 129–32

Borg 2005
Borg, Alan, *The History of the Worshipful Company of Painters, Otherwise Painter-Stainers*, London 2005

Bristow 1996
Bristow, Ian C., *Interior House-Painting: Colours and Technology 1615–1840*, New Haven 1996

Bristow 1996
Bristow, Ian C., *Architectural Colour in British Interiors 1615–1840*, New Haven 1996

Brough 1995
Brough, Janet, 'Chinese Export Oils at the Royal Pavilion', *The Picture Restorer*, no. 7, Spring 1995, pp. 14–17

Brough 1999
Brough, Janet, 'The Significance of Sheen: Surface Finish as an Important Aspect of Early Nineteenth Century Interiors', in C.V. Horie (ed.), *The Conservation of Decorative Arts*, London 1999, pp. 1–10

Brough 2013
Brough, Janet, *Colour in the Regency: Identification of Regency Pigments Used in the Original Decorations of the Royal Pavilion*, Brighton 2013

Carlyle 2001
Carlyle, Leslie, *The Artist's Assistant. Oil Painting Instruction Manuals and Handbooks in Britain 1800–1900*, London 2001

Chang 2010
Chang, Elizabeth Hope, *Britain's Chinese Eye: Literature, Empire, and Aesthetics in Nineteenth-Century Britain*, Stanford, California 2010

Cheang 2008
Cheang, Sarah, 'What's in a Chinese Room? 20th Century Chinoiserie, Modernity and Femininity', in Beevers 2008, pp. 75–81

Conner 1979
Conner, Patrick, *Oriental Architecture in the West*, London 1979

Conner 2009
Conner, Patrick, *The Hongs of Canton: Western Merchants in South China 1700–1900, As Seen in Export Paintings*, London 2009

Conner 2024
Conner, Patrick, 'From China Trader to Architect: William Chambers, His Pagodas, and Chinese Export Paintings', *Arts of Asia*, Spring 2024, pp. 102–113

Conner and Legouix Sloman 1981
Conner, Patrick and Susan Legouix Sloman, *William Alexander: An English Artist in Imperial China*, Brighton 1981

Conrad 2022
Conrad, Stephen, 'The Chamber Floor of the Royal Pavilion, Brighton, 1815–45', *The Burlington Magazine*, vol. 164, no. 1435, October 2022, pp. 986–99

Conrad 2023
Conrad, Stephen, 'Queen Victoria's Life in Brighton and the Royal Pavilion 1837–1845', *The Court Historian*, vol. 28, no. 3, 2023, pp. 220–36

Cornforth 1992
Cornforth, John, 'Picked out in Silver', *Country Life*, 6 August 1992, pp. 54–5

Croft-Murray 1962–70
Croft-Murray, Edward, *Decorative Painting in England 1537–1837*, London and Feltham, Middlesex 1962–70

Crossman 1991
Crossman, Carl L. *The Decorative Arts of the China Trade*, Woodbridge 1991

Daniels 1999
Daniels, Stephen, *Humphry Repton: Landscape Gardening and the Geography of Georgian England*, New Haven and London 1999

De Bellaigue 1967
De Bellaigue, Geoffrey, 'The Furnishings of the Chinese Drawing Room, Carlton House', *The Burlington Magazine*, vol. 109, no. 774, September 1967, pp. 518–28

De Bellaigue 1991
De Bellaigue, Geoffrey, *Carlton House: The Past Glories of George IV's Palace*, London 1991

De Bellaigue 1993
De Bellaigue, Geoffrey, 'A Royal Mise-en-Scène: George IV's Coronation Banquet', *Furniture History*, 1993, pp. 174–83

De Bruijn 2017
De Bruijn, Emile, *Chinese Wallpaper in Britain and Ireland*, London 2017

De Bruijn 2023
De Bruijn, Emile, *Borrowed Landscapes: China and Japan in the Historic Houses and Gardens of Britain and Ireland*, London 2023

De Bruijn, Bush and Clifford 2014
De Bruijn, Emile, Andrew Bush and Helen Clifford, *Chinese Wallpapers in National Trust Houses*, Newcastle upon Tyne 2014

De Mézières 1992 [1780]
De Mézières, Nicolas Le Camus, *The Genius of Architecture; or, The Analogy of that Art with Our Sensations*, trans. David Britt, with introduction by Robin Middleton, Santa Monica and Chicago 1992 [1780]

Dinkel 1983
Dinkel, John, *The Royal Pavilion*, London 1983

Dinkel 1987
Dinkel, John, 'The Re-creation of the Music Room Carpet', *The Royal Pavilion, Libraries & Museums Review*, Brighton 1987, no. 1, pp. 2–3

Doderer-Winkler 2013
Doderer-Winkler, *Magnificent Entertainments: Temporary Architecture for Georgian Festivals*, New Haven and London 2013

Erredge 1862
Erredge, John Ackerson, *History of Brighthelmston, or: Brighton as I View and Others Knew It*, Brighton 1862

Feeser et al. 2013
Feeser, Andrea, Beth Fowkes Tobin and Maureen Daly Goggin (eds), *The Materiality of Color: The Production, Circulation, and Application of Dyes and Pigments, 1400–1800*, Farnham and Burlington 2013

Ferrey 1861
Ferrey, Benjamin, *Recollections of A.N. Welby Pugin, and his Father, Augustus Pugin; With Notices of Their Works*, London 1861

Gage 1995
Gage, John, *Colour and Culture: Practice and Meaning from Antiquity to Abstraction*, London 1995

Gage 2000
Gage, John, *Colour and Meaning: Art, Science and Symbolism*, London 2000

Gaillard 2011
Gaillard, Emmanuelle and Walter, Marc, *A Taste for the Exotic: Orientalist Interiors*, London 2011

Gibbs 2013
Gibbs, Elaine M., 'Colors and Techniques of Eighteenth Century Chinese Wallpaper: Blair House as Case Study', in Feeser et al. 2013, pp. 247–63

Gow 1984
Gow, Ian, 'The First Intellectual Housepainter', *The World of Interiors*, May 1984, pp. 17–22

Grant 2005
Grant, Gordon, 'Out of the Blue: The Re-discovery of a Lost Ceiling Design', *The Royal Pavilion, Libraries & Museums Review*, Brighton July 2005, pp. 5–6

Harley 2001
Harley, R.D., *Artists' Pigments c.1600–1835: A Study in English Documentary Sources*, 2nd ed., London 2001

Heard and Jones 2019
Heard, Kate and Kathryn Jones (eds), *George IV: Art and Spectacle*, exh. cat., London 2019

Hobhouse 1995
Hobhouse, Hermione, *Thomas Cubitt: Master Builder*, Cirencester 1995

Impey 1977
Impey, Oliver, *Chinoiserie: The Impact of Oriental Styles on Western Art and Decoration*, London and Oxford 1977

Inskip 2004
Inskip, Peter, 'Moggerhanger, 1808–1812', *The Georgian Group Journal*, vol. 14, 2004, pp. 235–9

Jennings 1885
Jennings, Louis J. (ed.), *The Croker Papers: The Correspondence and Diaries of the Late Right Honourable John Wilson Croker, LLD, FRS* (3 vols), London 1885

Jones 2005
Jones, Mike, *Set for a King: 200 Years of Gardening at the Royal Pavilion*, Brighton 2005

Kiby 1990
Kiby, Ulrika, *Die Exotismen des Kurfürsten Max Emanuel in Nymphenburg: eine kunst- und kulturhistorische Studie zum Phänomen von Chinoiserie und Orientalismus im Bayern und Europa des 16. bis 18. Jahrhunderts*, Hildesheim, Zürich and New York 1990

Koldeweij 2000
Koldeweij, Eloy, 'Gilt Leather Hangings in Chinoiserie and Other Styles: An English Speciality', *Furniture History*, vol. 36, 2000, pp. 61–101

Koppelkamm 1987
Koppelkamm, Stefan, *Exotische Architekturen im 18. und 19. Jahrhundert*, Berlin 1987

Koppelkamm 2015
Koppelkamm, Stefan, *Imaginary Orient: Exotic Buildings of the 18th and 19th Centuries in Europe*, London 2015

La Monica 2016
La Monica, Marcella, *La Palazzina Cinese di Palermo. Tra decorazione e simbolismo*, Milan 2016

Lang 1990
Lang, Gordon, 'The Royal Pavilion Brighton: The Chinoiserie Designs by Frederick Crace', in Aldrich 1990, pp. 42–50

Langer 2000
Langer, Brigitte, *Die Möbel der Schlösser Nymphenburg und Schleißheim*, ed. Gerhard Hojer, Munich and New York 2000

Lewis 1865
Lewis, Lady Theresa (ed.), *Extracts of the Journals and Correspondence of Miss Berry from the Year 1783 to 1852*, 3 vols, London 1865

Lomax 2008
Lomax, James, 'Chinoiserie Silver in Britain', in Beevers 2008, pp. 39–54

Loske 2018
Loske, Alexandra, 'Cuvilliés Amalienburg – Kühler Traum in Silber und Farbe', in: Vorherr 2018, pp. 101–31

Loske 2019
Loske, Alexandra, 'The Female Influence on George IV's Taste and Collecting Habits', in Heard and Jones 2019, pp. 152–9

Loske 2021
Loske, Alexandra (ed.), *A Cultural History of Color in the Age of Industry*, New York and London 2021

Loske 2022
Loske, Alexandra, 'A Teapot Prince and His Enchanted Palace: The Royal Pavilion, Brighton', in Martin 2022, pp. 146–52

Lühr 2008
Lühr, Hans-Peter, (ed.), *Im Banne Ostasiens – Chinoiserie in Dresden. Dresdner Hefte: Beiträge zur Kulturgeschichte*, vol. 96, no. 4, Dresden 2008

Lyons 2024
Lyons, Rebecca, '"You Will Not Think Me a Bad Architect": George IV and the Image of British Royalty', in Aslet and Salmon 2024, pp. 186–207

Manji 2021
Manji, Fatima, *Hidden Heritage: Rediscovering Britain's Lost Love for the Orient*, London 2021

Markley 2006
Markley, Robert, *The Far East and the English Imagination, 1600–1730*, Cambridge and New York 2006

Marlowe 1990
Marlowe, Alan James and H.A. Crosby Forbes, *Chinese Export Silver*, London 1990

Martin 2022
Martin, Meredith, *Reimagining the Ballet des Porcelaines: A Tale of Magic, Desire, and Exotic Entanglement*, Turnhout, Belgium 2022

Marschner 2017
Marschner, Joanna (ed.), *Enlightened Princesses: Caroline, Augusta, Charlotte, and the Shaping of the Modern World*, New Haven and London 2017

Measom 1853
Measom, George, *The Official Illustrated Guide to the Brighton and South Coast Railways*, London 1853

Morley 1982
Morley, John, 'Early Chinoiserie Interiors at Brighton Pavilion', *Apollo*, September 1982, pp. 156–62

Morley 1984
Morley, John, *The Making of the Royal Pavilion, Brighton*, London 1984

Musgrave 1946
Musgrave, Clifford, *The Regency Festival: The Regency Exhibition Catalogue, The Royal Pavilion*, Brighton 1946

Musgrave 1951
Musgrave, Clifford, *The Royal Pavilion: A Study in the Romantic*, London 1951

Musgrave 1959
Musgrave, Clifford, *The Royal Pavilion: An Episode in the Romantic*, London 1959

Oakey 2019
Oakey, David, 'The Construction, Decoration and Demolition of George IV's Carlton House', in Heard and Jones 2019, pp. 69–88

Osterhammel 2018
Osterhammel, Jürgen, *Unfabling the East: The Enlightenment's Encounter with Asia*, Princeton and Oxford 2018

Page 1875
Page, Thomas, *Page's Handbook to Brighton and its Vicinity, With Short Tours in Sussex*, new ed., Brighton 1875

Parissien 2001
Parissien, Steven, *George IV: The Grand Entertainment*, London 2001

Parissien 2009
Parissien, Steven, *Interiors: The Home Since 1700*, London 2009

Payne 1919
Payne, Francis Loring, *The Story of Versailles*, New York 1919

Port 2013
Port, M. H., 'John Nash and the Royal Palaces', in Tyack 2013, pp. 125–52

Porter 2002
Porter, David, 'Monstrous Beauty: Eighteenth-Century Fashion and the Aesthetics of the Chinese Taste', *Eighteenth-Century Studies*, vol. 35, no. 3, 2002, pp. 395–411

Porter 2010
Porter, David, *The Chinese Taste in Eighteenth-Century England*, Cambridge 2010

Pückler-Muskau 1957
Prince Pückler-Muskau, *A Regency Visitor: The English Tour of Prince Pückler-Muskau, Described in his Letters 1826–1828*, trans. Sarah Austin, ed. E.M. Butler, London 1957

Quennell 1937
Quennell, Peter (ed.), *The Private Letters of Princess Lieven to Prince Metternich 1820–1826*, London 1937

Ribeyrol and Winterbottom 2023
Ribeyrol, Charlotte and Matthew Winterbottom (eds), *Colour Revolution: Victorian Art, Fashion and Design*, Oxford 2023

Roberts (Henry) 1939
Roberts, Henry D., *A History of the Royal Pavilion, with an Account of its Original Furniture and Decoration*, London 1939

Roberts (Hugh) 2000
Roberts, Hugh '"Quite appropriate for Windsor Castle": George IV and George Watson Taylor', *Furniture History*, vol. 36, 2000, pp. 115–37

Roberts (Hugh) 2007
Roberts, Hugh, 'Thrones Revisited', *Furniture History*, vol. 43, 2007, pp. 43–54

Roberts (Jane) 1987
Roberts, Jane, *Royal Artists: From Mary Queen of Scots to the Present Day*, London 1987

Roberts (Jane) 2001
Roberts, Jane (ed.), *George III and Queen Charlotte: Patronage, Collecting and Court Taste*, London 2001

Rogers 1978
Rogers, Derek, 'A.C. Pugin's Drawings of the Royal Pavilion at Brighton', *The Connoisseur*, June 1978, pp. 118–23

Rogger 2007
Rogger, André, *Die Red Books des Landschaftskünstlers Humphry Repton*, Worms 2007

Rogger 2007
Rogger, André, *Landscapes of Taste: The Art of Humphry Repton's Red Books*, London and New York 2007

Rumford 1875
Rumford, Count [Benjamin Thompson], 'Conjectures Respecting the Principle of the Harmony of Colours', in *The Complete Works of Count Rumford*, vol. 4, Boston 1875, pp. 63–71

Rutherford 1990
Rutherford, Jessica, 'Redecoration and Restoration: The Crace Firm at the Royal Pavilion, Brighton, 1863–1900', in Aldrich 1990, pp. 42–50

Rutherford 1992
Rutherford, Jessica, '"As Full of Lamps as Hancock's shop": Lighting in the Royal Pavilion 1815–1900', in Christopher Gilbert et al., *Country House Lighting, 1660–1890*, Leeds 1992, pp. 28–34

Rutherford 2003
Rutherford, Jessica, *A Prince's Passion: The Life of the Royal Pavilion*, Brighton 2003

Schinkel 1986
Schinkel, Karl Friedrich, *Reise nach England, Schottland und Paris im Jahre 1826*, ed. Gottfried Riemann, Berlin 1986

Schinkel 1993
Schinkel, Karl Friedrich, *'The English Journey': Journal of a Visit to France and Britain in 1826*, trans. F. Gayna Walls, ed. David Bindman and Gottfried Riemann, New Haven and London 1993

Setterwall et al. 1974
Setterwall, Åke, Stig Fogelmarck and Bo Gyllensvärd, *The Chinese Pavilion at Drottningholm*, Malmö 1974

Sitwell and Barton 1944 [1935]
Sitwell, Osbert and Margaret Barton, *Brighton*, London 1944 [1935]

Sloboda 2014
Sloboda, Stacey, *Chinoiserie: Commerce and Critical Ornament in Eighteenth-Century Britain*, Manchester 2014

Smith 1999
Smith, E.A., *George IV*, New Haven and London 1999

Sowden 1992
Sowden, Anne, 'The Restoration of the South Galleries at the Royal Pavilion', in *The Royal Pavilion and Museums Review*, no. 1, 1992, pp. 1–5

Sugden 1926
Sugden, Alan Victor and J.L. Edmondson, *A History of English Wallpaper, 1509–1914*, London 1926

Suebsman and Belz 2019
Suebsman, Daniel and Thomas Belz, *Alle Farben Chinas! Glasurenvielfalt aus über 1.000 Jahren / All the Colours of China! Myriads of Glazes from over 1,000 Years*, Düsseldorf 2019

Tarling 2018
Tarling, Judy, '"Not a Tittle Shall be Altered": The Story of Betrayal at Brighton', in Batty 2018, pp. 86–95

Ten-Doesschate Chu and Ding 2015
Ten-Doesschate Chu, Petra and Ning Ding (eds), *Qing Encounters: Artistic Exchanges between China and the West*, Los Angeles 2015

Thomas 2015
Thomas, Greg M., 'Chinoiserie and Intercultural Dialogue at Brighton Pavilion', in Ten-Doesschate Chu and Ding 2015, pp. 232–47
The Times, 7 June 1805

Tyack 2013
Tyack, Geoffrey (ed.), *John Nash: Architect of the Picturesque*, Swindon 2013

Vollmer 2002
Vollmer, John E., *Ruling from the Dragon Throne: Costume of the Qing Dynasty (1644–1911)*, Berkeley and Toronto 2002

Vorherr 2018
Vorherr, Albrecht (ed.), *François de Cuvilliés: Rokokodesigner am Münchner Hof*, Munich 2018

Wappenschmidt 1989
Wappenschmidt, Friederike, *Chinesische Tapeten für Europa: Vom Rollbild zur Bildtapete*, Berlin 1989

Wappenschmidt 1990
Wappenschmidt, Friederike, *Der Traum von Arkadien – Leben, Liebe, Licht und Farbe in Europas Lustschlössern*, Munich 1990

Watkin 2008
Watkin, David, 'The Reform of Taste in London: Hope's House in Duchess Street', in David Watkin, David and Philip Hewat-Jaboor, *Thomas Hope: Regency Designer*, New Haven and London 2008, pp. 23–43

Watkin 2013
Watkin, David, 'Nash in Context: Links with Schinkel, Percier and Fontaine, Soane and Cockerell', in Tyack 2013, pp. 169–81

Welich 2003
Welich, Dirk, *Der chinesische Pavillon im Schlosspark Pillnitz*, Dresden 2003

Welich 2008
Welich, Dirk, 'Pillnitz – ein chinoises Gesamtkunstwerk', in Lühr 2008, pp. 30–39

Welich and Kleiner 2010
Welich, Dirk and Anne Kleiner (eds), *China in Schloss und Garten: Chinoise Architekturen und Innenräume*, Dresden 2010

Wells-Cole 1983
Wells-Cole, Anthony, *Historic Paper Hangings from Temple Newsam and Other English Houses*, Temple Newsam Country House Studies, no. 1, Leeds 1983

Wells-Cole 1986
Wells-Cole, Anthony, 'Another Look at Lady Hertford's Chinese Drawing Room', *Leeds Arts Calendar*, no. 98, 1986, pp. 16–22

Wilmott 1850
Wilmott, Charles, *A Descriptive Guide to the Palace and Gardens of the Royal Pavilion at Brighton*. Brighton 1850

Wilmott 1851
Wilmott, Charles, *A Descriptive Guide to the Palace and Gardens of the Royal Pavilion at Brighton. A New Edition, with Illustrations of the State Apartments*, Brighton 1851

Wilson 1972
Wilson, Joan, 'A Phenomenon of Taste: The China Ware of Queen Mary II', *Apollo*, vol. 96, no. 3, 1972, pp. 116–23

Wilton-Ely 1993
Wilton-Ely, J. 'Pompeian and Etruscan Tastes in the Neo-Classical Country-House Interior', in Gervase Jackson-Stops et al., *The Fashioning and Functioning of the British Country House*, exh. cat., National Gallery of Art, Washington DC, 1993, pp. 51–71

Wood (Frances) 1998
Wood, Frances, 'Closely Observed China: From William Alexander's Sketches to His Published Works', *British Library Journal*, vol. 24, no. 1, London 1998, pp. 98–121

Wood (Heather) 1993
Wood, Heather, 'Old Blocks for New: The Reprinting of the Dragon Wallpaper', *The Royal Pavilion, Libraries & Museums Review*, no. 1, 1993, pp. 7–10

Index

Picture Credits

All images other than those listed below are courtesy of Brighton & Hove Museums.

Courtesy of Cooper Hewitt, Smithsonian Design Museum in New York 1.58, 1.59, 2.14, 2.36, 2.39, 2.41, 2.43, 3.26, 3.27, 3.34

Courtesy of Alexandra Loske 1.93, 3.2 (Photo: Clive Boursnell), 3.3 (Photo: Clive Boursnell) 3.29

Courtesy of Stephen Roberts-Pratt 2.11

Royal Collection Enterprises Limited © 2025 | Royal Collection Trust 1.98, 1.99, 2.2, 2.22, 2.23, 2.24, 2.25, 3.46

Acknowledgements

This book would not have been possible without the commissioning editor Mark Eastment at Yale University Press. It was his vision that made it happen, with the help of an outstanding team: Daphne Fordham-Smith, Leonie Kellman and Mia Husband. Thank you all for being kind, patient, and strict when necessary. It has been a joy working with you.

At the Royal Pavilion (Brighton & Hove Museums) I am indebted to many colleagues past and present, with particular thanks to Gordon Grant and David Beevers for factchecking and proofreading, as well as Janet Brough, Katie Hobbs, Nicola Coleby, Chloe Tapping, the entire current conservation team, our guides, duty managers and security team, and all front-of-house staff. Hedley Swain, thank you for believing in this project and my ability to deliver it. At the Royal Collection Trust, I am particularly grateful to Caroline de Guitaut, Kate Heard, Kathryn Hughes, Nicola Turner Inman and David Wheeler.

Special thanks are due to a small circle of friends and colleagues outside the Royal Pavilion, whose knowledge and expertise I value greatly and whose input has been invaluable, among them Emile de Bruijn, Patrick Conner, Stephen Conrad, Maurice Howard, Martin Levy, Neil Parkinson, Charlotte Ribeyrol and the *Chromotope* team, and Sir Simon Schama.

My immediate family and close friends have been as supportive and patient as ever: Jeremy Page, Flora Loske-Page, Renate Klauck-Neils and my late godfather Klaus Neils, Franky Bulmer, Eva Bodinet, Jenny Gaschke, Shân Lancaster, Lilian McFetridge, Jacqueline Rietz and Chandra Wohleber. Thank you, too, to my late father, Peter Loske who showed me the Märchenkönig's palaces Neuschwanstein, Linderhof and Herrenchiemsee when I was a small child. He may have caused all this.

The appendix of Pugin drawings in this book was made possible through the generous support of the Annie Burr Lewis Fund and the Albert Dawson Educational Trust.

The biggest and final thank you is due to Stephen Pavey, who, as a patron of the Royal Pavilion, has financed and supported the writing and promotion of this book with extraordinary generosity and trust.